Social Change and the Coming of Post-Consumer Society

Consumer society is an unquestionably complex social construct. However, after decades of unremitting dominance there are signs emerging that it is starting to falter, both as a coherent and durable system of social organization and as a strategy for societal advancement. Debates concerning how we can transition beyond present energy- and materials-intensive consumer society are beginning to gain greater salience.

Social Change and the Coming of Post-Consumer Society aims to develop more complete appreciation of the relevant processes of social change and to identify effective interventions that could enable a transition to supersede consumer society. Bringing together leading interdisciplinary experts on social change, the book identifies and analyzes several ongoing small- and modest-scale social experiments. Possibilities for macro-scale change from the interlinked perspectives of culture, economics, finance, and governance are then explored. These contributions expose the systemic problems that are emblematic of the current condition of consumer society, specifically the unsustainability of prevailing consumption practices and lifestyles and the persistence of inequalities. These observations are summarized and extended in the final chapter of the book.

This volume will be of great interest to students and scholars of sustainable consumption, sustainability transitions, environmental sociology, and sustainable development.

Maurie J. Cohen is Professor of Sustainability Studies and Director of the Program in Science, Technology, and Society in the Department of Humanities at the New Jersey Institute of Technology, USA.

Halina Szejnwald Brown is Professor of Environmental Science and Policy at Clark University and a Fellow at the Tellus Institute, USA.

Philip J. Vergragt is Professor Emeritus of Technology Assessment at Delft University, the Netherlands, and currently a Fellow at the Tellus Institute and a Research Fellow at Clark University, USA.

Routledge – SCORAI Studies in Sustainable Consumption

Comprising edited collections, co-authored volumes and single author monographs, *Routledge-SCORAI Studies in Sustainable Consumption* aims to advance conceptual and empirical contributions to this new and important field of study. In particular, this series will explore key issues such as the emergence of new modes of household provisioning, the evolution toward post-consumerist systems of social organization, novel approaches to consumption governance and innovative business models for sustainable lifestyles.

The Sustainable Consumption Research and Action Initiative (SCORAI) is an international knowledge network of approximately 1000 scholars and policy practitioners working at the interface of material consumption, human well-being, and technological and cultural change. For more information about SCORAI and its activities please visit www.scorai.org.

Series Editors:

Maurie J. Cohen, Professor of Sustainability Studies and Director of the Program in Science, Technology, and Society in the Department of Humanities at the New Jersey Institute of Technology, USA.

Halina Szejnwald Brown, Professor of Environmental Science and Policy at Clark University and a Fellow at the Tellus Institute, USA.

Philip J. Vergragt, Professor Emeritus of Technology Assessment at Delft University, Netherlands, and currently a Fellow at the Tellus Institute and a Research Fellow at Clark University, USA.

Titles in this series include:

Social Change and the Coming of Post-Consumer Society
Theoretical advances and policy implications
Edited by Maurie J. Cohen, Halina Szejnwald Brown and Philip J. Vergragt

"This fine collection focuses on the relationship between consumption and satisfaction, demonstrating how the economic culture of consumerism causes ecological damage, wasteful use of resources, and mindless yearning for distinction that is mistaken as the utter enjoyment of 'freedom.' The book explores examples and strategies of 'interstitial' change unfolding in the niches of consumer societies, the pursuit of which is driven by both economic crises affecting households and radical ideas of socioeconomic change as well as change of lifestyles. With a balanced focus on both novel practices of consumption and the policies needed to facilitate and nurture them, this volume maps roads toward post-consumerism."

Claus Offe, Professor Emeritus of Political Sociology,
Hertie School of Governance, Germany

"If we want a sustainable and healthy environment, it is essential to shift decisively from a hyper-consumerist society. However, we live in a capitalist economy and stable capitalism depends on consumerism. What is to be done in the face of such a sharp contradiction? *Social Change and the Coming of Post-Consumer Society* explores a wide range of approaches to this question. This book marks an important contribution to this area of inquiry."

Erik Olin Wright, Professor of Sociology, University of Wisconsin and former
President of the American Sociological Association, USA

"How do we transform political and economic structures in order to allow everyone to live meaningful lives with less intensive forms of consumption? Where do we start, and who will do the job? These are defining questions during an era of secular stagnation and impending climate disaster, and this book provides an important contribution in the quest for viable solutions."

Giorgos Kallis, ICREA Professor, ICTA-Autonomous
University of Barcelona, Spain

"Based on multiple case studies and theories of change, this book argues that the foundational pillars of consumer society are faltering. Drawing on a shared set of theories—from transition management to Karl Polanyi's embeddedness theorems—the volume contends that without deep changes in macroeconomic and political orientations, and mechanisms that escape current lock-ins, it will not be possible to achieve broad sociocultural change. The message is not of certainty or desperation, but rather of hope. By appealing to deeper values, broad change is possible. A must read for activists as much as for sustainability and consumption researchers."

Joachim Spangenberg, Vice-Chair, Sustainable Europe Research Institute, Germany

"Climate change, water shortages, and toxins in our food, air, and water. Loneliness and depression. Erosion of traditional values. These are among the problems that experts tell us we must solve for humanity to thrive, or even survive. However, these threats are symptoms of a deeper pathology, namely the desire for endless growth in consumption and the substitution of material goods for human relationships. This book sets out theory to understand how this came to be and what might be done about it, from an explicitly multidisciplinary perspective. The book also provides compelling accounts of exciting experiments in sustainable consumption now underway as people around the world seek to live within the limits of our finite planet, and in so doing, restore and heal our environment, our institutions, our communities, and ourselves."

John D. Sterman, Jay W. Forrester Professor of Management and Director of the System Dynamics Group, Sloan School of Management, Massachusetts Institute of Technology, USA

Social Change and the Coming of Post-Consumer Society

Theoretical advances and policy implications

Edited by Maurie J. Cohen,
Halina Szejnwald Brown, and
Philip J. Vergragt

Routledge
Taylor & Francis Group

LONDON AND NEW YORK

from Routledge

2017 : 12819

$\mathcal{D}4$

First published 2017

by Routledge
2 Park Square, Milton Park, Abingdon, Oxon OX14 4RN

and by Routledge
711 Third Avenue, New York, NY 10017

Routledge is an imprint of the Taylor & Francis Group, an informa business

British Library Cataloguing-in-Publication Data
A catalogue record for this book is available from the British Library

Library of Congress Cataloging-in-Publication Data
Names: Cohen, Maurie J., editor. | Brown, Halina Szejnwald, editor. | Vergragt, Philip, editor.
Title: Social change and the coming of post-consumer society : theoretical advances and policy implications / edited by Maurie J. Cohen, Halina Szejnwald Brown and Philip J. Vergragt.
Description: Abingdon, Oxon ; New York, NY : Routledge, 2017. | Series: Routledge studies in sustainable consumption
Identifiers: LCCN 2016040971| ISBN 9781138642058 (hb) | ISBN 9781315630168 (ebook)
Subjects: LCSH: Consumers. | Consumption (Economics)--Social aspects. | Social change.
Classification: LCC HC79.C6 S6293 2017 | DDC 306.3--dc23
LC record available at https://lccn.loc.gov/2016040971

ISBN: 978-1-138-64205-8 (hbk)
ISBN: 978-1-315-63016-8 (ebk)

Typeset in Goudy
by Saxon Graphics Ltd, Derby

Printed and bound in Great Britain by
TJ International Ltd, Padstow, Cornwall

13.12.2017 / 139,90 euro

Contents

List of figures and tables

Figures

Tables

Contributors

Julia Backhaus is a Doctoral Researcher at the International Centre for Integrated Assessment and Sustainable Development at Maastricht University. Her background is in science and technology studies, and her research focuses on social innovation, social practices, sustainable consumption, and theories of social change and transformation. She is Co-founder and a Steering Committee member of the European branch of the Sustainable Consumption Research and Action Initiative.

Tom Bauler is Professor and Chair of Environment and Economy at Université Libre de Bruxelles and is affiliated with the Centre d'Etudes du Développement Durable. He is an ecological economist and works from a political economy perspective on issues related to the governance of societal alternatives including beyond-GDP indicators, social innovation, and socio-environmental inequalities.

Halina Szejnwald Brown is Professor of Environmental Science and Policy at Clark University and Fellow at the Tellus Institute. She also is a Fellow of the International Society for Risk Analysis, a Fellow of the American Association for the Advancement of Science, and Co-founder and a Board Member of the Sustainable Consumption Research and Action Initiative. She received a PhD in Chemistry from New York University and has authored four books and over sixty scientific articles.

Maurie J. Cohen is Professor of Sustainability Studies and Director of the program in Science, Technology, and Society at the New Jersey Institute of Technology and Associate Fellow at the Tellus Institute. He is Co-founder and a Board Member of the Sustainable Consumption Research and Action Initiative and Editor of the journal *Sustainability: Science, Practice, and Policy*. His most recent book is *The Future of Consumer Society: Prospects for Sustainability in the New Economy*.

Predrag Cvetičanin is Assistant Professor in the Faculty of Arts at the University of Niš and Director of the Centre for Empirical Cultural Studies of Southeast Europe. He has coordinated a large number of national and international research projects on cultural participation, household strategies, informal practices, and social stratification in southeastern Europe.

Anders Hayden is Associate Professor in the Department of Political Science and the College of Sustainability at Dalhousie University. He is a member of the Editorial Board of the journal *Sustainability: Science, Practice, and Policy* and his most recent book is *When Green Growth is Not Enough: Climate Change, Ecological Modernization, and Sufficiency*.

Cindy Isenhour is Assistant Professor of Anthropology and Cooperating Faculty with the Climate Change Institute and Senator George J. Mitchell Center for Sustainability Solutions at the University of Maine. She is a member of the Board of Directors for the Society for Economic Anthropology and Advisor to the Sustainable Consumption Research and Action Initiative. Her most recent book is *Sustainability in the Global City: Myth and Practice* (with Melissa Checker and Gary McDonogh).

Tally Katz-Gerro is Reader in the Department of Sociology and Research Fellow in the Sustainable Consumption Institute at the University of Manchester. She was previously Associate Professor in the Department of Sociology at the University of Haifa, and her recent projects have focused on environmental habitus in Israel, Korea, and the United States and environmental tastes and ecosystem services.

Emily Huddart Kennedy is Assistant Professor of Environmental Sociology in the Department of Sociology at Washington State University. She is a Board Member of the Sustainable Consumption Research and Action Initiative and co-editor of *Putting Sustainability into Practice: Applications and Advances in Research on Sustainable Consumption* (with Maurie J. Cohen and Naomi T. Krogman).

Adrian Leguina is Research Associate with the Understanding Everyday Participation project in the Department of Sociology at the University of Manchester. His work is at the intersection of social statistics, stratification, and the sociology of cultural consumption and taste. As a quantitative methodologist and social scientist, his research contributes to empirical dialogues between perspectives and methods.

Derk A. Loorbach is Professor of Socio-economic Transitions and Director of the Dutch Research Institute for Transitions at Erasmus University Rotterdam. Since 2001, he has been among the first researchers to develop the field of transition management for sustainability. He has published extensively on sustainability transitions and serves as lead editor for the Springer book series on *Theory and Practice of Urban Sustainability Transitions*.

Bonno Pel is a Postdoctoral Researcher at the Centre d'Etudes du Développement Durable of the Université Libre de Bruxelles and works on the TRANSIT (Transformative Social Innovation Theory) research project. He received a degree in spatial planning and political philosophy from the University of Amsterdam and in 2012 completed a dissertation on system innovation processes in traffic management at Erasmus University Rotterdam. His research focuses on the governance and politics of system innovation and sustainability transitions, and he has published in *Technological Forecasting and Social Change*, the *Journal of Environmental Policy and Planning*, and *Ecology and Society*.

Inge Røpke is Professor of Ecological Economics in the Department of Development and Planning at Aalborg University, Copenhagen. She has published widely on ecological economics, technology in everyday life, and the relationship between consumption and the environment. She is presently working on a project on ecological macroeconomics and sustainability transitions. An article from this initiative appears in the journal *Ecological Economics*.

Marlyne Sahakian is Senior Researcher in the Faculty of Geosciences and the Environment at the University of Lausanne. She is currently coordinating national and European research projects on household energy and food consumption. Her research focuses on understanding natural resource consumption patterns and practices, especially in relation to environmental promotion and social equity, and identifying opportunities for transitions toward more "sustainable" societies. She is also a founding member of the European branch of the Sustainable Consumption Research and Action Initiative.

Juliet B. Schor is Professor of Sociology at Boston College and a member of the MacArthur Foundation Connected Learning Research Network for which she is leading a six-year project on the "sharing economy." Her PhD is in economics, which she taught at Harvard University from 1984 to 1995. She is the author of *True Wealth: How and Why Millions of Americans Are Creating a Time-Rich, Ecologically Light, Small-Scale, High-Satisfaction Economy* and several other books. She is the recipient of the Leontief Prize, the Herman Daly Prize, Guggenheim and Radcliffe fellowships, and the American Sociological Association's Public Understanding of Sociology Award.

Philip J. Vergragt is Professor Emeritus of Technology Assessment at Delft University of Technology, Fellow at the Tellus Institute, and Research Professor at Clark University. He is Co-founder and a Board Member of the Sustainable Consumption Research and Action Initiative and has written more than eighty scientific publications and four books. Vergragt obtained a PhD in Chemistry from the University of Leiden.

Robert Wengronowitz is a Teaching Fellow and PhD candidate in the Department of Sociology at Boston College. He is also a member of the MacArthur Foundation Connected Learning Research Network, and his research is funded by the United States Department of Agriculture. His dissertation uses a Bourdieusian lens to examine strategy and power in climate-change activism. Wengronowitz earned prior degrees from the University of Chicago and the University of Illinois at Urbana-Champaign.

Richard Wilk is Distinguished Professor and Provost's Professor of Anthropology at Indiana University, where he co-directs the Food Institute. He has also taught at the University of California, New Mexico State University, and University College London, and has held visiting professorships at Gothenburg University, the University of Marseille, and the University of London. His initial research on the cultural ecology of indigenous Mayan farming and family organization was followed by work on consumer culture and sustainable consumption, energy consumption, globalization, television, beauty pageants, and food. Much of his recent work has turned toward the global history of food and sustainable consumption. His most recent book is *Teaching Food and Culture* (co-edited with Candice Lowe Swift).

Jeffrey Wilson teaches ecological economics in the School for Resource and Environmental Studies at Dalhousie University and is Senior Associate with the Genuine Wealth Institute. He has played a key role in development of well-being and socio-economic indicator metrics in Canada and was involved in designing the Nova Scotia Genuine Progress Index and the Alberta Genuine Progress Indicator, two pioneering indicator projects in Canada.

Foreword

Richard Wilk

Historian Jackson Turner announced the closing of the American frontier in 1893, just at the cusp of an even greater historical change—the advent and triumph of mass consumer culture. During the following century, a cultural economy based on consumption has dominated the globe, meting out abundant wealth and goods to one segment of the planet, while impoverishing others through the exploitation and commodification of labor and raw materials. Today the expansion of consumer culture continues to accelerate, turning more and more people into "consumers," while scientists, citizens, and politicians have begun to realize that this growth cannot continue. The same engine that produces abundance and comfort for the consuming class is now destroying the physical conditions that made it possible in the first place.

Consumer culture is dependent upon the combustion of carbon-based fossil fuels, liberating the carbon slowly sequestered over hundreds of millions of years by living organisms. The entire biosphere is in the midst of a massive uncontrolled experiment to find out what happens to the atmosphere of a small planet when we add huge quantities of water vapor, carbon dioxide, methane, and nitrous oxide. The results are only now becoming clear; changes in climate and weather, rising sea levels, and mass extinction of plant and animal life. The results may surpass in their impact, the effects of the meteor that ended the Cretaceous period. After centuries of increased carbon emissions in the name of modernity, science now recognizes that we need to end the experiment, and embark on another, to see if the process is reversible, or if it will end in a catastrophic feedback cycle.

The contributors to this book are building on years of research in the emerging field of "sustainable consumption" which has established the connection between consumer culture and climate change. From this work we have learned a great deal about the interactions involving culture, politics, and technology that drive the growth of consumer culture at an ever-increasing rate. The authors also build on important advances in theories of social change, which provide a common language and set of intellectual tools for understanding the relationships among the economy, technology, and society. Poaching ideas from many different disciplines, these theories help us understand the inner workings of the "runaway train" of consumer capitalism (to borrow ecological economist Brian Czech's

(2000) metaphor). They also recognize the limitations of the over-specialized and fragmented scholarship on consumerism among the many fields and disciplines that touch on consumer culture. The result is a kind of inquiry we might call *post-disciplinary*, based on recognition that the project of changing consumer society is huge, encompassing, complex, and "wicked."

This book marks the emergence of "sustainable consumption" as a mature field that is turning to the serious question of "what is to be done?" The introduction and conclusion argue that it is not enough to visualize post-consumerist utopias; we need to think about practical actions that can move a massive and entrenched system into a more sustainable direction. These contributions to the volume collectively realize that we cannot depend on the slow and uneven growth of "green consumerism," which often ends up just substituting one kind of harmful practice for another. The corporate world has been very adept at absorbing and coopting each successive effort to create alternative economies, turning dissent into a commodity (Frank and Weiland, 1997). At the same time, the marketing industry has refined and grown the tools needed to keep people consuming, even when they have filled their houses, garages, attics, and storage lockers with stuff they never have time to use (Arnold et al., 2012).

Despite many movements aimed at finding alternatives to consumer culture, people continue to chase the dream of abundance and wealth. No matter how educated we may be, we still fall for the same old tricks. Conspicuous consumption still puts us on an endless treadmill of conformity and individualism, commensality and competition. Marketers find yet more ways to absorb new categories of goods into endless fashion cycles, converting durables into consumables, and inventing entirely new forms of material culture; for example, the development of gourmet food and cosmetics for dogs. Leisure is commercialized, play requires expensive equipment, and even after work is over we engage in forms of productive consumption like do-it-yourself home improvement and home cooking. Every kind of health and safety is driven by fear and hope into the marketplace. Consumer culture acts as a parasite on social life, turning important social relationships, every form of generosity or altruism into a reason to buy more things, from the diamond wedding ring to the elaborately painted, hermetically sealed coffin. Genuine concerns about health and safety are appropriated and used to create new niches and product categories.

It takes courage and fortitude to even imagine challenging a system that motivates almost $600 billion on advertising and publicity every year. How could we imagine effective action in the face of such an overwhelming force? The editors and authors of this book understand the complexity and difficulty of their task, and the chapters in this volume seek out the weaknesses, vulnerable spots, and cracks in consumer culture, the places where social action can make a difference. Their post-disciplinary science is infused with the search for practical activism, strategies that can open new pathways toward a post-consumer society.

Whatever the difficulty and risk, I cannot imagine a more important task. Climate change is the defining issue of this era, the most fundamental and important challenge our young species has ever faced. If we are not going to leave a shattered and damaged world to our descendants, there is no time to waste.

References

Arnold, J., Graesch, A., Ragazzini, E., and Ochs, E. (2012) *Life at Home in the Twenty-First Century: 32 Families Open Their Doors*. Los Angeles, CA: Cotsen Institute of Archaeology Press.

Czech, B. (2000) *Shoveling Fuel for a Runaway Train: Errant Economists, Shameful Spenders, and a Plan to Stop Them All*. Berkeley, CA: University of California Press.

Frank, T. and Weiland, M. (eds.) (1997) *Commodify Your Dissent*. New York: W. W. Norton.

Preface

This book has been inspired by our discussions over the last few years with affiliates of the Sustainable Consumption Research and Action Initiative (SCORAI). Established in 2008, SCORAI is an international knowledge network of professionals working at the interface of material consumption, human well-being, and technological and cultural change. Its aims are to foster a transition beyond the currently dominant consumer society; to understand the drivers of the consumerist economy in affluent technological societies; to formulate and analyze options for post-consumerist lifestyles, social institutions, and economic systems; and to provide the knowledge for emergent grassroots innovations, social movements, and public policies. SCORAI has experienced steady growth since its inception and now comprises nearly one thousand people around the world. It is anchored by organizational nodes in North America, Europe, China, and Israel and its activities are facilitated by a website, a listserv for online discussions, a monthly newsletter, and a regular series of thematic workshops, conferences, colloquia, and publications.[1] Members of the SCORAI Board serve on a voluntary basis and the network as a whole and its activities are supported by occasional grants and in-kind contributions by sponsoring institutions.

The specific concerns that gave rise to this volume centered on how to transition beyond the present energy- and materials-intensive consumer society. We began by contemplating how the voluminous literature on social change—both in terms of retrospective explanations and prospective inquiries—could help us to understand the dynamics of such a transformation and if there were ways to influence its underlying processes. Of course, we were aware of the extensive work conducted on social movements, sociotechnical transitions, and other theories of social change, but we found that most of it was not directly germane to questions pertaining to consumer society. We were also familiar with many grassroots initiatives and other social experiments, but this work was not particularly salient with respect to the linkages between macroscale transition and consumerism.

As we discuss in detail in the introductory chapter, consumer society is unquestionably a complex social construct. Its constituent infrastructures, practices, and institutions have developed over an extended period of time, but did not become fully entrenched until the decades following World War II, first in the United States and then in many other parts of the world. After several decades of unremitting dominance and formidable influence, consumer society is starting to falter, both as a coherent and durable system of social organization and a strategy for societal advancement. Widening cracks and unintended consequences are becoming evermore apparent, from ecological impacts to income inequality to inability to deliver secure lifestyles and sufficient well-being.

Our primary motivation in this project has been to develop a more complete appreciation of relevant processes of social change and to identify effective interventions that could enable a transition to supersede consumer society. Innovation of new technologies and social practices to manage consumption will be, after all, critically important for reducing greenhouse-gas emissions as well as for alleviating other environmental problems including diminishing soil fertility, declining biodiversity, ongoing toxic contamination of humans and ecological systems, and increasing scarcity of various natural resources. In addition to these familiar biophysical problems, the economy, the political system, and the culture of present-day consumer society are responsible for widening disparities in income and wealth and for exacerbating poverty even in rich countries. Under these circumstances, sustainable consumption is not only about curtailing the energy and materials throughput of affluent consumers, but is also focused on ensuring a decent standard of living for all.

As we continued to enhance our understanding of the relationship between social change and consumption, a proposal emerged to organize a year-long series of seminars over the course of a twelve-month period spanning 2014 and 2015. We invited prominent scholars interested in large-scale social change—mostly from outside of our own circle of research on sustainable consumption, alternative lifestyles, and social experimentation—to create opportunities for fruitful dialogue on a range of pertinent issues. We are delighted that Dorothy Holland, Douglas Holt, Claus Offe, George Ritzer, Juliet Schor, David Snow, John Sterman, and Erik Olin Wright accepted our invitation to participate in this colloquium and, in some instances, for accommodating scheduling adjustments due to snowstorms and other unanticipated incidents. Video recordings of all sessions comprising the colloquium are accessible on the SCORAI website.[2]

To synthesize the diverse perspectives presented during these seminars, and to apply them specifically to the challenges of a transition beyond consumer society, we then organized a two-day workshop in Boston in October 2015. Most of the contributions that comprise this book were originally presented in draft form at this event and then subsequently revised for publication. Participants in the workshop included Erik Assadourian, Jeffrey Barber, Tom Bauler, Joshua Farley, James Goldstein, Tally Katz-Gerro, Emily Huddart Kennedy, Anders Hayden, Cindy Isenhour, Michele Lamont, Derk Loorbach, James Meadowcroft, Claus Offe, Inge Røpke, Marlyne Sahakian, Juliet Schor, Adrian Smith, Jennie Stephens, John Stutz, Vanessa Timmer, and Richard Wilk. Ruby Woodside and Tiy Chung, both graduate students at Clark University at the time, provided excellent administrative and technical support and Robert Orzanna expertly edited and posted the video recordings on the SCORAI website. We thank the V. Kann Rasmussen Foundation for financial support.

The Tellus Institute hosted both the colloquium and the workshop and we are grateful for this collaboration as well as for more general institutional assistance that SCORAI has received over the years. A special word of thanks to John Stutz who has been an especially valued colleague and friend. We also appreciate the help of David McAnulty who for the last several years has skillfully looked after the network's finances. At Routledge, Margaret Farrelly and Annabelle Harris have been in equal parts patient and helpful throughout the incubation of this volume. We are indebted to Janice Baiton and Elizabeth Spicer for careful assistance during the final stages of production.

Finally, we would be remiss if we did not acknowledge that this book reflects the presentations and discussions during the colloquium and the collegial exchanges that took place at the workshop, as well as the incisive scholarship of the contributors. Of course, we realize that we have not been able to generate answers to all of our questions and that many issues still remain to be explored. We hope that in coming years others will take up study of the unfolding transition to post-consumer society and add to this body of knowledge.

In terms of its organization, this volume is divided into two main themes. Following our introductory chapter, an initial section identifies and analyzes several ongoing small- and modest-scale social experiments. The second theme explores possibilities for macro-scale change from the interlinked perspectives of culture, economics, finance, and governance. These contributions expose the systemic problems that are emblematic of the current condition of consumer society, specifically the unsustainability of prevailing consumption practices and lifestyles and the challenges of a pending transition. We summarize and cautiously extend these observations in the final chapter of the book.

MJC, HSB, and PJV,
Princeton, NJ and Wellfleet, MA
August 2016

Notes

1   Further details on SCORAI are at www.scorai.org.
2   See http://scorai.org/colloquium-on-consumption-and-social-change.

Part I

Consumption and social change

An introductory discussion and synthetic framework

1 Introduction

Halina Szejnwald Brown, Philip J. Vergragt, and Maurie J. Cohen

Even a casual glance at the daily news provides ample evidence that we are living through an era of profound challenges including ecological crises, mass migrations, growing wealth inequalities at different geographic scales, and political extremism. Individually, but even more dramatically when taken in combination, these developments indicate that underlying systems of social organization are under profound stress. In recent years, a growing number of observers—from a wide array of political vantage points—have begun to sense that sweeping changes in the dominant order may be approaching (see, e.g., Mason, 2015; Monbiot, 2016; Reich, 2016; Angus, 2016; Levin, 2016).

Those seeking to understand the current trajectory of generally affluent countries in the world today have looked at processes of change through a variety of analytic frames including the shifting role of labor in the economy, the instability of contemporary political arrangements, the evolving role of globalized capital, and the advent of revolutionary technologies (Lanier, 2013; Ford, 2015; Brynjolfsson and McAffee, 2016; King, 2016; Gordon, 2016; Streeck, 2016). While each of these points of departure has potential to open up important lines of discussion, this book considers social change through the prism of consumer society—the system of social organization that in the years following World War II became in many countries the synthesizing logic for societal cohesion, economic development, institutional design, and power relations. The concept of consumer society is, of course, not an unproblematic notion, and it has been variously invoked over the years, often for polemical or provocative purposes (e.g., Galbraith, 1958; Packard, 1960; Scitovsky, 1976; see also Horowitz, 2005). Below we clarify what we mean before moving to the core questions of this book.

The *Oxford English Dictionary* defines consumer society as "a society in which the buying and selling of consumer goods and services is the predominant social and economic activity."[1] The first acknowledged usage of the term was in 1920 and during the intervening decades the scale of consumption, as well as its influence on political discourse and ideology, cultural meanings, and major institutions has only become more pervasive and entrenched.[2]

The transition that brought consumer society to its currently dominant position commenced and quickly accelerated in the United States in the years following 1945 and, through the efforts of government, industrial firms, and organized labor, in a span of not much more than a single generation came to be the principal organizing logic of contemporary life. The leaders of these institutions shrewdly recognized a unique window of opportunity created by the confluence of several auspicious factors—the post-Depression craving for more materially comfortable lifestyles, the vast scale of the country's post-war industrial overcapacity, the national euphoria over uncontested American political and economic primacy (and the endless possibilities it afforded), the demographic surge that gave rise to the "baby boom" generation, and the technological advances and industrial resourcefulness that made an abundance of novel consumer goods more accessible than ever (Glickman, 1999; Cohen, L., 2003; Brown and Vergragt, 2016; Cohen, M., 2017). The resultant transformation ushered in a historically unprecedented period of national economic growth and led to sweeping redefinition of predominant living arrangements across large parts of the country (Brown, 1995; Collins, 2002; Gordon, 2016).

The diffusion of consumerist lifestyles also prompted a cultural shift whereby mass consumption became societally entrenched as a ubiquitous system of artifacts, symbols, and shared understandings. Consumer goods also came to be the centerpiece of social practices, leisure time, communal rituals, and celebrations in everyday life, as well as inseparably conflated with potent political ideals such as freedom, independence, and democracy. Equally important, a symbiotic relationship developed between mass consumption and the status of the economy. While the United States was at the forefront of these developments during the post-war period, it did not take long for Western Europe, Japan, and other countries to similarly remodel themselves and strike out on the same trajectory (Strasser et al., 1998; de Grazia, 2005; Garth, 2010; Garon, 2011; Francks and Hunter, 2012; Shrivastava and Kothari, 2012; Pulju, 2013).

In short, consumer society has evolved into a complex system of technology, culture, institutions, markets, and dominant business models. It is driven by belief in the feasibility and inherent desirability of limitless consumption-led growth and is justified by the creed of neoliberalism that has powerfully shaped political and economic life in the United States and elsewhere over the last several decades (Harvey, 2007; Ventura, 2012). Relentless emphasis on consumption has also fundamentally colored prevalent understanding of human betterment and well-being. To consider a transition beyond consumer society is to interrogate this entire system and to expose the tensions among different worldviews, political ideologies, and class conflicts. It is our contention that we can learn a great deal about the underlying mechanisms of contemporary social organization by examining the workings of consumer society and specifically how it functions and reproduces itself. It thus follows that efforts to address the challenges that affluent countries face and to transition beyond consumer society are deeply intertwined endeavors.

Over the past decade it has become increasingly common to examine the efficacy of consumer society and to speculate on its ultimate durability (e.g., Humphery 2010; Lewis, 2013; D'Alisa et al., 2015; Cohen, 2016). Numerous scholars and activists have become engaged in searching for leverage points and promising interventions to steer presumptive harbingers of social change in directions that are ecologically and socially sustainable, politically stable, and capable of providing decent livelihoods. This rapidly cumulating body of knowledge and experience covers a wide spectrum of potential mechanisms and plausible agents—from the role of small scale, out-of-the-mainstream social innovations and experiments (Brown and Vergragt, 2008; Seyfang, 2009) to more instrumental approaches to altering human motivations through explicit government policies (Lorek and Fuchs, 2013; Spangenberg, 2014; Schäpke and Rauschmayer, 2014). Researchers have also considered the transformational potential of evolving social practices (Shove et al., 2007; Halkier, 2013; Spaargaren, 2013), insurgent sociotechnical changes (Geels and Schot, 2007; Kemp and Van Lente, 2013), and business models less calibrated for continual expansion (Kelly, 2012; Wells, 2013). Other areas of emphasis have included macro-level policies premised on alternatives to the economic growth paradigm (Victor, 2008; Jackson, 2009; Kallis, 2011; Harris, 2013), new fiscal policies like carbon taxes (Parry et al., 2014), and social movements committed to bringing forward different types of economic organization, institutions, and ethics (Raskin, 2011; Therborn, 2013). Additionally notable are numerous future visions and scenarios developed over the last two decades (Green and Vergragt, 2002; Raskin et al., 2002; Quist and Vergragt, 2006; Quist et al., 2011; Mont et al., 2014; Doyle and Davies, 2013; Speth, 2015).[3]

As ambitious as many of these efforts have been, less emphasis has been devoted to formulating a conceptual framework for understanding how such recommendations might be actualized, or more to the point, how systemic social change occurs. Without adequate comprehension, the search for effective strategies within state and civic domains is essentially a hit-or-miss exercise. The leading questions for this book then are: How might we interpret the potential of societal developments unfolding at the macro-, meso-, and micro-scales to foster a transition beyond consumer society? Do widely accepted theories of social change allow us to recognize—and possibly facilitate—incipient innovations as precursors of a prospective transformation?

It is an unfortunate truism that most scholarship devoted to explicating social change aims to speak primarily to members of distinct disciplinary specialties. Sociologists tend to focus on social movements, popular mobilization, and institutional change as the most relevant factors. Political scientists favor the lens of power relations and concentrate their attention on "opportunity structures." Economists organize their understanding of social change around systems of production, natural resource endowments, international trade, and supply and demand of labor while cultural anthropologists direct their scrutiny to broadly shared belief systems, values, understandings, and norms. For all of their importance and insight, these disciplinary perspectives confront serious obstacles when trying to describe fundamental change in consumer society and to recognize its nascent signs. For one thing, it takes knowledge from all of these angles to get a handle on a complex system such as consumer society. Furthermore, the change processes presently transpiring are interdependent, with non-linear causal relationships and feedback loops (see especially Sterman, 2012). The hallmark of reductionist science—understanding the whole by assembling the understandings of changes in individual societal parts—is clearly inadequate when applied to multi-causal progressions of social change because of the co-evolutionary relationships that exist among the various domains.

For that reason, we find that it is more productive to draw on a suite of complementary conceptual perspectives. Below, we highlight four such approaches, beginning with Erik Olin Wright's concept of interstitial social transformation. We then turn our attention to the multi-level perspective on sociotechnical transitions that originated among scholars of technological innovation in the Netherlands during the 1990s and has been advanced in subsequent years by a large network of primarily European researchers. The third formulation that we consider is the theory of strategic action fields articulated by Neil Fligstein and Doug McAdam. Our final theoretical perspective draws on several enduring ideas initially described by political economist Karl Polanyi. These four approaches are corresponding and jointly form a conceptual framework for exploring different aspects of the core questions of this volume.

In his recent book *Envisioning Real Utopias*, sociologist Erik Olin Wright (2010) considers alternatives to the capitalist system of social organization and the possible routes for reaching them. Specifically, he seeks prospective arrangements that would be grounded in civic empowerment over the state and the economy. By calling these different systems "real utopias," Wright draws attention to the need to combine a commitment to deeply democratic, egalitarian, and just values and aspirations while devoting serious attention to the problem of how institutions really work and how attempts at social engineering can produce unintended perverse consequences.

As numerous observers have remarked over the years, the capitalist system, which is tightly bound up with consumer society, and in many respects supplies its commanding logic and propulsive engine, has proven to be remarkably resilient over time. This is partly because of the powerful forces that have successfully reproduced it, most notably coercion, institutional rules, ideology, culture, and material interests. However, the prevailing order also has built-in fault lines that derive from its very complexity as well as from its inefficiency, rigidity, and path dependency. Opportunities for radical social transformation may occur when these cracks widen as a result of either unintended side-effects arising from actions people take or purposeful projects of social change.

Wright considers three broad strategies for achieving radical social change. He dismisses the first option, what he terms "ruptural change," in essence an intentionally organized socialist revolution that starts with destruction of powerful incumbent institutions. The second means of radical social change is symbiotic and entails alternative movements challenging existing structures and culture and seeking to solve certain practical problems through social empowerment that effectively takes over and repurposes existing institutions and power structures. However, Wright finds greater promise in a third pathway predicated on "interstitial" strategies. This approach aims to nurture novel modes of social organization in the fractures of the dominant system, in niches where they do not seem to pose any immediate threat to dominant classes and institutions. While leaders of these small-scale activities do not usually regard their interventions as being focused on undermining the larger system, they deliberately work to build new organizational forms and to foster novel social relations beyond the customary reach of the state.

Wright argues that such interstitial processes have historically played a central role in large-scale social change. Most dramatically, capitalism developed in the apertural spaces of feudal society and grew in due course to a scale at which point it was able to supplant its predecessor (Lefebvre et al., 1985; Braudel, 1995). These niche activities, often invisible and unacknowledged during their early phases of gestation, may provide the groundwork for future ruptural transformations that in time are unavoidable and lead the way toward alternative forms of social organization. Proponents of such transitions work to formulate innovative visions, to foster social and technical learning, and to build social capital.

Wright's theory of social change through interstitial processes is in several respects closely related to, and complementary with, the so-called multi-level perspective (MLP) on sociotechnical transitions. The MLP approach was initially developed by Dutch scholars working in the field of innovation studies to describe large-scale shifts in sociotechnical systems of production and consumption (Kemp, 1994; Geels, 2002; Geels and Schot, 2007; Markard et al., 2012; see also Smith et al., 2005; Shove and Walker, 2007). The concept of a sociotechnical system denotes, on the one hand, a relatively stable configuration of techniques and artifacts and, on the other hand, an array of institutions, rules, practices, and networks that determine the "normal" developments and uses of technologies in a particular area of provisioning to satisfy human needs (Kemp and Rotmans, 2005; Smith et al., 2005). Accordingly, an operative sociotechnical system (or "regime" in the language of its associated research community) constitutes an amalgam of social and technological components and fulfills a socially valued function such as generating electricity from fossil fuels or providing urban mobility on the basis of widespread automobile ownership. It also embodies strongly held convictions and interests concerning particular lifestyles, institutions, and power relations, all of which are co-dependent and continually co-evolving. Stability, complexity, and resilience are central characteristics of established sociotechnical systems and this means that change is invariably slow, involving both innovations in science and technology and changes in social practices, professional norms, belief systems, and other factors.

The MLP conceptualizes change in complex sociotechnical regimes as resulting from accumulated transformations occurring at three nested levels. In addition to the regime described above, the macro-level (or the "landscape") comprises broad dominant ideas, large-scale social currents, and historical trends on the scale of a country, region, or the world. Illustrative examples include widespread recognition of anthropogenic climate change, urbanization and growth of megacities, mass migration and terrorism, economic globalization, and diffusion of the Internet. Change at the landscape level is typically gradual, but can occasionally be sharp and sudden, much like a powerful earthquake. Regardless of the specific pace, transformation in landscape conditions can have profound implications on the continued viability of extant sociotechnical system.

To complete the typology of the MLP, micro-level innovations occur in niches which are spaces that enable individuals and groups to experiment with new technologies, social arrangements, production techniques, and consumption routines. Particularly salient examples at present include electric vehicles, organic urban gardens, locally owned renewable energy generation, and some manifestations of the "sharing economy" (Raven and Verbong, 2009; van Bree et al., 2010; Bell and Cerulli, 2012; Martin et al., 2015). Niche activities generally seek to grow and could potentially come to challenge and perhaps even supersede the incumbent sociotechnical system which operates on and is anchored in the meso-level. Like the dominant mode of social organization addressed by Wright, the established regime also contains structural fault lines that are created by internal contradictions, complexity, institutional cumbersomeness, and technological shortcomings. Movement at either the landscape or niche levels (and especially at both of them) may destabilize incumbent arrangements, and large-scale social change is imputed to occur when emergent activities in niches, regimes, and landscapes are "aligned" temporally and spatially. While these developments generally mature slowly, the actual transition from the existing to an alternative sociotechnical regime may be quite rapid. A classic instance (and one that is extensively cited in the MLP literature) is the replacement of horse-drawn carriages with the combustion-powered automobile, a development that followed a "latency" period of several decades but that became manifest in the course of a few years as a profound "ruptural" social change (Geels, 2005).

Wright's formulation and the MLP share an emphasis on niches as the space for experimentation and for their capacity to destabilize the dominant complex system. Both approaches stress the processes of reproduction that give the prevailing configuration its resilience and durability, the incumbent power structures that benefit from it and provide protection, and the integral, strategically exploitable tensions that are inherent characteristics. The MLP though adds an important element to the social transformation theory of Wright by emphasizing technology as a key element in producing and changing complex societal systems and by pointing out how technical know-how, culture, and institutions co-evolve. It also enriches that understanding by articulating the concept of a landscape and highlighting technological innovation as a potential trigger of change taking place across different scales. At the same time, the social transformation conception puts more emphasis on the role of power in both the stability and the change of complex systems.

The similarity (and in some respects complementarity) of the two approaches also includes their limited attention on the unavoidable dynamics of contestation among social actors, both in competing niches and at the niche-regime interface that are typically conspicuous during periods of disruption. While the MLP emphasizes the importance of "aligning" destabilizing changes at the levels of the landscape and niches, as well as the growing stress within the regime, both frameworks devote less attention to how some interstitial processes might lead to radical systemic transformation while others fall short. The result is that from an empirical perspective neither approach offers much assistance on how to recognize the early signs of approaching change in a dominant system of social organization.

The contemporary work of sociologists Neil Fligstein and Doug McAdam (2012) and the enduring insights of political economist Karl Polanyi (2001) confront these issues by focusing on the behavior and mutual relations of key social actors who are guided by, respectively, self-interest and ideology. Fligstein and McAdam's influential theory of strategic action fields strives to explain how stability and change are achieved by social actors in specific arenas (fields). They synthesize scholarship produced by a wide array of political sociologists, political scientists, economic sociologists, social movement scholars, and organizational sociologists and seek to interpret empirical phenomena of interest to researchers working in these domains.

A strategic action field is a constructed social order in which actors (individual and collective) routinely interact with each other on the basis of overlapping interests, shared understandings about the purpose of the field, relationships to each other, and rules governing legitimate actions. So defined, strategic action fields are fundamental units of collective interaction in society. They are, even when stable over long periods of time, dynamic structures where gradual social changes occur continuously as a result of activities undertaken by incumbents, challengers, and the state. Viewed through the lens of the MLP's typology of niches, regime, and landscape, connectivity within a strategic action field occurs at various levels of aggregation and co-evolution is also an intrinsic feature of related strategic action fields.

According to Fligstein and McAdam, incremental changes are prevalent and transformative changes are less common. The latter could happen when the stable order in a strategic action field—the institutionalized rules of the game, the shared understandings about incumbent-challenger relations and prevailing distribution of power, the appropriate use of technology, and other constitutive elements—become destabilized by changes or prompted by external events in other fields. Borrowing terminology from the MLP, pressures from niches, changes in a landscape, and strains in the incumbent regime may spatially and temporally converge and briefly come into alignment. Under such circumstances, field actors rearrange their mutual connections and power relationships adapt accordingly, followed or accompanied by changes in other domains of the system that the field represents.

This theory offers a broad lens for analyzing and understanding social change by examining developments in multiple fields and accounting for their resultant impacts on one another. Using two cases from the United States—changes in racial politics between 1932 and 1980 and restructuring of the mortgage market between 1969 and 2011—Fligstein and McAdam demonstrate that radical change in a field is the result of strategic actions within that field as well as the destabilizing effects produced by changes in other closely relevant ("proximate") strategic action fields.

From the perspective of research design, examining social change in accordance with the theory of strategic action fields pushes analysts to define the purpose of the field and to identify its key actors and their mutual relationships and institutional rules. It also entails indicating the external fields—state and non-state—that are most important for the reproduction of a particular field and the maintenance of its stability. It is furthermore important to pay attention to the events and processes that are likely to destabilize the field, the challengers who come to the fore to exploit the vulnerable situation, the insurgent alternative visions of the field that are circulating, the social skills with which to pursue incipient agendas, and the actions taken by all parties to affect a new condition of dynamic equilibrium.

The theory of strategic action motivates treatment of consumer society as an assemblage of fields, including the growth-impelled financial system, the marketing industry, the mortgage and home-construction sectors, the transportation infrastructure, and numerous others. Destabilization can occur at various levels—micro, meso, and macro—within a field as well as due to, as noted above, events in other proximate fields. One can also conceptualize a large-scale social change occurring as a result of significant concurrent changes in multiple interlinked fields. From a research perspective, this means that to identify the signs of transformative social change it is useful to map out the relevant strategic actions fields, as well as the field that most directly represents the heart of the incumbent system, and to consider the likelihood and extent of changes within and between them.

In addition to self-interest, ideology plays an important role in motivating, directing, and justifying the behavior of social actors, whether viewed through the lenses of Wright's concept of transformative social change, the MLP, or Fligstein and McAdam's strategic action fields. Normative commitments also set the stage for the actions taken by the state, often with far-reaching consequences at all societal levels. As we observed earlier, the emergence of consumer society was enabled by the widely shared conviction that consumer capitalism was a superior system for generating and distributing societal wealth and for nurturing democracy. In addition, the overall project was informed by a particular interpretation of Keynesianism, namely that mass consumption should be the pillar on which to build a virtuous cycle of economic growth. In the second half of the twentieth century, neoliberalism provided the ideological justification for allowing markets to mediate societal aspirations and problem-solving, thus increasing dependence on economic growth and consumption as the interlinked engines of social progress. The seminal work of Karl Polanyi (2001; see also Block and Somers, 2014) is helpful in conceptualizing the role of ideology—and specifically its political economic expressions—as a driver of social change.

According to Polanyi, all economic systems known up to the end of feudalism in Western Europe were deeply embedded in society and organized around the principles of redistribution, reciprocity (gift-giving), or householding (self-provisioning) and guided by strong social norms. The emergence of a market economy (and eventually of a consumer society) was greatly facilitated by "disembedding" the economy from its social, cultural, and political contexts. In other words, the economic realm increasingly came to be conceptualized as autonomous and separate from other societal realms. This is a false and misleading conception, as economies are always enmeshed in wider organizational systems and guided by government regulations. Polanyi regarded this idea to be utopian and asserted that pursuit of it would inevitably lead to disaster.

Disembedding means in practical terms to turn everything into a marketable good governed by the forces of supply and demand (see also Granovetter, 1985 and Giddens, 1990). To make this work, Polanyi contended, it was necessary to commodify human labor, land, and money (he called these "fictitious commodities" and noted that this practice contributed to exploitation of human labor and land). Commodification also gave rise to the creation of the reductionist concept of *homo economicus*, which refers to an individual who acts in the marketplace strictly according to her own perceived economic self-interest. The ascendency of this notion resulted in replacement of the "embedded" actors who had previously valued cooperation, community, and mutual support and were emblematic of preceding stages of socioeconomic development. In the second half of the twentieth century, neoliberal ideology emerged as a direct descendant of the interlinked processes of disembedding and commodification and the concept of *homo economicus* and gave rise to economic and social policies that triggered the Great Recession of 2008 and are responsible for growing income inequality and other harmful social conditions.

Polanyi further introduced the concept of the "double movement" to describe processes of social change from the perspective of political economy. The disembedding of the economy from the political and social realms and the pervasive belief in the power of a self-correcting free market as the driver of human progress—which Block and Somers (2014) refer to as market fundamentalism—is known as the "first movement." This movement in its purest form leads to human suffering, ecological degradation, and other adverse outcomes. The "second movement" is a reaction to these excesses, usually by way of collective action in the political sphere. The state then responds by means of legislation and policies designed to protect people from the consequences of the first movement.

The recent political economic history of Europe illustrates this progression. From the early nineteenth century onward, the ideology of "self-regulating markets" had the upper hand as a guiding logic for national economic policies. The second movement at the time consisted of organized actions to fight the most horrific impacts of industrialization, but was not successful to sufficiently counteract the first movement. After a "hundred year peace" in the nineteenth century, the political, economic, and social orders collapsed in 1914 because of the internal contradictions of the first movement (exemplified by the gold standard). In the years following World War I, history in essence repeated itself. After a brief struggle with various socialist experiments (for instance, "Red Vienna"), the first movement reasserted itself, a development that initially led to the 1929 economic collapse and its aftermath and, in due course, to World War II.

According to Block and Somers (2014), Polanyi wrote his "Great Transformation" in 1944 to influence the post-war political economic settlements and to try to avoid the mistakes made thirty years earlier, including re-establishment of the gold standard. The Keynes-inspired Bretton Woods agreements, which created a supranational governance structure (the World Bank and the International Monetary Fund) promoting the goals of full employment and a regulated free market, largely reflected his warnings.[4] Social democratic policies in Western Europe and the New Deal-inspired policies like Kennedy's New Frontier and Johnson's Great Society in the United States thrived in this context as the first three post-war decades (roughly 1945 to 1975) witnessed relative social peace and an extraordinary reduction in inequality with respect to income, wealth, and social relations.

However, Keynes' rather technocratic approach—which led to the establishment of similarly technocratic policy institutions—did not sufficiently address the more fundamental issue of a disembedded economy. As a consequence, starting in the mid-1970s, market fundamentalism regained legitimacy and prominence in the form of neoliberalism (after Polanyi and Keynes mistakenly thought that they had been buried once and for all). The results were disastrous for the relatively young movement toward more egalitarianism as well as for the global ecosystem increasingly threatened by mass consumption and economic financialization.

While Polanyi does not focus explicitly on consumerism as the bulwark of modern capitalism, his conceptual contribution to the theme of this book derives from recognition of the importance of political economic ideology in social change. In particular, the systemic tensions created by neoliberal ideology—as illustrated by apparent inseparability between economic growth and sustainability—need to be taken into account when contemplating development of a new system of social organization.

Taken together, the quartet of conceptual approaches outlined above helps us to understand how social change beyond consumer society might transpire and how the contributions comprising this volume constitute a coherent conceptual vision. Some authors explicitly draw on one or more of these four theories while others are more implicit in how they embrace this ensemble of approaches. In the remainder of our discussion, we summarize the chapters that follow and, where appropriate, highlight the connections to the previously outlined synthesis.

The content of this book is organized into three subsequent sections. The next section, entitled "Niches of social innovation," offers case studies of initiatives aimed at modifying familiar systems of production and consumption. These social experiments highlight the role of niche activities in interstitial processes, niche-regime interactions, and strategic action fields and shed light on the activities of key actors in a number of different provisioning domains.

In Chapter 2, Juliet Schor and Robert Wengronowitz analyze the recently emergent sharing economy through a cultural lens. The authors seek to understand the extent to which new forms of platform-based economic exchange might be the seedbed of nascent post-consumer lifeways that are more egalitarian, communal, and environmentally sustainable. Drawing on the work of sociologist

Pierre Bourdieu, they introduce the concept of eco-habitus, which entails a preference for "authentic" localism, an emphasis on manual skills rather than abstract thinking, and an affinity for small-scale production and do-it-yourself (DIY) activities. Eco-habitus also celebrates the community and social relationships. The authors contend that "high cultural capital" consumers have been the early adopters of platform-economy innovation and are the primary embodiment of eco-habitus. Notably, this development represents a striking inversion of the traditional values distinguishing conventionally high and low cultural capital consumers. The former have traditionally shied away from manual work, locally made products, and sharing with strangers in favor of abstraction, individualized consumption, and cosmopolitan shopping.

Schor and Wengronowitz's findings, consistent with the work of political economist Karl Polanyi on the social embeddedness of the economy, highlight the power of free-market ideology even among proponents of social change who purport to reject these currently dominant values. The result is that in the strategic action field of the sharing economy incumbent actors have had little difficulty reorienting some of these new business models in ways that make them consistent with notions of "platform capitalism" rather than the "sharing economy." Looking toward the future of more collaborative modes of consumption, Schor and Wengronowitz see two competing possibilities: the business-as-usual scenario will continue the trajectory of translating and absorbing sharing into dominant forms of market exchange or we will see a radical departure where this mode of consumption contributes to a refashioned economy that is more embedded in society. The emerging progressive movement within the sharing economy that advocates for radical, anti-capitalist alternatives gives some credence to the latter scenario.

Chapter 3 by Marlyne Sahakian continues this discussion of the sharing economy and she, too, draws on insights originally developed by Karl Polanyi to amplify the distinction between commodified modes of collaboration and forms of exchange that enhance social cohesion. This contribution formulates a typology that brings into sharper focus provisioning practices consistent with the social and solidarity economy and draws on fieldwork involving affiliated enterprises in Geneva and its surrounding area. Sahakian profiles six organizations in western Switzerland including a mobility cooperative, an electronic platform that matches drivers with underutilized parking spaces, a public bicycle program, a creative scheme that enables neighbors to exchange household objects via their personal mailboxes, a project that retrofits newspaper-vending machines as micro-sized sharing depositories, and a website that facilitates the mutual exchange of various goods and services. While these cases are mostly very small-scale experiments, the chapter points to the importance of the Internet in enabling these alternative consumption routines and the ways in which new social norms become instantiated. Resonating with the MLP's notion of niches as "protected spaces," Sahakian emphasizes the importance of government support for these initiatives, especially regarding the apportionment of risk, if they are to gain wider relevance in terms of scale and replicability.

In Chapter 4, Emily Huddart Kennedy examines a related case pertaining to the "eat-local" movement. Using social practice theory and extensive empirical research, she describes the political narratives that circulate in the Canadian local food movement and inquires whether they might hold potential for transformative social change. This chapter demonstrates that the most visible figures within the strategic action field of local food increasingly realize that they have to confront the powerful incumbent system of industrial food production if further progress is to be made. Awareness of this challenge is creating tension between a politically astute leadership and others in the movement who, for the most part, hold to strongly rooted twin beliefs that food activism should be apolitical and that any political intent should be expressed through individualized market behavior. Despite the very real prospect of alienating adherents—and thus undermining economic influence—some leaders in the Canadian local food movement evince increasing willingness to engage with the political and ideological domains. They have begun to openly discuss the shortcomings of the dominant agro-food system and, in particular, to shed light on the social inequities it generates. Kennedy's work highlights the process of contestation among actors in this strategic action field and the conscious deployment of interstitial strategies by its frontrunners through the framing of the eat-local movement as a collective political agent.

Chapter 5 by Tom Bauler, Bonno Pel, and Julia Backhaus focuses on social innovation which is a topic that has attracted increasing attention over the last few years among European academics, activists, and policy makers as an important complement to top-down government interventions. The "transformative" variant of this approach challenges dominant institutions, leading to "irreversible, persistent adjustment in societal values, imaginaries and behaviors." Echoing themes discussed elsewhere in this book, Bauler et al.'s contribution examines the vulnerability of these projects to capture by incumbent institutions. The authors report on two cases that seek to promote radical changes in economic and social relations: the International Network of Social and Solidarity Economy (generally known by its French acronym, RIPESS) and the Basic Income Earth Network (BIEN).

The ideologically motivated ambitions of the two organizations can be understood as part of what Polanyi referred to as the "second movement." By examining the strategic action fields of each case, Bauler and his colleagues describe the tensions inherent in pursuing transformative social change between, on the one hand, domesticating radical ideas and, on the other hand, remaining ideologically consistent but politically marginal. This is the crucial dilemma for strategists seeking to infiltrate the interstitial spaces of the dominant system. In the RIPESS case, the social and solidarity principles have been successfully translated into specific locally relevant schemes, but mostly in attenuated form. With respect to BIEN, next to strident proponents of basic income are other more pragmatic actors in the broader movement who advocate on behalf of policies such as tax-exemption or flexible social security as useful social experiments that constructively advance the debate. Notably, the chapter's authors observe that although capture leads to less transformative changes, a certain degree of concerted engagement enables long-term transformative change.

In Chapter 6, Tally Katz-Gerro, Predrag Cvetičanin, and Adrian Leguina demonstrate how a sharp and protracted economic crisis can destabilize prevailing consumption practices and, under certain circumstances, set them on a trajectory toward greater environmental sustainability. They focus specifically on four countries in the greater Balkan region of southeastern Europe (Serbia, Bosnia-Herzegovina, Croatia, and Slovenia) which have been seriously affected by the economic contraction and subsequent stagnation triggered by the financial meltdown that began in 2007. This chapter synthesizes and builds on a growing body of research on how economic crises variously affect household consumption practices and contribute to the instigation of novel routines. Not surprisingly, socioeconomic status, educational attainment, and geographic residency (urban vs. rural) are key factors in understanding the unevenness of these processes, but also salient is each country's developmental condition and degree of integration into the global economy in terms of reliance on consumer-oriented lifestyles. Katz-Gerro and colleagues develop a taxonomy that delineates five strategies for how households cope with the strain of economic crisis and contribute to social change: proactive self-provisioning, passive endurance, consumption reduction, proactive with no consumption curtailment, and mixed forms of adjustment.

The third section of this volume entitled "Post-consumerist transitions" turns attention toward more macro-level analyses of social change. Chapter 7, by Cindy Isenhour, employs an anthropological perspective to argue that economic exchange is tightly bound up with culture, as well as social and political systems and historical circumstances. Considering the recent history of consumer culture, she "understands culture not as a thing but as a process deeply influenced by the material and structural elements of society, the strong ideational pull of past human experiences, and our encounters with new natural, economic, political, or intellectual environments." A transition beyond the culture of consumption therefore requires more than a change in values and practices as is often presupposed by leading critics of contemporary consumerism. Social change at this scale rather requires transformation of the underlying and prefiguring economic, institutional, and political domains. Isenhour then draws on Polanyi's work to hypothesize on the possible trajectory of a shift beyond consumer society. She highlights growing societal tensions around the impoverishment of many socioeconomic groups in the United States, the lack of opportunity that households encounter, the extent of environmental degradation, and the degree to which the costs of growth are externalized on society's most vulnerable populations and future generations—all outcomes that are largely attributable to the hegemony of market fundamentalism in the country over the past forty years. This strain may signal the cresting of the "first movement" and open a political space for the "second movement" which would entail expressions of collective civil outrage and subsequent state-lead institutional changes aimed at constraining or undermining the social and economic structures that enable consumer capitalism.

In Isenhour's rendition, the second movement would make explicit the connections between unregulated consumer capitalism, dramatic inequalities, environmental degradation, and overconsumption, thus bringing together the hitherto relatively separate social justice and ecological movements. Both would draw on already existing strong cultural values in the United States of equal opportunity and justice which may be the only way to challenge powerful neoliberal appeals to freedom and abundance.

Inge Røpke in Chapter 8 focuses on reform of the financial sector which will invariably be important for any transition beyond consumer society. Most recent literature on the sustainability dimensions of finance highlights consumer credit, protections from predatory lending, and pensions and insurance. In contrast, she takes a wider view and stresses the role of the financial system as a driver of unsustainable consumption and, indirectly, a contributing factor to many ecological problems. During the first three decades following World War II, the economic growth model was based on strong linkage between, on the one hand, productivity and wages and, on the other hand, the state's commitment to full employment and public investment. The financial sector was, in a Polanyian sense, embedded in the macroeconomy and served to support it. As the post-war model was supplanted by neoliberal ideology, the economy became increasingly disembedded from society and the financial system lost its attachment to the real economy. Røpke emphasizes that these process entailed struggles over ideology and economic power and were further propelled by the advent of several key technological innovations.

The resulting financialization of the economy enabled increasingly risky speculation while the allure of large profits in the housing market generated incentives in the United States and elsewhere to build ever larger, more luxurious, and thus more profitable homes. Along the way, materials and energy consumption increased upward while easy credit drew even people with modest means into the game. The human suffering and dislocation during the subsequent Great Recession and the successful preclusion of radical reforms by powerful incumbent actors have been amply documented. These developments are eerily reminiscent of the "first movement" described by Polanyi before the outbreak of the two world wars during the twentieth century.

Røpke proposes several reforms of the financial system directed toward increasing systemic resilience, reducing risks and complexity, redirecting credit and investments, and creating disincentives for speculation. The overarching goal of these recommendations is to re-embed the financial system in the macroeconomy. If (and this is a big if) these reforms could be successfully implemented, one could readily envision a future where there is less upward pressure on consumption.

Chapter 9 by Anders Hayden and Jeffrey Wilson discusses the technocratic approach of seeking to induce social change through government adoption of so-called beyond gross domestic product (GDP) indicators of societal progress. Drawing on the Canadian and UK experiences, the authors analyze the reasons for the relative lack of success with formal implementation of various GDP alternatives. When originally introduced in 1937 by Nobel laureate Simon Kuznets, and first applied by policy makers during following years, GDP reflected the widely shared belief that economic growth was the surest way to improve human well-being. The ongoing and largely unreflective deployment of this particular policy tool is a testament to the remarkable appeal of this narrative. The conclusion that proponents of GDP alternatives derive from this experience is that the most effective strategy for a change in priorities—from economic growth to other more multifaceted understandings of societal progress—is to move to a new set of indicators.

Research by Hayden and Wilson sheds important light on the behavior of actors in this strategic action field and shows how they have been unable to speak with one voice and incapable of influencing the state or mobilizing a popular bottom-up demand for change. The reasons for failure include the multiple and inconsistent visions and agendas advanced by proponents, the difficulty communicating this seemingly powerful idea to actors in other fields, and the political and ideological strength of skeptics and other opponents. While it is obviously not presently possible to determine whether the interventions proposed by the Beyond GDP Movement will in the future become marginally important technocratic policy tools or fizzle out altogether, more transformative scenarios are also plausible. For example, popular social movements built on currently growing societal discontent may usher in a new narrative about human well-being. Alternatively, politicians may find themselves unable to deliver on public expectations of ever-increasing GDP, as some analysts anticipate is emerging to be the case for the developed world (Costanza et al., 2014; Gordon, 2016; see also Irwin, 2016). Under such circumstances, they would be obliged to look to other means to substantiate their political performance. When such interstitial spaces open up, the GDP alternatives may provide a powerful mechanism for affecting social change.

In Chapter 10, Derk Loorbach uses the MLP to explore what types of governance might advance a radical transition beyond consumer society and its commitment to increasing economic growth. He takes as a starting point the historical transformation that brought about the era of modernization—a process that was impelled by the need to address persistent societal problems such as hunger, inadequate healthcare, unevenly allocated political rights, and others. Loorbach conceptualizes this radical systemic social change as the outcome of a "family of transitions" in various subsystems. These lower order transitions share a number of characteristics that constitute the design principles of the modern state: centralized coordination, linear innovation, and inexpensive fossil fuels. A radical transition to transcend consumer society would have to fundamentally challenge this ideology of incumbent institutions, markets, and practices. Loorbach stresses the importance of three emergent forces for change—self-organization, renewable energy, and systemic innovation—and proposes "panarchy governance" as an overarching concept. He defines this model as "the context in which multiple forms or regimes of governance co-exist and develop in an unplanned or centrally coordinated way" and emphasizes that transformative institutions capable of dealing with diversity, surprise, and uncertainty would compete without prescribing specific solutions. Panarchy, somewhat paradoxically, would require strong government, clear boundaries, guiding sustainability principles, capacity for systematic development of skills, and conditions to enable broad participation.

The final section of the book is entitled "Social change toward post-consumer society" and in Chapter 11 we revisit the full span of this volume to assess what we have learned. We conclude that broad sociocultural changes to transcend consumer society are unlikely to occur without deeper reorganization of the macroeconomy and political priorities. To get the transition under way, there is a great need to develop a coherent "second movement," which might arise to counteract the problems that have been created by prevalent modes of market fundamentalism. While the obstacles to such mobilization are considerable, there are signs that the foundational pillars of consumer society are faltering and it may not be possible for much longer to pacify intensifying civic discontent with neoliberal sloganeering. This book is conceived out of a desire to prepare for that moment.

Notes

1   The word "consume" derives from the Latin *consumere* formed from *con* meaning "altogether" and *sumere* "take up." The OED finds that the first published use of the term "consumer society" appeared in a 1920 book by Norman Hapgood entitled *The Advancing Hour* in which he wrote "The consumer is the principal person considered, and the worker, employee or producer, within the consumer society, has had thus far little special representation." Hapgood was a New York City-based journalist, editor, and author and he helped to promote establishment of the League of Nations. He was appointed by President Woodrow Wilson to serve as American ambassador to Denmark and was an early writer to denounce Henry Ford for anti-Semitism.

2   Historians of consumption have variously traced the emergence of contemporary consumerist practices to fourteenth-century China, fifteenth-century Italy, and elsewhere. Mass consumption in these societies, though, tended to be limited to a fairly narrow segment of the population and large-scale material acquisition was not regarded as a central feature of societal organization as became the case in the United States and other countries during the years after 1945. For extremely useful reviews of the international history of consumption, see Stearns (2006) and Trentmann (2016).

3   See also the SPREAD Sustainable Lifestyles 2050 project which was conducted between January 2011 and December 2012 with financial support from the European Commission's Seventh Framework Funding Scheme. Details at www.sustainable-lifestyles.eu.

4   Although the World Bank and International Monetary Fund are portrayed by Block et al. (2014) as manifestations of the "second movement," they quickly developed into pillars of advancing free-market ideology and practices, especially in developing countries. These developments, and eventual emergence of the World Trade Organization, led to divisive protests in Seattle in 1999 and establishment of a vibrant anti-globalization social movement (often referred to as "Another World is Possible") and creation of the World Social Forum which can be considered as more credible manifestations of the second movement.

References

Angus, I. (2016) *Facing the Anthropocene: Fossil Capitalism and the Crisis of the Earth System*. New York: Monthly Review Press.

Bell, S. and Cerulli, C. (2012) "Emerging community food production and pathways for urban landscape transitions," *Emergence: Complexity and Organization* 14(1):31–44.

Block, F. and Somers, M. (2014) *The Power of Market Fundamentalism: Karl Polanyi's Critique*. Cambridge, MA: Harvard University Press.

Braudel, F. (1995) *A History of Civilizations*, Richard Mayne, trans. New York: Penguin.

Brown, C. (1995) *American Standards of Living, 1918–1988*. Hoboken, NJ: Wiley-Blackwell.

Brown, H. and Vergragt, P. (2008) "Bounded socio-technical experiments as agents of systemic change: the case of zero-energy residential building," *Technological Forecasting and Social Change* 75(1):107–130.

Brown, H. and Vergragt, P. (2016) "From consumerism to wellbeing: toward a cultural transition?" *Journal of Cleaner Production* 132:308–317.

Brynjolfsson, E. and McAfee, A. (2016) *The Second Machine Age: Work, Progress, and Prosperity in a Time of Brilliant Technologies*. New York: W. W. Norton.

Cohen, L. (2003) *Consumers' Republic: The Politics of Mass Consumption in Postwar America*. New York: Vintage.

Cohen, M. (2017) *The Future of Consumer Society: Prospects for Sustainability in the New Economy*. New York: Oxford University Press.

Collins, R. (2002) *More: The Politics of Economic Growth in Postwar America*. New York: Oxford University Press.

Costanza, R., Kubiszewski, I., Giovannini, E., Lovins, H., McGlade, J., Pickett, K., Ragnarsdóttir, K., Roberts, D., De Vogli, R., and Wilkinson, R. (2014) "Time to leave GDP behind," *Nature* 505(7483):283–285.

D'Alisa, G., Demaria, F., and Kallis, G. (eds.) (2015) *Degrowth: A Vocabulary for a New Era*. New York: Routledge.

De Grazia, V. (2005) *Irresistible Empire: America's Advance Through Twentieth-Century Europe*. Cambridge, MA: Belknap Press.

Doyle, R. and Davies, A. (2013) "Towards sustainable household consumption: exploring a practice oriented, participatory backcasting approach for sustainable home heating practices in Ireland," *Journal of Cleaner Production* 48:260–271.

Fligstein, N. and McAdam, D. (2015) *A Theory of Fields*. New York: Oxford University Press.

Ford, M. (2015) *Rise of the Robots: Technology and the Threat of a Jobless Future*. New York: Basic Books.

Francks, P. and Hunter, J. (eds.) (2012) *The Historical Consumer: Consumption and Everyday Life in Japan, 1850–2000*. New York: Palgrave Macmillan.

Galbraith, J. (1958) *The Affluent Society*. New York: Houghton Mifflin.

Garon, S. (2011) *Beyond Our Means: Why America Spends While the World Saves*. Princeton, NJ: Princeton University Press.

Garth, K. (2010) *As China Goes, So Goes the World: How Chinese Consumers Are Transforming Everything*. New York: Hill and Wang.

Geels, F. (2002) "Technological transitions as evolutionary reconfiguration processes: a multi-level perspective and a case-study," *Research Policy* 31(8–9):1257–1274.

Geels, F. (2005) "The dynamics of transitions in socio-technical systems: a multi-level analysis of the transition pathway from horse-drawn carriages to automobiles (1860–1930)," *Technology Analysis & Strategic Management* 17(4):445–476.

Geels, F. and Schot, J. (2007) "Typology of sociotechnical transition pathways," *Research Policy* 36(3):399–417.

Giddens, A. (1990) *The Consequences of Modernity*. Palo Alto, CA: Stanford University Press.

Glickman, L. (1999) *A Living Wage: American Workers and the Making of Consumer Society*. Ithaca, NY: Cornell University Press.

Gordon, R. (2016) *The Rise and Fall of American Growth: The U.S. Standard of Living Since the Civil War*. Princeton, NJ: Princeton University Press.

Granovetter, M. (1985) "Economic action and social structure: the problem of embeddedness," *American Journal of Sociology* 91(3):481–510.

Green, K. and Vergragt, P. (2002) "Towards sustainable households: a methodology for developing sustainable technological and social innovations," *Futures* 34(5):381-400.

Halkier, B. (2013) "Sustainable lifestyles in a new economy: a practice theoretical perspective on change behavior campaigns and sustainability issues," in Cohen, M., Brown, H., and Vergragt, P. (eds.), *Innovations in Sustainable Consumption: New Economics, Socio-technical Transitions, and Social Practices*. Northampton, MA: Edward Elgar, pp. 209–228.

Harris, J. (2013) "The macroeconomics of development without throughput growth," in Cohen, M., Brown, H., and Vergragt, P. (eds.), *Innovations in Sustainable Consumption: New Economics, Socio-technical Transitions, and Social Practices*. Northampton, MA: Edward Elgar, pp. 31–47.

Harvey, D. (2007) *A Brief History of Neoliberalism*. New York: Oxford University Press.

Horowitz, D. (2005) *The Anxieties of Affluence: Critiques of American Consumer Culture, 1939–1979*. Amherst, MA: University of Massachusetts Press.

Humphery, K. (2010) *Excess: Anti-consumerism in the West*. Malden, MA: Polity Press.

Irwin, N. (2016) "We're in a low growth world. How did we get here?" *New York Times*, August 6.

Jackson, T. (2009) *Prosperity Without Growth: Economics for a Finite Planet*. London: Earthscan.

Kallis, G. (2011) "In defence of degrowth," *Ecological Economics* 70(5):873–880.

Kelly, M. (2012) *Owning Our Future: The Emerging Ownership Revolution*. San Francisco, CA: Berrett-Koehler.

Kemp, R. (1994) "Technology and the transition to environmental sustainability: the problem of technological regime shifts," *Futures* 26(10):1023–1046.

Kemp, R. and Van Lente, H. (2013) "The dual challenge of sustainability transitions: different trajectories and criteria," in Cohen, M., Brown, H., and Vergragt, P. (eds.), *Innovations in Sustainable Consumption: New Economics, Socio-technical Transitions, and Social Practices*. Northampton, MA: Edward Elgar, pp. 115–132.

Kemp, R. and Rotmans, J. (2005) "The management of the co-evolution of technical, environmental and social systems," in Hemmelskamp, J. and Weber, M. (eds.) *Towards Environmental Innovation Systems*. Berlin: Springer, pp. 33–56.

King, M. (2016) *The End of Alchemy: Money, Banking, and the Future of the Global Economy*. New York: W. W. Norton.

Lanier, J. (2013) *Who Owns the Future?* New York: Simon and Schuster.

Lefebvre, G., Procacci, G., Merrington, J., Hill, C., Hobsbawm, E., Dobb, M., Sweezy, P., and Takahashi, K. (1985) *The Transition from Feudalism to Capitalism*. New York: Verso.

Levin, Y. (2016) *The Fractured Republic: Renewing America's Social Contract in the Age of Individualism*. New York: Basic Books.

Lewis, J. (2013) *Beyond Consumer Capitalism: Media and the Limits to Imagination*. Malden, MA: Polity Press.

Lorek, S. and Fuchs, D. (2013) "Strong sustainable consumption governance: precondition for a degrowth path?" *Journal of Cleaner Production* 38:36–43.

Markard, J., Raven, R., and Truffer, B. (2012) "Sustainability transitions: an emerging field of research and its prospects," *Research Policy* 41(6):955–967.

Martin, C., Upham, P., and Budd, L. (2015) "Commercial orientation in grassroots social innovation: insights from the sharing economy," *Ecological Economics* 118(1):240–251.

Mason, P. (2015) *Postcapitalism: A Guide to Our Future*. New York: Farrar, Straus and Giroux.

Monbiot, G. (2016) *How Did We Get Into This Mess? Politics, Equality, Nature*. New York: Verso.

Mont, O., Neuvonen, A., and Lähteenoja, S. (2014) "Sustainable lifestyles 2050: stakeholder visions, emerging practices and future research," *Journal of Cleaner Production* 63:24–32.

Packard, V. (1960) *The Waste Makers*. New York: D. McKay.

Parry, I., Veung, C., and Heine, D. (2014) *How Much Carbon Pricing is in Countries' Own Interests? The Critical Role of Co-Benefits*. Washington, DC: International Monetary Fund. www.imf.org/external/pubs/cat/longres.aspx?sk=41924.0.

Polanyi, K. (2001 [1944]) *The Great Transformation: The Political and Economic Origins of Our Time*. Boston, MA: Beacon Press.

Pulju, R. (2013) *Women and Mass Consumer Society in Postwar France*. New York: Cambridge University Press.

Quist, J. and Vergragt, P. (2006) "Past and future of back-casting: the shift to stakeholder participation and a proposal for a methodological framework," *Futures* 38(9):1027–1045.

Quist, J., Thissen, W., and Vergragt, P. (2011) "The impact and spin-off of participatory backcasting: from vision to niche," *Technological Forecasting and Social Change* 78(5):883–897.

Raskin, P., Banuri, T., Gallopin, G., Gutman, P., Hammond, A., Kates, R., and Swart, R. (2002) *Great Transition: The Promise and Lure of the Times Ahead*. Boston: Global Scenario Group.

Raskin, P. (2011) "Imagine all the people: advancing global citizens movement," *Kosmos: A Journal for Global Transformation*, Spring/Summer. www.kosmosjournal.org/article/imagine-all-the-people-advancing-a-global-citizens-movement.

Raven, P. and Verbong, G. (2009) "Boundary crossing innovations: case studies from the energy domain," *Technology in Society* 31(1):85–93.

Reich, R. (2016) *Saving Capitalism: For the Many, Not the Few*. New York: Vintage.

Schäpke, N. and Rauschmayer, F. (2014) "Going beyond efficiency: including altruistic motives in behavioral models for sustainability transitions to address sufficiency," *Sustainability: Science, Practice, and Policy* 10(1):29–44.

Scitovsky, T. (1976) *The Joyless Economy: An Inquiry into Human Satisfaction and Consumer Dissatisfaction*. New York: Oxford University Press.

Seyfang, G. (2009) *The New Economics of Sustainable Consumption: Seeds of Change*. New York: Palgrave Macmillan.

Shove, E. and Walker, G. (2007) "CAUTION! Transitions ahead: politics, practice, and sustainable transition management," *Environment and Planning, A* 39(4):763–770.

Shove, E., Watson, M., Hand, M., and Ingram, J. (2007) *The Design of Everyday Life*. New York: Berg.

Shrivastava, A. and Kothari, A. (2012) *Churning the Earth: The Making of Global India*. New York: Viking.

Smith, A., Stirling, A., and Berkhout, F. (2005) "The governance of sustainable socio-technical transitions," *Research Policy* 34(10):1491–1510.

Spaargaren, G. (2013) "The cultural dimension of sustainable consumption practices: an exploration in theory and policy," Cohen, M., Brown, H., and Vergragt, P. (eds.), *Innovations in Sustainable Consumption: New Economics, Socio-technical Transitions, and Social Practices*. Northampton, MA: Edward Elgar, pp. 229–251.

Spangenberg, J. (2014) "Institutional change for strong sustainable consumption: sustainable consumption and the degrowth economy," *Sustainability: Science, Practice, and Policy* 10(1):62–77.

Speth, G. (2015) *Getting to the Next System: Guideposts on the Way to a New Political Economy*. Washington, DC: The Next System Project. http://thenextsystem.org/wpcontent/uploads/2015/10/GettingToTheNextSystem.pdf.

Stearns, P. (2006) *Consumerism in World History: The Global Transformation of Desire*. New York: Routledge.

Sterman, J. (2012) "Sustaining sustainability: creating a systems science in a fragmented academy and polarized world," in Weinstein, M. and Turner, R. (eds.), *Sustainability Science: The Emerging Paradigm and the Urban Environment*. New York: Springer, pp. 21–58.

Strasser, S., McGovern, C., and Judt, M. (eds.) (1998) *Getting and Spending: European and American Consumer Societies in the Twentieth Century*. New York: Cambridge University Press.

Streeck, W. (2016) *How Will Capitalism End?* New York: Verso.

Therborn, G. (2013) *The Killing Fields of Inequality*. Malden, MA: Polity Press.

Trentmann, F. (2016) *Empire of Things: How We Became a World of Consumers, From the Fifteenth Century to the Twenty-First*. New York: HarperCollins.

Van Bree, B., Verbong, G., and Kramer, G. (2010) "A multi-level perspective on the introduction of hydrogen and battery-electric vehicles," *Technological Forecasting and Social Change* 77(4):529–540.

Ventura, P. (2012) *Neoliberal Culture: Living with American Neoliberalism*. New York: Routledge.

Victor, P. (2008) *Managing Without Growth: Slower by Design, Not Disaster*. Northampton, MA: Edward Elgar.

Wells, P. (2013) *Business Models for Sustainability*. Northampton, MA: Edward Elgar.

Wright, E. (2010) *Envisioning Real Utopias*. New York: Verso.

Part II
Niches of social innovation

2 The new sharing economy
Enacting the eco-habitus

Juliet B. Schor and Robert Wengronowitz

Introduction

The emergence of the "sharing economy," a sprawling entity that ranges from local clothing swaps to the global rental platform Airbnb, has spawned a heated debate between proponents and critics (Schor, 2014). On the one hand, what we call the new sharing economy, also known as "collaborative consumption," is seen as a progressive, disruptive force that makes economies more efficient and distributes value to consumers (Botsman, 2010; *The Economist*, 2013; Geron, 2013). It is also thought to reduce ecological footprints while creating economic opportunities and decentralized collaboration, including for ordinary people (Gansky, 2010; Sperling, 2015). Many see peer-to-peer (P2P) consumption as more genuine than the de-personalized culture of the mainstream consumer sector. These kinds of exchanges harken back to an era when people did more provisioning for themselves, lived in denser connection with others, and were less motivated by money. Collaborative consumption meshes well with an emerging consumer ethos that rejects mass production in favor of personalization, artisanal work (rather than factory labor), local economies (over global ones), authenticity (over a culture of plastic), and deeper engagement with the material world (Carfagna et al., 2014). It feels "real," a term that came up repeatedly in our research sites. To borrow Schumacher's (1973) phrase, the new sharing economy seems small and beautiful, as if people really mattered.

In contrast, progressives tend to a more dystopian view (Baker, 2014; Scholz, 2016b; Slee, 2014, 2015, 2016). Influential political economist Robert Reich (2015) has dubbed it a "share the scraps" economy. Like other critical commentators, his concerns center around providers and the sporadic, often low-paid, on-demand "gig" work that characterizes some platform labor (Henwood, 2015; Kessler, 2014; Scholz, 2016b). Anthony Kalamar (2013) coined the term "sharewashing" to describe a new form of "greenwashing" in which companies capture the symbolic value of ethical or altruistic sharing for material benefit while engaging in exploitative labor practices and ecologically intensive activities. Others argue that the autonomy of producers is weakened via software that creates a "Big Brother" surveillance dimension, strongly associated with the continually operating, always nearby "smart" phone (Davies, 2015; Rosenblat,

2015). Progressives also argue that the entrance of venture capital into the sector has led to cooptation, turning what began as a progressive, socially transformative idea (sharing) into "platform capitalism" (Lobo, 2014). Critics point to the enormous wealth being extracted by founders and early investors (Scholz, 2016b).

While these important questions have dominated the popular debate, this chapter focuses on another set of issues that we believe will influence the trajectory of this sector: the cultural values and practices of platform participants. As the activities continue to expand, it is vital to understand the social forces within the field and their influence on consumer culture more broadly: does collaborative consumption represent something "new under the sun" or is it evolving into normative consumer culture? This focus reflects our belief that not only economic factors but also cultural ones influence social outcomes, particularly in the consumer arena. By normative consumer culture, we refer to the dominant consumer culture in the United States, a social construction that has been described in a large historical and sociological literature (Firat and Dholakia, 1998; Schor, 1998; Cohen 2003). While it is beyond the scope of this chapter to elaborate the nature of contemporary consumer culture, for our purposes aspects of normative consumer culture which differ from collaborative consumption are the importance of ownership (versus access to goods), the value of branded products, individualist approaches to consumption, relatively impersonal retail interactions, indifference to environmental impacts and the backstory of products, and shopping as a leisure activity. Collaborative consumption aims to remake consumption relations to render them more personal, ecologically sustainable, and communal.

Our discussion is based on five years of qualitative research that began in 2011, an early stage in the emergence of the sector. A team of sociologists from Boston College and Boston University has conducted the research reported on here.[1] We have completed seven cases in the collaborative consumption space. Three are nonprofits: a time bank in which participants trade services and each member's time is equivalent in value regardless of the service being performed; a food swap where members prepare foods and exchange them with others; and a makerspace where members share a workspace and tools and engage in various types of production ranging from high-tech robots to handcrafted furniture. Three of our cases are for-profit platforms. Airbnb matches travelers with hosts who rent out spare rooms or entire apartments and houses. Turo (formerly RelayRides) is a similar platform but for automobiles—participants rent their personal cars to individual consumers. TaskRabbit is a platform for service provision—peers rent out their labor for anything from furniture assembly to data entry. Our last case (open education) includes nonprofits and for-profits in the education space where participants teach one another skills and knowledge outside of formal educational institutions (e.g., Coursera, SkillShare). (For more detailed findings on a number of our cases refer to Carfagna, 2014; Attwood-Charles and Schor, 2015; Schor and Fitzmaurice, 2015a; Schor et al., 2016.)

While we have conducted a number of discourse analyses on the new sharing sector, the bulk of our data comes from interviews and surveys. We have interviewed and surveyed approximately 250 users and conducted hundreds of hours of participant observations. Interviews ranged from 45 to 90 minutes and included respondents' personal narratives, how they became involved in the platform, their motives, attitudes toward risk, and the nature of their experiences with these platforms and sites. Our interviews were concentrated in an urban area in the northeastern United States, though several were conducted elsewhere. Our participants are in the 18–34 age range. We chose this group because they are the early adopters and innovators in this sector, as well as its most active participants (Rossa, 2015).

We begin by making a number of general points to situate the sector historically. The chapter then turns to our cultural analysis, which is centered on the idea of a specific "ecological" habitus that we find among our participants. After describing this particular habitus we explain our findings. We conclude with consideration of the sector's potential contribution to progressive, sustainable social change.

A brief history of the new sharing economy

Types of sharing initiatives

Following Schor and Fitzmaurice (2015a), we characterize collaborative consumption as consisting of five major categories: re-circulation of goods, increasing the utilization of durable assets, exchange of labor services, sharing of productive assets, and a hybrid model that combines service and goods provision. (We exclude crowdfunding, which is an important related practice.) We trace the origins of the sharing sector to 1995 and the creation of eBay and Craigslist (Schor and Fitzmaurice, 2015a), both of which have become mainstream consumer outlets.[2] These sites were constituted as secondary markets for consumer goods, although they have now expanded to include a variety of goods and services.

The second category of sharing platform involves optimizing the use of durable goods and other economically productive assets. This is often referred to as "collaborative consumption." In this segment, the historic forerunner has been tool-libraries; in the digital space, Zipcar. In lodging, Couchsurfing was first, followed by Airbnb. Numerous other assets are also now available for rental: garages, attics, parking spaces, and residential lawns. Nonprofits are furthermore mobilizing idle capacity in publicly owned assets, such as fruit trees. In their peer-to-peer versions, these innovations provide people with low-cost access to goods and allow owners to earn money or acquire goods. In general, the economic effects of the 2009 recession provided a huge boost to these platforms, and can be credited with launching the sector overall.

The third type of sharing practice is the exchange of labor services. The historic pioneer is time banking, which, in the United States, began in the 1980s, as a way to provide work for unemployed people (Cahn and Rowe, 1992; Seyfang, 2004; Collom, 2011; Collom et al., 2012). In contrast to some of the other originating platforms, time banks have not scaled. Among the for-profits, there have been many entrants to monetized service exchanges: TaskRabbit, Postmates,

Favor, Uber, and Lyft. (Based on common convention, we exclude MTurk, Upwork, and similar sites. This exclusion is hard to explain analytically. However, the sharing economy was originally consumption based, and is still largely made up of companies that are consumer oriented. By contrast MTurk, Upwork and similar sites are used by businesses.) While Uber and Lyft have grown rapidly, due largely, we believe, to the presence of significant rents in the taxi industry on account of the legal barriers to entry, by contrast, the platforms focusing on errands and delivery have been less successful. There is a lot of competition in the errands and delivery sites, they are selling services that many consumers are used to doing for themselves, and the remuneration tends to be rather low on many platforms.

The fourth segment involves sharing productive assets. Examples include co-working-, hacker-, and makerspaces. Lending libraries for books, tools, and other goods also fit within this category. Cooperatives are the historic corollary. Coops have been operating in the United States since the nineteenth century, with upticks in formation in the 1970s and again during the last decade (Alperovitz, 2011). While cooperatives do not entail stranger sharing (see below) they are increasingly considered part of the sharing economy. Recently there has been considerable energy for a movement of "platform cooperativism" (Scholz, 2014; Schneider and Scholz, 2015).

A final category is a hybrid of goods and service provision and involves the exchange of home-produced goods, such as food, crafts, and clothing. The craft marketplace Etsy is the largest of these sites. The food category has many platforms—for example, Feastly, Kitchensurfing, and EatWith. There are also many small, predominantly offline initiatives in this category, such as the food swap that we have been studying. These offline spaces tend to focus on the creation of more social connection and social experience, while also providing a useful service.

Historical notes

The discourse surrounding the sharing economy tends to overemphasize novelty; therefore, we note a few historical points before turning to our findings. First, there is a strong link between collaborative consumption and the earlier open-source and free-software movements, which have harnessed the mostly volunteer labor of software engineers to write code and to solve problems collectively (Benkler, 2004, 2006). The success, in particular, of the open-source movement paved the way for other kinds of peer-produced and shared-online content such as file sharing, video posting, and music swapping, or crowdsourcing of information in cases such as Wikipedia. While in the United States these activities are not generally credited as part of the sharing economy, there is a strong historical and global connection between the emergence of online P2P efforts and the digital sharing platforms that we research.

A second historical point is to recognize that sharing has long been a part of human social relations. There has been a tendency in the discourse about collaborative consumption to assert or assume that sharing is a new practice. Participants employ a discourse of innovation, trendiness, and technological progress. This characterization suffers from class and race myopia, as well as what historians call "presentism" (blindness to the past and judging it based on the values and ideas of the present) (Hull, 1979). Humans have always collaborated and shared—it is one of our defining characteristics as a species and is traceable to our foraging ancestors (Gintis et al., 2005). Sharing reproduces social relations and solidifies cultural practices (Gell, 1986; Belk, 2007, 2010).

Furthermore, sharing is not just a relic of pre-modern societies. In the United States, Carol Stack's (1974) classic ethnography of the dense relations of reciprocity and interdependence among poor black urbanites showed how important sharing was to survival even a few decades ago. By contrast, more recent work by Hochschild (2012) on the growth of outsourced services among middle-class whites suggests lower and declining levels of sharing. Thus, the presumption of novelty ignores the higher levels of sharing that working-class, poor communities, and communities of color have maintained in the face of an increasingly marketized society. For this reason, we prefer the term the "new" sharing economy, to distinguish it from earlier forms.

However, there *are* innovative aspects of the collaborative consumption space. We note three: "stranger sharing," reliance on digital technologies, and participation of "high cultural capital" consumers (Schor, 2014; Schor and Fitzmaurice, 2015a). Although there are exceptions (such as elite travelers in ancient Greece), historically, people have tended not to share with strangers (individuals outside of their social networks). By contrast, today's sharing platforms facilitate sharing among people who are not acquainted and do not share personal social connections. This makes trust a key aspect of these exchanges (Bicchieri et al., 2004).

Trust relates to the second novel aspect of collaborative consumption—the role of digital technologies. As noted, stranger sharing entails risk, especially because many of these platforms involve intimate, and unregulated, situations—sharing one's home or car, going into strangers' homes for service work or eating foods prepared by unknown cooks. Digital platforms are thought to decrease the risk involved in stranger sharing because they crowdsource information on users via the use of ratings and reputations systems. This can make the platforms more appealing, especially as a critical mass is approached or reached.

A growing literature and some of our data, however, suggest ratings do not always convey useful information. For instance, Lee and colleagues (2015) contend ratings may be relatively unimportant on Airbnb. Research by Zervas and colleagues (2015) finds that Airbnb ratings are inflated relative to similar properties on TripAdvisor (see also, Hu et al., 2009). This does not mean that ratings on Airbnb and other platforms are inaccurate, but there is evidence that users do give higher ratings than they believe justified. Producers and consumers understand that digital reputations matter a great deal, so low ratings generally require malfeasance, tardiness, or very poor service. There are also concerns on some platforms that ratings are not bilateral, meaning that consumers hold power over producers (Bolton et al., 2013). Dillahunt and Malone (2015) found the uni-directionality of ratings proved to be a problem for a group of low-income, low-education providers on a variety of platforms. These users were wary of putting their trust in the technology. But bilateral ratings can also produce inaccuracies. In our research, we found that people on Airbnb may be reluctant to rate others poorly, in part because of fear of retaliation.

We suspect that the relatively low rates of malfeasance that currently characterize the platforms are less a function of ratings systems and more a result of the honest motives of early adopters. This raises the possibility that as usage spreads, the prevalence of malfeasance may rise. Research from New York City suggests that some providers are being targeted by customers to engage in illicit activities (Ravenelle, 2015). Nevertheless, these ratings systems have been sufficient to entice large numbers of people to enter into unknown situations with unknown people. In fact, for some platforms, such as Couchsurfing and to a lesser extent Airbnb, the chance to meet new people has been an important part of the appeal. Whether these exchanges create more social trust and friendship, and are thus a means to rebuild frayed social capital, is a question that we address below. Our research also suggests that while ratings and reputational data matter, providers develop other ways of gaining information to reduce potential risks from unknown others.

Finally, we note that the sociological composition of participants in this sector is disproportionately oriented to people with high levels of education and cultural capital. We discuss this issue in the next section. Here we merely note that many of our respondents share out of choice rather than necessity. This differs from sharing as a survival strategy.

We turn now to a discussion of the sociology of the collaborative consumer.

Sociologically situating the collaborative consumer

Collaborative consumption has become popular among a diverse group of techno-enthusiastic, ecologically concerned, and social justice-inspired individuals (Orsi and Doskow 2009; Gansky, 2010; Chase, 2015; McLaren and Agyeman, 2015). One reason is that these groups share a similar "habitus," or consumer sensibility. This term is rooted in consumption scholarship in the tradition of French sociologist Pierre Bourdieu (1977, 1984, 1990). In order to situate our findings, we begin with a short description of Bourdieu's concept of habitus and the consistency of our findings with his analysis. Next, we contrast the habitus of our participants with those of trendsetters from the 1990s. Here, we describe our participants' sensibilities as an "eco-habitus" (Carfagna et al., 2014).

Bourdieu argued that consumer tastes and practices are ingrained in a habitus—a semi-conscious, often embodied sense of what people like and do not like, a matrix of tastes and behaviors that people carry with them. The word connotes habituation, routine, almost automaticity. The habitus is developed in the family and then further shaped in early adulthood. For Bourdieu, a key point about the habitus is that it varies strongly with socioeconomic position, which he conceptualized in terms of two key types of capital: economic capital (understood straightforwardly as economic resources, money, and assets) and cultural capital (which is a more complex idea, and consists of both family upbringing in matters of taste and manners as well as formal schooling, which inculcates cultural capital). People with more cultural capital have different tastes than those from the working class, the poor, or the newly rich, who often have economic assets but not cultural ones.

Bourdieu also recognized that consumer trends are often driven by people with high levels of cultural capital but less economic capital. This group includes artists, style-makers, intellectuals, and cultural actors. They may be members of the avant-garde, and they are frequently young. They are highly educated and their tastes lead mass consumer tastes. Bourdieu situates these groups within the dominant class, although they are in what he terms the dominated pole of this class. For Bourdieu, much of the dynamism within consumer culture is attributable to struggles between this group and more culturally conservative groups, such as employers and managers, who possess high levels of economic assets, but less cultural capital. In our work, we have found that early participants in the sharing economy are located within the high cultural capital, lower economic capital (HCC/LEC) segment of the dominant class. In order to understand our participants' tastes and preferences as they are rooted in their habitus, we contrast them to HCC consumers from past decades.

In his magisterial work *Distinction*, Bourdieu (1984) argued that people with higher cultural capital have a global and cosmopolitan outlook, valorize abstraction and idealism, and display a strong orientation toward mental work and against manual labor. In an influential study from the mid-1990s, which applied Bourdieu's findings to the United States, Holt (1998) found that HCC consumers largely conformed to Bourdieu's characterization. Holt identified a number of binary oppositions between his low and high cultural capital informants, which largely reproduced Bourdieu's categories. Three of these binaries are central to our work: global/local, ideal/material, and mental/manual. Holt found that low cultural capital consumers preferred local consumption rather than global, were more grounded in the concrete and material rather than the abstract and ideal, and were inclined toward manual work rather than mental work. By contrast, he found that HCC individuals disparaged manual labor, preferring to engage in the realm of the abstract, mental, and ideal.

The taste patterns of our HCC participants suggest an evolution over the decades since Bourdieu's and Holt's research (Carfagna et al., 2014). Our HCC consumers favor the qualities previously identified with low cultural capital: localness, materiality, and manual work. For example, our HCC informants prefer local production and consumption to global consumer culture, as the popularity of local microbrews, farm-to-table restaurants, and "locavore" eating attests. Similarly, they are interested in the material aspects of goods, such as the textures of food and clothing, and even the feel of soil. They seek experiences that feel "real," by which they include a sense of the tactile, an almost palpable resonance with the energy of objects. Finally, they are also oriented to the manual, rather than idealistic and abstract aspects of culture.

We argue this reconfiguration is rooted in an "eco-habitus" (Carfagna et al., 2014). What we mean by this is that our participants frequently call upon ecological or environmental values to explain their consumer practices. Their eco-habitus represents an affinity for small-scale production and consumption, which serves to align with ecological consciousness while also creating distance from mass production. There is also a tendency to celebrate community and authentic social relationships, which often fits seamlessly with environmental predilections. The eco-habitus leads them to an affinity for do-it-yourself (DIY) activities. They enjoy creating things with their hands, as though it were "natural." Our respondents seek to reclaim their grandparents' skills and practices: they sew and mend clothes, can foods, and listen to the radio (digitally, often through podcasts). Other popular activities include darning socks, working with wood, and otherwise getting their hands dirty. They are attentive to the sourcing of goods and their materiality. Our participants are concerned with production processes, both on account of their ecological effects and due to the ethical issues raised in working environments. When they express their preferences for eating in tune with local seasonality and connecting to local farms, they are drawing on both ecological and social rationalities.

Because habitus is a "semi-conscious" characteristic, objective measures of the environmental impacts of these consumers' lifestyles will reveal inconsistencies. Therefore it is important to note that in developing the concept of an eco-habitus, we are not claiming that participants minimize their ecological footprints, nor are we suggesting that those with larger quantities of cultural capital are responsible for less ecological damage. Some of our respondents do focus on the environmental impacts of their activities, especially their carbon consumption, and they engage in low-intensity practices (e.g., local eating, bicycling, purchasing used goods, and sharing). Furthermore, many have relatively low economic capital and spend less than higher income consumers, which generally produces a comparatively low ecological footprint. However, we also discover that some of the practices we are studying seem to lead to higher carbon footprints. For example, we find that Airbnb hosts travel more because their rental earnings make it possible to do so. Furthermore, by making travel generally less expensive we find that both hosts and guests report traveling more frequently. Similarly, there is now evidence that ride-sharing platforms such as Uber and Lyft are used as substitutes for public transportation, an effect which likely raises the carbon footprint of riders (Rayle et al., 2014).

Rather, our claim is that HCC consumers in the collaborative consumption space make judgments using environmental criteria and deploy discourses of ecological impact. If sometimes only as part of a consumer myth (Thompson and Coskuner-Balli, 2007), our participants ponder how their actions affect the environment and what other actions might reduce those effects. They tend to identify—more so discursively than in practice—with an ecological consciousness, what Leopold (1949) described as a "land ethic" where each human is but a "plain member and citizen" of the "land-community" as opposed to its conqueror (see also Kirschenmann, 2010). Haluza-Delay (2008) describes an eco-habitus as "the practices of living socially and ecologically well in place" which could be a powerful end goal for environmental social movements (see also Haluza-DeLay, 2006; Haluza-DeLay and Berezan, 2013). We agree, however, we find that actually enacting ecological practices is difficult for our participants and that even some of the most ecologically oriented individuals increase their footprints as a result of sharing economy practices.

As our HCC respondents enact the eco-habitus, they do so in typically high cultural capital ways. For example, their localism is of a cosmopolitan variety. Their practices of making and creating are infused with high-tech tools and knowledge. They are not adopting the habits and tastes of lower cultural capital consumers; rather, they creatively reconfigure and transform them. Furthermore, the enactment of an eco-habitus is part of a strategy of distinction, Bourdieu's signature concept for understanding how consumers act within the field of consumption. Engaging in distinguishing practices is a key strategy for gaining status within a field. Such practices are critical for the reproduction of social class because their subtlety effectively enacts class power on a daily basis. As our participants live out ecologically oriented, high-status tastes, they are typically claiming distinction and the status positions associated with successful distinctive performances. Indeed, participating in the new sharing economy itself became a source of distinction as this new sector emerged in the late 2000s. With this background in mind, let us turn more specifically to consider the sector of collaborative consumption.

Enacting the eco-habitus: our findings

We turn now to participants' experiences on the platforms and the new kinds of consumer experiences being practiced. A first point concerns the economic benefits of these sites. We find that earning money is an important motive for participating in many of the platforms that are part of the collaborative consumption economy (Schor, 2015). Consumers appreciate the low cost/high value of many of the services. Providers on some sites are able to make considerable sums. For example, a few of the Airbnb providers we interviewed have earned more than $30,000 a year by renting out their own apartments (Schor, 2015). However, the economics of the platforms are only part of the story. The ability to enact the eco-habitus is also important to the success of the sector. This enactment occurs largely via the reconfigured binaries that we discussed above. Our participants display a sophisticated sense of the local, embody a discursively bedazzled materiality, and orient themselves to the manual. Nevertheless, they maintain distance from necessity. These three characteristics can be situated under two broad headings: practicing authenticity and social connection via locality.

Practicing authenticity

We find that a central feature of the experience in the new sharing economy is the ability to combine aspects of authenticity: localness, materiality, personalization, and "real" social interactions (for a discussion of authenticity in relation to food, see Johnston and Baumann (2007). Our respondents articulate a desire for authentic relations, both with other people and with products. They find this on the sharing sites. This is particularly true of Airbnb, which provides cheaper and more diverse accommodation than the chain hotels. Our respondents tell us that with Airbnb, the ability to stay in a neighborhood rather than a downtown city center is a major part of the appeal. So, too, is access to insider information, or a real story about a neighborhood or city, including the consumer culture to be found within it. On ridesharing sites, sitting in the front with the drivers and learning their stories is an appealing feature. Users are interested in the more personalized dimensions of these platforms and appreciate this sociability. We also believe another important aspect of personalization is the fact that the monetary transaction is socially distant from the interpersonal interaction. With Airbnb the money is paid in advance, through the site or the app. On TaskRabbit, although payment is made after the task, it is done through the app, which imparts social distance to the transaction. With ridesharing platforms, the same is true, and for Uber, there is no tipping.

In our nonprofit sharing sites, the eco-habitus is prominent. These consumers emphasize local production, artisanal work, and connection to the land. Food swappers often use their community farm shares to create their offerings—and they make certain others are aware of their connections to these farms. The material dimensions of what is being offered are central. The time bank organizes P2P sharing of time, with many preferring manual services. Overall, conformity to the eco-habitus attracts many of our respondents, and almost all of the HCC participants.

Furthermore, participants used their activities on sharing platforms to enact moral practices in line with the eco-habitus. One RelayRides owner purchased a hybrid vehicle with the intention of renting it out, in order to improve renters' fuel efficiency and to demonstrate the technology to people who might not otherwise know about it. An Airbnb host reported not wanting to earn more than she paid in rent because that would not be "fair" to the landlord. Many talked about the social and ecological impacts of their activities with great passion and commitment.

We also find an important role for the eco-habitus in reshaping the meaning of work. Many of these sites involve HCC providers doing work that has been associated with lower status. Highly educated, high-status individuals are taking on a variety of blue- and pink-collar tasks: driving, housecleaning, delivery and errands, or running a small lodging enterprise. Our HCC informants create discourses and symbolic meanings so that this work does not violate their class identity—work that is constructed as socially "beneath" a person's status must be reconfigured to make it palatable. In doing so, they discursively project aspects of the eco-habitus onto their activity. This eliminates the symbolic denigration that would ordinarily occur when high-status individuals engage in low-status work. Furthermore, the rhetoric of novelty, technological efficiency, and innovation that pervade the sector also erase the symbolic contamination of low-status work.

In the nonprofits, such as the food swap and makerspace, the authenticity and realness of the work is particularly evident. Swappers are highly attuned to the ingredients used, the kinds of packaging, and the textures of the foods and sensory aspects of the offerings that are brought to the swap. The foods that are offered are made by hand, at home. Similarly, at the makerspace, production is done by hand (albeit with the help of tools and machines). But there is a premium placed on one-of-a-kind products, the materials that are used, and the individual creativity and artisanship that are deployed. Our makers are critical of mass-produced consumer goods. One informant remarked: "Why would I buy it if I could make it?", a sentiment shared by quite a few at the space. Makerspace members are also highly averse to waste, often using scrap materials in their creative endeavors.

Social connection via locality

As we have argued, the eco-habitus is rooted in a valorization of the "local." While this is most evident in preference for local food and supporting local businesses, the local is also enacted via the search for P2P connection. Our participants desire connection with local others. And in the case of lodging platforms, they seek to incorporate distant others (e.g., travelers) into their local networks. They express strong desires to build community and social connection, whether it is via swapping food, trading services, hosting guests, or participating in a shared workspace. On Airbnb about half of our hosts report having significant social interactions with their guests, and guests also find the interpersonal contact to be important.

This desire for connection comes at a time when there is considerable debate among scholars about trends in social connectivity (for a recent review, see Parigi and Henson, 2014). While some argue that social isolation has risen over time (McPherson et al., 2006), other research is more skeptical of this claim (Fischer, 2011). In addition, some contend that while new technologies have enabled an increase in social connections, these contacts may be ephemeral or shallow (Turkle, 2012). Many of our respondents are nostalgic for a time when people knew their neighbors and were more firmly embedded in robust social networks. Their participation in collaborative consumption is partly motivated by the hope of building stronger social connections, especially in comparison to the sociability they gain from conventional market exchanges. Participants on both sides of the market articulate a desire to meet people, make friends, and get to know others. While not all our respondents reported being able to achieve these outcomes, many did. Furthermore, they hold out the hope that collaborative consumption will lead to a genuine, local, person-to-person consumer culture that supplants the impersonal and foreign culture of corporate chains.

Are their hopes being realized? There is definitely evidence of a friendlier, more sociable consumer experience. The site that has been most successful at creating new social ties is Airbnb. Among just over half the Airbnb hosts we interviewed, social interaction was not only part of their practice, but also an important motivation in bringing them to the platform. Our hosts socialized with their guests by eating with them, taking them around town, and in a small number of cases, even creating lasting friendships. To a somewhat lesser extent, the TaskRabbits we interviewed also cited social connection as an important component of their experience, though few are motivated to become Rabbits for this reason. Some discussed the creation of new social networks they could now rely on. Others noted the opportunity to meet people they would not have met otherwise. In general, Rabbits were generally satisfied with their social interactions. A sizeable number noted that their experiences would not be possible or would be less likely via conventional labor arrangements.

On some sharing sites, the desire for social connection is a central dimension of the experience. Parigi and State (2014) examined Couchsurfing and found that participation resulted in new friendships, at least initially. However, they also found that over time, the ability of the platform to create these connections, especially close ones, declined. Users become "disenchanted" as the relationships they form are now more casual and less durable. That disillusion may also be connected to a change in Couchsurfing's business model, or to the growth of competitor Airbnb. This research raises the issue of whether the social benefits of sharing sites will endure as they lose novelty and the user group expands from what may be a unique assemblage of first-stage participants.

It is becoming apparent that many sites do little to create social connections, even when there may be consequences associated with not building trust. For example, a study by the P2P car-rental site RelayRides found that renters maintained automobiles better when they met the owners, and that both parties rated experiences more highly when there was an in-person interaction (Chernova, 2013). However, our respondents on this site reported sporadic social interaction and said that meeting people is not a motive for participation.

We also found that in the not-for-profit time bank and food swap we studied sharing largely failed to produce the social connection that participants and founders desired. This was surprising to us because these sites aspire to create social ties, via nonmonetized trading. Even when people wanted to develop new friends, they found it difficult to do so. Furthermore, many were unsatisfied with the connections they did form, likely associated with their high expectations. At the food swap, there was not only an inability to create social ties, but even the more basic task of trading foodstuffs proved elusive. Despite being launched with good intentions, considerable enthusiasm, and robust participation, the food swap atrophied and eventually ceased to operate over the months we examined it (Schor and Fitzmaurice, 2015b).

We believe these failures are largely because participants at these sites engage in a great deal of status-positioning via distinguishing practices (Schor et al., 2016). At the food swap, for example, HCC participants rejected trade offers from people who brought items prepared with mass-produced, store-bought ingredients. HCC food swappers made their offerings with produce from their farm-share or another alternative market. They felt strongly about the inadequacy of some of the items produced by those possessing insufficient "foodie" cultural capital (Johnston and Baumann, 2007).

Finally, in the makerspace we studied, social ties developed, but they were highly segmented (Attwood-Charles and Schor, 2015). When high-status actors exchanged labor or materials, their preferred currency was beer or a favor. With lower-status makers, however, the highly positioned actors requested money or simply refused to collaborate. Their time was seen as too valuable for working with those located in "the suburbs," as the lower-status spaces were termed in this hierarchical makerspace. We were not expecting such high levels of exclusionary behavior in a sharing site that discursively promotes a horizontal, nonhierarchical identity.

Our findings from the nonprofit cases especially (makerspace, time bank, food swap) reveal that while the eco-habitus leads people to desire social connection, the fact that it is part of a HCC habitus operates in the other direction. It is important to recognize that while the specific values of the eco-habitus may enhance desirable features of consumer culture, such as more genuine social connection or a vibrant DIY practice, they frequently do so in a socially exclusionary way. This exclusionary behavior, while not unusual among HCC actors, can be limiting when these participants also aspire to create social change. In our nonprofit cases, all of the sites embraced social missions of democratic, participatory, and empowering change of one type or another. Indeed, the discourse of the collaborative consumption sector emphasizes the possibilities of change via these economic innovations. The exclusionary behaviors we found at these sites undermined their ability to function effectively and by extension, to create new economic structures and practices, a point we have argued in more detail elsewhere (Schor et al., 2016).

Conclusion: eco-habitus, democratic sharing, and the emergence of a true peer-to-peer economy?

In the introduction to this chapter we asked whether the new consumer practices that make up the sharing economy would lead to a transformation of consumer culture in a more ecologically sustainable and socially egalitarian direction. One view, present in the more dystopian literature, argues that this sector represents a hyper-capitalist, neoliberal development (e.g., Slee, 2015; Scholz, 2016b). It is platform capitalism, rather than democratic sharing (Lobo, 2014). We also wonder whether the mainstreaming of the sector, resulting in a reduction in the segment of HCC participants with an eco-habitus, will lead these sites to become far more normative in terms of the dominant consumer culture. By contrast, there are numerous actors in the sector who seem determined to retain its early ideological commitments to creating social connection and building a more just, accessible, and humane economy. Whether they will prevail in the face of powerful normalizing pressures remains to be seen.

Platform structure may be key to how the sector evolves. Founders and investors extract significant portions of the total value produced. This value could instead go to producers and consumers. In a democratized space, providers and users would have a real say in how the platform operates. Such changes would help platforms function not just more efficiently and innovatively, as is celebrated, but also in a way that prioritizes benefits to users (Orsi and Doskow, 2009; see also Edelman and Geradin, 2015). There is now an increasing chorus of voices arguing for change along these lines (Chase, 2015; Scholz, 2016b).

The economics of this sector may favor a more cooperative and democratic structure because the value provided by the platform itself is likely to decline over time. Unlike traditional businesses that produce and sell a product, platforms act as intermediaries with participants producing the services. The intermediary role is not without value, but there are reasons to believe that the first wave of platforms may lose their current advantage in providing services (see Schor, 2015 for an argument along these lines). In labor services, with the exception of the ridesharing companies, the existing platforms are relatively weak. A number of sites, such as Zaarly, Homejoy, and TaskRabbit, have either closed down or radically changed their business models, some several times. None has a dominant enough position that a new entrant would be unfeasible. As noted above, a new movement called platform cooperativism seeks to democratize ownership by turning producers and consumers into platform owners, and this effort is gaining traction (Schneider, 2014; Scholz 2014, 2016a; Chase, 2015). Orsi (2013) has identified approaches that current users, company managers, and investors may find useful as they convert to cooperative structures.

However appealing for environmentalists and progressives, these approaches remain emergent, or even marginal. User ownership and control, a sharing paradigm, genuine attention to ecological impact, and a rejection of commercial exchanges are aspirations rather than realities. Therefore, we conclude by suggesting that the answer to the question of whether collaborative consumption represents a new consumer culture or merely business-as-usual (BAU) is as yet unanswerable. On the one hand, there are aspects of the for-profit platforms that indicate they are already BAU entities, or are converging in that direction. These include the strong value orientation; the rise of dominant, maybe even monopoly platforms, in a number of markets; the role of financial investors; and the ways in which mainstreaming seems to dilute the early, principled values of the sector. On the other hand, the eco-habitus in its current form is oriented to both a different type of economy (more local, less corporate, more sustainable) as well as a strong desire for social connection. There is also a progressive movement developing within the sharing sector that explicitly challenges its drift toward BAU, and advocates for a radical, anti-capitalist alternative (Slee, 2015; Scholz, 2016a). The relative strength of these trends remains an open question.

Notes

1   In addition to the authors, the research team includes doctoral students Will Attwood-Charles, Mehmet Cansoy, Luka Carfagna, Isak Ladegaard, and Connor Fitzmaurice. The MacArthur Foundation generously funded this research. More information on the project is available at http://clrn.dmlhub.net/projects/connected-consumption.
2   According to the first national random sample survey of the sharing economy in the United States, which the first author helped to field, more than half of all Americans

reported using Craigslist and similar sites. More than 70 percent purchased used goods offline. In contrast, newer platforms such as Airbnb and bicycle sharing have between 8 percent and 12 percent usage. The highest participation of "new" sharing practices reported was the non-profit activity of tool-lending, with over 12 percent reporting having participated (Center for a New American Dream and PolicyInteractive, 2014).

References

Alperovitz, G. (2011) *America Beyond Capitalism: Reclaiming Our Wealth, Our Liberty, and Our Democracy*. Boston, MA: Democracy Collaborative Press/Dollars and Sense.

Attwood-Charles, W. and Schor, J. (2015) Distinction at work: status practices in a community production environment. Unpublished paper, Boston College.

Baker, D. (2014) "Don't buy the 'sharing economy' hype: Airbnb and Uber are facilitating rip-offs." *The Guardian*, May 27. www.theguardian.com/commentisfree/2014/may/27/airbnb-uber-taxes-regulation.

Belk, R. (2007) "Why not share rather than own?" *The Annals of the American Academy of Political and Social Science* 611(1):126–140.

Belk, R. (2010) "Sharing," *Journal of Consumer Research* 36(5):715–734.

Benkler, Y. (2004) "Sharing nicely: on shareable goods and the emergence of sharing as a modality of economic production," *Yale Law Journal* 114(2):273–358.

Benkler, Y. (2006) *The Wealth of Networks: How Social Production Transforms Markets and Freedom*. New Haven, CT: Yale University Press.

Bicchieri, C., Duffy, J., and Tolle, G (2004) "Trust among strangers," *Philosophy of Science* 71(3):286–319.

Bolton, G., Greiner, B., and Ockenfels, A. (2013) "Engineering trust: reciprocity in the production of reputation information," *Management Science* 59(2):265–285.

Botsman, R. (2010) *What's Mine Is Yours: The Rise of Collaborative Consumption*. New York: Harper Business.

Bourdieu, P. (1977) *Outline of a Theory of Practice*. New York: Cambridge University Press.

Bourdieu, P. (1984) *Distinction: A Social Critique of the Judgement of Taste*. Cambridge, MA: Harvard University Press.

Bourdieu, P. (1990) *The Logic of Practice*. Palo Alto, CA: Stanford University Press.

Cahn, E. and Rowe, J. (1992) *Time Dollars: The New Currency That Enables Americans to Turn Their Hidden Resource-Time-into Personal Security and Community Renewal*. Emmaus, PA: Rodale Press.

Carfagna, L. (2014) *Beyond Learning-as-Usual: Connected Learning Among Open Learners*. Irvine, CA: Digital Media and Learning Research Hub. http://dmlhub.net/wp-content/uploads/files/BeyondLearningAsUsual_v3.pdf.

Carfagna, L., Dubois, E., Fitzmaurice, C., Ouimette, M., Schor, J., and Willis, M. (2014) "An emerging eco-habitus: the reconfiguration of high cultural capital practices among ethical consumers," *Journal of Consumer Culture* 14(2):158–178.

Center for a New American Dream and Policy Interactive (2014) *Analysis Report: New American Dream Survey 2014*. Charlottesville, VA: Center for a New American Dream. http://newdream.s3.amazonaws.com/19/d9/7/3866/NewDreamPollFinalAnalysis.pdf.

Chase, R. (2015) *Peers Inc.: How People and Platforms Are Inventing the Collaborative Economy and Reinventing Capitalism*. New York: Public Affairs.

Chernova, Y. (2013) "RelayRides learns lesson: car sharers want personal connection, not anonymity," *Venture Capital Dispatch*. November 25. http://blogs.wsj.com/venture

capital/2013/11/25/relayrides-learns-lesson-car-sharers-want-personal-connection-not-anonymity.

Cohen, L. (2003) *A Consumers' Republic: The Politics of Consumption in Postwar America.* New York: Knopf.

Collom, E. (2011) "Motivations and differential participation in a community currency system: the dynamics within a local social movement organization," *Sociological Forum* 26(1):144–168.

Collom, E., Lasker, J., and Kyriacou, C. (2012) *Equal Time, Equal Value: Community Currencies and Time Banking in the US.* Burlington, VT: Ashgate.

Davies, S. (2015) "The hard work of figuring out an odd-job revolution," *The Financial Times*, February 19.

Dillahunt, T. and Malone, A. (2015) "The promise of the sharing economy among disadvantaged communities," *Proceedings of the 33rd Annual ACM Conference on Human Factors in Computing Systems*, pp. 2285–2229. http://dl.acm.org/citation.cfm?doid=2702123.2702189.

Edelman, B. and Geradin, D. (2015) *Efficiencies and Regulatory Shortcuts: How Should We Regulate Companies like Airbnb and Uber.* Cambridge, MA: Harvard Business School. www.benedelman.org/publications/efficiencies-and-shortcuts-2015-11-24.pdf.

Firat, A. and Dholakia, N. (1998) *Consuming People: From Political Economy to Theaters of Consumption.* New York: Routledge.

Fischer, C. (2011) *Still Connected: Family and Friends in America Since 1970.* New York: Russell Sage Foundation.

Gansky, L. (2010) *The Mesh: Why the Future of Business Is Sharing.* New York: Portfolio Penguin.

Gell, A. (1986) "Newcomers to the world of goods: consumption among the Muria Gonds," in Appadurai, A. (ed.), *The Social Life of Things: Commodities in Cultural Perspective*, New York: Cambridge University Press, pp. 110–140.

Geron, T. (2013) "Airbnb and the unstoppable rise of the share economy," *Forbes*, February 11.

Gintis, H., Bowles, S., Boyd, R., and Fehr, E. (eds.) 2005. *Moral Sentiments and Material Interests: The Foundations of Cooperation in Economic Life.* Cambridge, MA: MIT Press.

Haluza-DeLay, R. (2006) "The practice of environmentalism: creating ecological habitus," *Conference Papers–American Sociological Association.* http://csopconsulting.tripod.com/sitebuildercontent/sitebuilderfiles/3RHDecological_habitus.pdf.

Haluza-DeLay, R. (2008) "A theory of practice for social movements: environmentalism and ecological habitus," *Mobilization* 13(2):205–218.

Haluza-DeLay, R. and Berezan, R. (2013) "Permaculture in the city: ecological habitus and the distributed ecovillage," in Lockyer, J. and Veteto (eds.), *Environmental Anthropology: Engaging Ecotopia, Bioregionalism, Permaculture, and Ecovillages.* New York: Berghahn Books, pp. 130–145.

Henwood, D. (2015) "What the sharing economy takes," *The Nation*, January 27.

Hochschild, A. (2012) *The Outsourced Self: Intimate Life in Market Times.* New York: Metropolitan Books.

Holt, D. (1998) "Does cultural capital structure American consumption?" *Journal of Consumer Research* 25(1):1–25.

Hu, N., Zhang, J., and Pavlou, P. (2009) "Overcoming the J-shaped distribution of product reviews," *Communications of the ACM* 52(10):144–147.

Hull, D. (1979) "In defense of presentism," *History and Theory* 18(1):1–15.

Johnston, J. and Baumann, S. (2007) "Democracy versus distinction: a study of omnivorousness in gourmet food writing," *American Journal of Sociology* 113(1):165–204.

Kalamar, A. (2013) "Sharewashing is the new greenwashing," *OpEdNews*. www.opednews. com/articles/Sharewashing-is-the-New-Gr-by-Anthony-Kalamar-130513-834.html.

Kessler, S. (2014) "Pixel and dimed: on (not) getting by in the gig economy," *Fast Company*, March 18. www.fastcompany.com/3027355/pixel-and-dimed-on-not-getting-by-in-the-gig-economy.

Kirschenmann, F. (2010) *Cultivating an Ecological Conscience: Essays from a Farmer Philosopher*, ed. C. Falk. Lexington, KY: University Press of Kentucky.

Lee, D., Hyun, W., Ryu, J., Lee, W., Rhee, W., and Suh, B. (2015) "An analysis of social features associated with room sales of Airbnb," *Proceedings of the ACM Conference on Computer Supported Cooperative Work 2015*, pp. 219–222. http://dl.acm.org/citation. cfm?id=2699011&dl=ACM&coll=DL&CFID=659225669&CFTOKEN=61721455.

Leopold, A. (1949) *A Sand County Almanac and Sketches Here and There*. New York: Oxford University Press.

Lobo, S. (2014) "S.P.O.N.—Die Mensch-Maschine: Auf Dem Weg in Die Dumpinghölle (S.P.O.N.—The man-machine: on the way to the dumping hell)," *Speigel Online*, March 9. www.spiegel.de/netzwelt/netzpolitik/sascha-lobo-sharing-economy-wie-bei-uber-ist-plattform-kapitalismus-a-989584.html (in German).

McLaren, D. and Agyeman. J. (2015) *Sharing Cities: A Case for Truly Smart and Sustainable Cities*. Cambridge, MA: MIT Press.

McPherson, M., Smith-Lovin, L., and Brashears, M. (2006) "Social isolation in America: changes in core discussion networks over two decades," *American Sociological Review* 71(3):353–375.

Orsi, J. (2013) "The sharing economy just got real," *Shareable*, September 16. www. shareable.net/blog/the-sharing-economy-just-got-real.

Orsi, J. and Doskow, E. (2009) *The Sharing Solution: How to Save Money, Simplify Your Life and Build Community*. Berkeley, CA: Nolo.

Parigi, P. and Henson, W. (2014) "Social isolation in America," *Annual Review of Sociology* 40(1):153–171.

Parigi, P. and State, B. (2014) "Disenchanting the world: the impact of technology on relationships," *Social Informatics* 8851:166–182.

Ravenelle, A. (2015) Hustle: The lived experiences of workers in the sharing economy: crime and exploitation. Unpublished paper, City University of New York.

Rayle, L., Shaheen, S., Chan, N., Dai, D., and Cervero, R. (2014) *App-Based, On-Demand Ride Services: Comparing Taxi and Ridesourcing Trips and User Characteristics in San Francisco*. Berkeley, CA: University of California Transportation Center. http://76.12.4.249/artman2/uploads/1/RidesourcingWhitePaper_Nov2014Update.pdf.

Reich, R. (2015) "The share-the-scraps economy," *The Huffington Post*, April 4. www. huffingtonpost.com/robert-reich/the-sharethescraps-econom_b_6597992.html.

Rosenblat, A. (2015) "Uber's phantom cabs," *Motherboard*, July 27. http://motherboard. vice.com/read/ubers-phantom-cabs.

Rossa, J. (2015) "The sharing economy: the workers," *Bloomberg Brief*, June 15. https:// newsletters.briefs.bloomberg.com/document/4vz1acbgfrxz8uwan9/the-workers-demographics.

Schneider, N. (2014) "Owning is the new sharing." *Shareable*, December 21. www. shareable.net/blog/owning-is-the-new-sharing.

Schneider, N. and Scholz, T. (2015) "The Internet needs a new economy," *The Next System Project*, November 8. http://thenextsystem.org/the-internet-needs-a-new-economy.

Scholz, T. (2014) "Platform cooperativism vs. the sharing economy," *Medium*, December 5. https://medium.com/@trebors/platform-cooperativism-vs-the-sharing-economy-2ea737f1b5ad.

Scholz, T. (2016a) *Platform Cooperativism: Challenging the Corporate Sharing Economy*. New York: Rosa Luxemburg Stiftung. www.rosalux-nyc.org/wp-content/files_mf/scholz_platformcooperativism_2016.pdf.

Scholz, T. (2016b). *Uberworked and Underpaid: How Workers Are Disrupting the Digital Economy*. Malden, MA: Polity Press.

Schor, J. (1998) *The Overspent American: Upscaling, Downshifting, and the New Consumer*. New York: Basic Books.

Schor, J. (2014) "Debating the sharing economy," *Great Transition Initiative*, October. www.greattransition.org/publication/debating-the-sharing-economy.

Schor, J. (2015) The sharing economy: reports from stage one. Unpublished paper, Boston College. www.bc.edu/content/dam/files/schools/cas_sites/sociology/pdf/TheSharing Economy.pdf.

Schor, J., Fitzmaurice, C., Attwood-Charles, W., Carfagna, L., and Dubois Poteat, E. (2016) "Paradoxes of openness and distinction in the sharing economy," *Poetics* 54:66–81.

Schor, J. and Fitzmaurice, C. (2015a) "Collaborating and connecting: the emergence of the sharing economy," in Reisch, L. and Thøgersen, J. (eds.), *Handbook of Research on Sustainable Consumption*. Northampton, MA: Edward Elgar, pp. 410–425.

Schor, J. and Fitzmaurice, C. (2015b) Handmade matters: the anatomy of a failed circuit of commerce. Unpublished paper, Boston College.

Schumacher, E. (1973) *Small Is Beautiful: Economics as If People Mattered*. New York: Harper and Row.

Seyfang, G. (2004) "Time banks: rewarding community self-help in the inner city?" *Community Development Journal* 39(1):62–71.

Slee, T. (2014) "Sharing and caring." *Jacobin*, January 24. www.jacobinmag.com/2014/01/sharing-and-caring.

Slee, T. (2015) *What's Yours is Mine: Against the Sharing Economy*. New York: OR Books.

Slee, T. (2016) "The sharing economy's dirty laundry," *Jacobin*, March 23. www.jacobinmag.com/2016/03/uber-airbnb-sharing-economy-housing-tech.

Sperling, G. (2015) *How Airbnb Combats Middle Class Income Stagnation*. Washington, DC: Sperling Economic Strategies. https://airbnb.box.com/shared/static/jrry0if4cgjr nvw1ykrpmw8ugivrx2mx.pdf.

Stack, C. (1974) *All Our Kin: Strategies for Survival in a Black Community*. New York: Harper and Row.

The Economist (2013) "The rise of the sharing economy," March 9.

Thompson, C. and Coskuner-Balli, G. (2007) "Countervailing market responses to corporate co-optation and the ideological recruitment of consumption communities," *Journal of Consumer Research* 34(2):135–152.

Turkle, S. (2012) *Alone Together: Why We Expect More from Technology and Less from Each Other*. New York: Basic Books.

Zervas, G., Proserpio, D., and Byers, J. (2015) "A first look at online reputation on Airbnb, where every stay is above average," *Social Science Research Network*, January 28. http://papers.ssrn.com/sol3/papers.cfm?abstract_id=2554500.

3 Toward a more solidaristic sharing economy

Examples from Switzerland

Marlyne Sahakian

Introduction

In the wake of recurrent financial crises and rising environmental and social concerns, new practices have begun to enter into popular usage to enable the sharing of resources, usually among peers and often associated with notions of increased solidarity and sense of community. Many of these forms of collaborative consumption are being facilitated through technological means that allow people to conduct provisioning transactions over the Internet and through mobile devices, allegedly reducing operating costs and facilitating exchanges (Botsman and Rogers, 2010; Gansky, 2010; Rifkin, 2014). The so-called sharing economy is currently being mobilized to describe a wide variety of activities in a range of sectors, from housing and transport to consumable goods and financial services. While there is a great deal of enthusiasm around the potential of the sharing economy to contribute to a more sustainable future, we need to pay closer attention to what proponents mean by "sharing" in terms of production, consumption, and financing, both in discourse and in practice. A dictionary consultation on the word "sharing" reveals its many shades: sharing can allude to dividing and distributing shares or portions, as in sharing land among heirs; but it can also imply an experience or type of usage, as in shared feelings or emotions. Sharing also refers to having something in common, as in sharing a passion.

This chapter explores opportunities presented by the sharing economy to go beyond customary consumerism and to support more solidaristic forms of interaction (see also Chapters 2 and 5). While the most prominent so-called sharing initiatives are primarily based on self-interest and profit accumulation, I build on an effort to conceptualize collaborative consumption in relation to communal exchange that occurs within the context of the social and solidarity economy (SSE) (Sahakian and Servet, 2016). The distinction here is between dividing up the proverbial pie for more individual profit or placing the pie in the commons and allocating resources on the basis of societal goals and democratic principles. Based on six examples from Switzerland, this chapter seeks to demonstrate that certain forms of sharing tend toward greater sustainability because they encourage social cohesion and environmental improvement while others are motivated primarily by personal advantage and pecuniary gain with little to no concern for social or environmental outcomes. The various Swiss illustrations fall into two main product and service categories: the sharing of personal goods and household items and the sharing of mobility services.

To highlight the notion of solidaristic sharing, I describe the development of the SSE over the past fifteen years and then present how its associated practices are presently playing out in the western part of Switzerland. Based on this background, I discuss the sharing economy by proposing analytical handles that distinguish sharing in solidarity from its other forms. I then present and analyze the Swiss sharing economy examples. What emerges from this research is the significance of the organizational frameworks that govern sharing services and ensure that solidaristic principles and practices are upheld over the longer term and at different scales. Clarifying institutional arrangements could lead to insights on how practices could be reconfigured to foster more sustainable forms of consumption. More solidaristic expressions of the sharing economy, through political reforms and policy support, could enable social change and foster transitions beyond the customary consumer society.

The social and solidarity economy in theory and practice

The contemporary social and solidarity economy originates out of the nineteenth-century social economy of Western Europe and emerged as a direct consequence of rapid industrialization and growing inequalities, particularly in urban areas. The early labor movement created communal enterprises at the time as "a tool in the struggle for the liberation of the working class" (Dubuisson-Quellier, 2013). For example, in France a law was enacted in 1867 to provide a legislative framework to establish the legitimacy of cooperatives. Throughout Europe and elsewhere, mutual organizations of various kinds were launched as an innovative and people-centered response to early forms of industrial capitalism, but were soon relegated to what would be termed the "third sector," distinguished from for-profit and governmental entities. As the state-sponsored welfare system assumed an increasingly prominent role in addressing social issues after World War II, there was a further waning of appeal for the social economy. It was only in the 1990s that interest in the social economy was rekindled, in the wake of recurring financial crises, rising environmental concerns, and the failure of the welfare state and international organizations to effectively address social inequalities.

Members of civil society from thirty-two countries gathered in Peru in 1997 to sign the Lima Declaration which sought to promote worldwide structural changes in existing economic systems. This initiative led to the creation of the RIPESS (Réseau Intercontinental de Promotion de l'Economie Sociale et Solidaire)—a transnational network to promote SSE.[1] The notion of "solidarity" was added to that of a "social economy," to differentiate this movement from the third sector. As further elaborated in Chapter 5, the concept of a solidarity-based economy is meant to "reinvigorate and radicalize the institutionalized, captured and diluted initiatives of the *social* economy." In 2001, participants at the first World Social

Forum in the Brazilian city of Porto Alegre rallied around the slogan "another world is possible," with the SSE poised to play a prominent role in this new world order. The goal of the SSE, in one concise definition, is to place "service to its members or to the community ahead of profit; autonomous management; a democratic decision-making process; the primacy of people and work over capital in the distribution of revenues" (Defourny et al., 2000). Activities could include some forms of social entrepreneurship, community currencies, or micro-credit programs, as well as certain worker, consumer, producer, and financial cooperatives. The SSE also encompasses community-supported agriculture, social reinsertion programs, community-operated exchange platforms, and some sharing initiatives. The common ground for all SSE activities is to put people above profit, or to ensure that human beings are at the center of economic and social life (ISGC, 1997). Financial gains are subject to limits, democratic processes are promoted, and organizations active in the SSE are expected to be self-managed and relatively independent from public support (Laville, 2003, 2011). From this brief introduction (described in greater detail in Sahakian, 2016), it is worth noting that all actors involved in the SSE are presumed to share certain values, such as limits to profit and the importance of democratic processes, yet the SSE is interpreted in different ways around the world (Fraisse, 2003). For instance, in France only mutual companies and cooperatives are considered to be part of the SSE, a distinction based on organizational legal status.

By contrast, in Switzerland any entity can be part of the SSE, including for-profit companies, so long as it works progressively toward upholding SSE principles. The main argument for this more permissive interpretation is that adopting a particular legal form does not guarantee that an organization lives up to SSE principles in practice (Defourny et al., 2000). In the Swiss context, the SSE was formally instituted in Geneva with the founding of the Chambre de l'Économie Sociale et Solidaire (APRES) in 2004, a development that in due course led to the creation of other chapters across the country.[2] A recent survey that compared members of the SSE in Geneva with firms in the market economy reported smaller differences between the highest and lowest salaries within organizations, higher average salaries for entry-level work, and larger proportions of people working on flexible schedules (APRES-GE, 2010). In the APRES Charter, which governs all members of the SSE in Geneva, respect for ecology is one of the main guiding principles. In practice, entities that sign on to the Charter must agree to progressively put into place management systems that promote environmental sustainability, such as sustainable procurement strategies. Not all companies in the SSE work in the environmental sector, with all sectors of the economy represented among the current 265 members, including health and social services, banking and insurance, housing, recycling services, food services, arts and leisure, training and education. For-profit entities can be part of the SSE, provided profit is not their sole aim.

Sharing in the social and solidarity economy

Based on the brief introduction to the SSE, this section focuses on how sharing that is motivated by social and solidaristic principles can be conceptually distinguished from other forms of sharing. I explore three interrelated themes: 1) the value system proposed in different types of economic activities, 2) forms of governance, both within organizations and in the economy overall, and 3) the relation to the dominant capitalist market economy.

First, the SSE proposes an explicit value proposition: people and societal well-being are more important than profit when it comes to defining economic activities. While enterprises in the SSE can be profitable, the accumulation of profit is not the sole motivation for action. What is more, in the SSE environmental considerations are also taken into account. Sharing in the SSE should entail reducing ecological impacts, along with material and energy throughputs, and not aiming solely for pecuniary gains. To understand what forms of sharing are aligned with solidaristic principles, understood here as promoting societal values and recognizing biophysical limits, the work of Elinor Ostrom (2002) is relevant. In contrast to claims of an inevitable tragedy of the commons or the necessity of strong government regulation to avoid overshoot, Ostrom suggests a third approach based on interdependent people organized to govern themselves while obtaining continual joint benefits. This involves placing resources in the commons, as well as making explicit a set of shared norms and expectations around usage. In recent work with Jean-Michel Servet, we used the term "communal sharing" to define forms of collaborative exchange predicated on identification of common needs and environmental limits rather than solely on individual needs (Sahakian and Servet, 2016). Relating value systems to sharing activities would therefore entail uncovering the importance that is given to societal and environmental values in contrast to competitive, individualistic, and financially remunerative motives. How the value proposition plays out in practice is another question, and one that I will not address directly in this chapter. I consider instead the ways in which activities present their value system as part of a discourse, for example in mission statements.

Second, a major assumption in the SSE is that modern, democratic governance systems are needed to support more equal and complementary relations. The SSE aims to play out in a democratic political setting, but also to promote participatory processes within organizations. SSE entities are usually self-managed, self-organized, and generally independent from state support. Proponents of the SSE envision this form of governance and decision-making as a way to advance sustainable development (Cretieneau, 2010). According to Laville (2003), the SSE is ultimately about promoting democracy on the local level through economic activity, or the "democratization" of the economy based on the participatory engagement of all citizens (see also Defourny and Develtere, 1999; Fraisse et al., 2007). This organizational feature implies that people have a more equal footing in solidarity-based sharing economy initiatives and are working toward a more inclusive economy overall.

The SSE would therefore distinguish sharing out of solidarity from sharing solely on the basis of need or when one is in dire straits. It is worth introducing the notion of reciprocity here, a much-debated concept that is conceptually close to notions of solidarity. Based mostly on the anthropological research of Richard Thurnwald and Bronislaw Malinowski, Karl Polanyi (1957) defined reciprocity as one of the oldest types of economic interaction, involving exchanges of mutual benefit, between symmetrical subgroups. This idea could also be extended to the relationship between a master and slave because not all forms of reciprocity are solidaristic. Reciprocity in the SSE entails complementary relations based on voluntary interdependence (Servet, 2007) or being "invested with the potential of solidarity, consciously interdependent on others" (Servet, 2009). This distinction stands in opposition to the notion of "demand sharing," or reciprocity based on unequal power relations (Peterson, 1993). Whether unequal or solidaristic sharing is taking place depends on the forms of interdependence between the relevant people and organizations. In other words, it is important to distinguish whether people are engaged out of "mechanical interdependence," constrained in their choices by price fluctuations or the scarcity of goods and services in a capitalist marketplace (Servet, 2007; Hillenkamp, 2013), or enmeshed in relationships premised on equal footing.

Finally, the notion of reciprocity raises the question of how a solidaristic sharing economy relates to the dominant market economy. Karl Polanyi (2001) proposed four economic ideal-types with the aim of encompassing all forms of production, exchange, and circulation of goods and services, as well as finance and final consumption: 1) the market economy, and non-market economies including, 2) reciprocity, 3) redistribution, and 4) householding. As the economy, for Polanyi, is embedded in social relations, these ideal types draw attention to the institutional arrangements, governance systems, and political settings in which the related economic activities play out. Governed by a host of regulations, a market economy is regulated by scarcity and price, with property as its "constitutive institution" (van Griethuysen, 2010). Despite the claims of neoliberal champions, the global market is far from value-neutral, but is in fact, as David Graeber (2001) writes, a "totalizing system that would subordinate everything—every object, every piece of land, every human capacity or relationship—on the planet to a single standard of value." Redistribution, primarily through state taxation on production (through income taxes) and consumption (through sales taxes), is also dependent on laws and regulations within a particular economic system. By contrast, reciprocity relies on community norms and social values that promote and define mutual relations. Sharing takes place in all of these economic forms: sharing through monetary exchanges or leasing in a market economy, sharing in the form of the redistribution of citizen wealth (taxation and welfare by the state) or through charitable organizations, and sharing through reciprocal relations.

I have more recently defined sharing as being closely related to the Polanyian ideal type of householding whereby groups of people working with different livelihood strategies navigate between capitalist and non-capitalist systems;

between, on the one hand, the marketplace and, on the other hand, forms of reciprocity and redistribution (Sahakian, 2017). Polanyi (2001) loosely defined householding as involving "a closed group" that aims toward "producing and storing for the satisfaction of the wants of the members of the group", which he considered to be a more sophisticated feature of economic life, appearing historically after redistribution and reciprocity (Halperin, 1991). He could not have imagined, at his time, the role that the Internet would come to play in creating virtual groups and promoting social networks of all kinds, both on- and offline. Today, people can become part of closed groups that extend over different geographic boundaries, for instance the members of the worldwide couchsurfing community.[3] An example would be a person who rents rooms in conventional hotels, as well as through Airbnb, and also engages in couchsurfing. While some people may participate exclusively in the market economy, others move back and forth between the system of monetized exchange and various modes of the sharing economy. In some cases, householding is a form of resistance to capitalism and dependence on the state (Halperin, 1991), which is evident in certain forms of sharing, such as co-using and repairing household appliances, rather than purchasing new equipment. But even in these cases, most people purchase certain items from the capitalist marketplace while also privileging noncompetitive market economies.

The economic ideal type of "householding" raises questions about the institutional arrangements that are needed to govern hybrid economic relations involving both public and private spheres, as is the case in the sharing economy today. For instance, how should we regulate sharing activities which involve goods and services that travel between a capitalist marketplace and more solidaristic forms of interaction? The cornerstone of the capitalist system, namely private property, is at the forefront of this issue: when sharing in a householding form, people can use, sell, exchange, or co-use their private property (such as a couch or an appliance), which is transferred back and forth between the private and public realm, raising a host of regulatory issues, as will be discussed later in this chapter.

Based on these proposed links between the SSE and the sharing economy, the goal of the following section is to further explore the degree of solidarity taking place in Swiss sharing initiatives and to test a framework for evaluating them in relation to solidaristic and sustainability principles. What follows is a brief overview of the six case studies. The interviews that I conducted with key actors involved in each case were guided by the three main conceptual handles discussed above and that organize the ensuing analysis: 1) the vision and mission behind the initiatives and how they relate to solidarity and environmental sustainability; 2) how the initiatives are governed and managed in practice; and 3) the interface between the sharing economy initiatives and the market economy.

The Swiss sharing economy and case studies

First mentioned in the general media only in recent years, the sharing economy in Switzerland is positioned as being "revolutionary," but faces several barriers including changing mindsets, limited economic incentives, and political hurdles (Delaye and Vakaridis, 2014). A more recent report by the consultancy Deloitte (Zobrist and Grampp, 2015) is more forthcoming: the firm expects that more than half of the Swiss population will participate in the sharing economy in the near future and that these activities represent a clear investment opportunity for domestic companies. All notions of altruism are set aside and the sharing economy is depicted as a "modern rendition of the market economy" (translated from French). Two emblematic global brands of the so-called sharing economy, Airbnb and Uber, are active in Switzerland. There is furthermore a long history of sharing in Switzerland, such as through Caritas, an association committed to helping socially disadvantaged people, or Emmaüs, working since 1957 in Geneva to address social inequity through shelters and second-hand shops.[4] Rather than discuss questionable global actors of the so-called sharing economy in Switzerland, or older examples of charitable endeavors, I focus in the subsequent discussion on more recent sharing economy initiatives that have originated specifically in Switzerland.[5]

Description of case studies

The first case study is the Lucerne-based Mobility cooperative, the main car-sharing service in Switzerland which celebrated twenty years of operation in 2007. Based on its annual report, 120,300 people used its services in 2014, an increase of 7.4 percent from the previous year.[6] The Mobility fleet is densely distributed across cities in Switzerland, with parking spaces at all major transit hubs; more than 2,700 vehicles can be accessed in 1,400 parking areas across the country. Using Mobility is generally cheaper than car ownership, provided users privilege public transport for longer trips. Early on, managers of the Swiss rail system recognized the potential of car-sharing as a way to increase transportation options by creating a shared car-to-rail service, thereby reducing reliance on private vehicles for longer routes (which are more expensive via Mobility). The close linkage that has subsequently developed between Mobility and public transportation systems means car-sharing does not generally compete with public transportation options in Switzerland. In August 2015, Mobility launched Swiss Pass, a single card for multi-modal transportation—including car-sharing, bicycle-sharing, and train travel—to further promote the links between private/public and motorized/non-motorized modes.

The second case study is Parku, headquartered in Zurich with activities also in the Netherlands and Austria. The idea behind the organization is that parking can be scarce and expensive, and that technology can be used to facilitate access to existing and underutilized spaces. Parku is a corporation with shareholders and one of the founders is also its main investor. The firm's offices are located in an industrial building with all the flair of a start-up including hardware and software development at its core. Inducing drivers to use the Parku application has not been as much of a challenge as getting people to share their parking spaces, as the financial incentive for renting spare places is not typically a strong motivating factor.[7] In addition to working with individual parking-space owners, Parku is approaching the public and private proprietors of parking facilities across Zurich, developing software that allows employees to share or rent out their leased corporate parking spaces when they are not using them. This arrangement provides a financial benefit to employees or firms that own underutilized parking lots.

The third case is the association Lausanne Roule (Lausanne Rolls), co-founded in Lausanne in 2004 by serial entrepreneur and avid cyclist Lucas Girardet. The goal of the organization is to promote bicycling in the city and the objective has been to get more cars off the roads and more people on bikes—in the most pragmatic way possible, by making shared bicycles more available on the streets of Lausanne.[8] When the initiative first launched in the city, the different tours and activities were organized to make it enjoyable for people to get to know Lausanne from a bicycle seat. When starting this initiative on the shared École Polytechnique Fédérale de Lausanne (EPFL) and the University of Lausanne campus, staffed bike depots were replaced with bike stations and a campus card (outfitted with a smart chip) that allowed students to directly access the bicycles. In the summer of 2009, Girardet announced his intention to take his idea national at a press conference and was approached by his technical partners at EPFL to transition his association to a for-profit-corporation. For Girardet, it was an opportunity to evolve Lausanne Roule into a much larger-scale initiative. Velopass, a for-profit corporation, was subsequently founded; after almost two years of negotiations, the company was sold to the Swiss Postal System and rebranded as PubliBike.

The fourth case, Pumpipumpe, is a sharing initiative founded by Lisa Ochsenbein (Zurich) and Ivan Mele (Bern), product and process designers respectively. In 2012, they came up with a novel idea for promoting the sharing of everyday household items.[9] Working at the level of neighborhoods, Pumpipumpe stickers are used on mailboxes to allow residents to promote everyday items that they are willing to share. The stickers are designed with illustrations of the actual household items (e.g., drill, ladder, books, toys), which can be ordered and customized via the Pumpipumpe website. More than 15,000 households in Switzerland, Germany, and Austria have acquired these stickers, yet how much sharing is actually taking place is not being tracked. Recently, Pumpipumpe launched an online map that allows people to view approximately 7,000 addresses where objects are available for sharing. In the future, Ochsenbein envisions an online application to facilitate exchanges, but prefers the "real, live network" of an offline, rather than online, community—as an opportunity to enhance social connectivity among neighbors.

The fifth case study is based on the work of Dan Acher, a social entrepreneur and cultural activist, managing several different businesses in Geneva under the Happy City Lab label, including two called Tako and 42 Prod.[10] Projects range from organizing an annual outdoor cinema program, to setting up sixty pianos in the streets of Geneva during a yearly musical festival. The case study is focused on one of Archer's sharing initiatives: the placing of neighborhood-exchange boxes on city streets which stemmed from a personal effort to give away his own stuff. After putting items out on the street and watching passersby collect them, he states, "I thought, how could I make it so that other people could give their stuff away and have that same experience of satisfaction?" He customized a box usually used for distributing newspapers, with instructions on the container explaining that anyone could take or leave what they wanted. Almost instantly, as he describes, "the box was adopted." The City of Geneva then financed the installation of additional units in 2012. After a few years, the containers were suffering from wear and tear; when Acher's team took them down to have them replaced, his organization received hundreds of messages along the lines of "What have you done with my box?" Acher underlines the sense of ownership people came to develop for these exchange boxes, explaining that each one is maintained and cared for by people living in the neighborhood.[11]

Finally, Tryngo is a recently established online platform, active mostly in Geneva and the surrounding area (including nearby France), but with the ambition of extending its services to other parts of France and the United Kingdom. The website helps people find and share services, activities, household items, and spaces. Launched in May 2015, Tryngo has received favorable press reviews and is slowly gaining traction, although it is too early to evaluate its success. Founder and CEO Umer Ali believes that a new type of collaborative consumption will replace the traditional form of consuming as an expression of ownership. For Umer, technology is about bringing people together toward sharing, which he sees as having both economic and social benefits. At present, the platform takes a commission on the exchange of products and services which are shared for modest fees (e.g., one Swiss franc per day for a digital voice recorder, 20 Swiss francs per hour for Japanese lessons).[12]

Analysis of case studies in relation to value propositions

None of the respondents in this study expressed moneymaking as their sole aim. Profitability is regarded as a necessary means to pay decent wages, for Tako for example, while it is considered crucial to advance business innovations and development, for others such as Parku and velopass. In terms of placing people above profit, sharing is seen as a way to improve certain societal services, such as mobility through car- or bike-sharing, but also a way to challenge notions of ownership. At Tryngo, the vision of the organization is: "share to change." Or as founder Ali put it: "through sharing we are creating a parallel model to that of the traditional model (of ownership), which will render the older model obsolete." As a designer by training, Pumpipumpe co-founder Ochsenbein believes that sharing could lead to new product and service design, reducing the negative environmental impacts of excessive stuff. "Sharing makes sense in the material world as we have it today and would make sense in a world where we have very intelligent products, which go back into recycling," she explained. Sharing could ultimately influence purchasing decisions, leading to less material throughput in the economy and reduced volumes of waste.

Sharing as a way to more efficiently use resources is a main theme across all six of the initiatives in Geneva that inform this chapter. For instance, achieving sustainability targets is a priority at Mobility. Unlike most examples of car-sharing around the world, the goal of Mobility is to reduce private car usage and to increase multi-modal transit through its historic and well-developed partnership with the Swiss rail system. Mobility economically penalizes long-distance travel and dedicated parking spaces at all main transit hubs mean that users can seamlessly move from private to public transport. Based on a 2013 study conducted among its users, Mobility calculated the effects of car-sharing on car ownership, claiming that one shared vehicle replaces nine privately owned vehicles and that Mobility customers drive 27% less, use 8.8 million litres less fuel, and generate 20,500 tonnes less carbon dioxide per year than private car owners. When asked about rebound effects, Sonia Roos at Mobility responded that some people who try car-sharing may not own their own vehicle (thus increasing private transport mileage through Mobility), and may go on to then purchase their own private cars, based on the Mobility experience. She finds that this negative rebound is abated through more positive rebound effects and that "[t]he majority of our clients drive less with a car and change their habits," such as giving up a second car, for example, or privileging rail for longer distances. The other compensating factor is the fuel efficiency and overall quality of the Mobility fleet. The extent to which car-sharing through Mobility contributes to reducing private mobility and privileging public transport needs be further studied. Ultimately, both Mobility and Parku promote mechanized forms of mobility, even if there are strong connections to public options through the Mobility network. The Lausanne Roule bike-sharing initiative started as an effort to foster just the opposite: to get more cars off the street and more people on bikes.

The three mobility services, Mobility, Parku, and PubliBike, all challenge customary notions of ownership, but are not devoted to enhancing social connectivity. Sharing via Tryngo is facilitated through an Internet platform, but the goal is for people to meet and exchange in person at different locations across the city. In the cases of Tako and Pumpipumpe, the neighborhood is the scale at which sharing occurs. Solidaristic sharing takes place when people exchange items through the boxes placed on city streets, which become part of the fabric of community life, or through the advertisements on their personal mailboxes. Participants report satisfaction with giving and receiving, but also are experiencing new forms of leisure, such as reading more or different books or sharing different kinds of toys with their children. In relation to social inclusion, Pumpipumpe works with unemployed and underprivileged groups through social reinsertion programs. While Ochsenbein was not familiar with the social and solidarity economy in Switzerland, the principles and practices of her association live up to solidaristic values, including environmental values. Both Tako and Tryngo are members of the SSE in Geneva.

Analysis of case studies in relation to democratic governance principles

Governance within organizations relates not only to their type of institutional structure—for-profit or cooperative for instance—but also to their size. For smaller entities such as Pumpipumpe, Tryngo, and Tako the question of governance is simply not top of mind. There is a scale of activity at which democratic decision-making happens naturally, but also a scale at which systems need to be put in place to ensure participatory forms of management. The Lausanne Roule example is a case in point and highlights how growing to a national scale and into a for-profit entity has meant foregoing some of the ideals that motivated the founding of the original association. Girardet explained that the legal status of an association had a nice quality about it and was a very simple structure to set up, but that for a second stage of development, the risks and financial turnover were such that another structure was needed. As he explained, "For Lausanne Roule there were committee meetings that said 'amen' twice a year to our activities, but it was a very fragile structure." However, the decision to transition to a corporation was a difficult one. Some of his team members supported this path, while others refused to be a part of the new venture—believing in the associative structure at all costs and breaking with the newly established company out of principle. Girardet described how he lost friends in this process, who saw this move as trading in ideology for profiteering. The for-profit entity velopass was eventually sold to the Swiss Postal System and rebranded as PubliBike. Yet he now seems to regret this sale. "They are no longer in the mindset of making bikes available," he confided in the interview. "It has become purely financial, to make money or perhaps to lose as little money as possible. All of the ideals have been lost."

Setting up an activity as an association is often the favored route for a new, small-scale sharing initiative, as the cooperative structure may be more complicated to put in place and is perceived as being a somewhat outdated model, based on these interviews. Yet cooperatives are predicated on democratic decision-making and participatory membership models and, according to Sonia Roos at Mobility, the cooperative structure is one of the keys to its success. She explained:

> With this form, we have the possibility to have a long-term sustainability strategy ... We don't need to send profit reports each month to our investors. We have the possibility to grow in a more sustainable manner and retain the profit. We reinvest the profit into business innovation and technology.

Through a system that engages with a broad membership network across Switzerland, Roos claims that the cooperative governance structure allows Mobility to be close to its end-users and continuously improve its services. Mobility is also part of a larger cooperative network in Switzerland called the Community of Interests for Cooperative Enterprises (IGG) founded in 2010 and aimed at providing counsel to companies organized on a cooperative basis.[13]

According to its website, IGG is the largest group of cooperative companies in Switzerland, accounting for approximately 16 percent of the country's gross domestic product (GDP). There can be a downside to a cooperative model relative to the market economy, however, as I will discuss in the next section.

To insure financial profit and access to different types of revenue streams, Tako founder Acher has created an association that serves the public interest and therefore gains access to public funds (and manages the neighborhood box-exchange project), while 42 Prod is a limited liability company, able to take on consulting projects that generate additional revenue for the team and for nonlucrative ventures such as the neighborhood box scheme. The management style across the other entities that are part of Acher's consortium is horizontal in that the eight staff members participate in the day-to-day decisions, yet the companies are organized with Acher as the final arbiter. He deplores the need for these different structures, as it increases his operating costs to manage multiple accounting systems, but he explained that the City of Geneva requested these various institutional forms.

Analysis of case studies in relation to the economic marketplace interface

What has emerged from the case studies, and in relation to Polanyi's economic types, is that actors in the sharing economy navigate between different economies, from the capitalist and competitive market economy to the social and solidarity economy based on reciprocity and democratic governance. What I am terming the "economic market interface" is meant to capture all of the moments when solidaristic sharing comes up against customary forms of commercial exchange focused on profit making, but also a competitive marketplace where capital investments and limited risks may be necessary to remain afloat, or where recruiting employees means competing with a labor market for attractive salaries.

At Mobility, Roos was not familiar with the formal notion of the SSE yet many of its guiding principles adhere to this framework.[14] For example, over the past two years, the scale of difference between the lowest and highest paid salary at Mobility has been no more than five. When asked whether these remuneration limits posed a problem in terms of attracting talent in a competitive employment market, Roos explained,

> We have no problems hiring good people because I would say it's getting more and more important to have a good job, rather than a high salary. We talk about the Generation Y that has other values. We have a very good reputation in this area.

A cooperative structure has its advantages, in terms of implementing long-term sustainability plans, but also presents certain drawbacks. While Mobility strives for transparency with its members, information such as user profiles is not shared publicly, for competitive reasons. There is also the question of Mobility International AG (MIAG), the limited liability company which develops the software and applications at the heart of this sharing enterprise. As Roos explained, there was a need to create a separate legal entity to protect the overall organization from the risks involved with technological developments, yet this subsidiary does not need to adhere to the same governance system as the cooperative.

With the objective of reducing the barriers to sharing and in partnership with other major cooperatives in Switzerland (La Mobilière and Migros), Mobility has invested in Sharoo, a peer-to-peer car-sharing service that could have potential in more rural areas where Mobility fleets are currently not available. Roos explains, "For the customer, the proximity is very important ... There's a mental barrier in getting to know the car-sharing system. We hope that all these sharing activities help to decrease the barriers for more people, toward more sharing." Another initiative launched by Mobility in 2015 in Basel is called Catch-a-Car, in the form of a limited liability corporation. The barriers to sharing have been further reduced, as no prior car reservation is needed and membership is expedited. Much like Uber but without the driver, this service allows a user to identify an available car in the immediate vicinity, access the vehicle using a smart card, and then drop it off at another location. Pilot projects, such as these examples, are also set up as limited liability corporations by Mobility—as they are able to attract more capital investment than what would be gained through a cooperative membership base, and are also able to protect the entities and individuals engaged in the pilot from financial risks. Here we can see how a cooperative governance structure must adapt in the face of the market economy. In a larger context of competitive and rapid technological developments, cooperatives in Switzerland are finding ways to adapt by creating for-profit spin offs to reduce risk and inject capital as needed.

Umer Ali would like Tryngo to be an economically viable sharing economy initiative, and for this to happen the start-up will need to be profitable. "I'm not afraid of being a corporation," he explains, suggesting that this stance is not comfortable to some members of the SSE who would rather "ignore the notion of profitability." Girardet, founder of Lausanne Roule, similarly indicated that for him, SSE members tend to shy away from profitability yet, as he put it, "If I take risks and am able to sell my company, why not [make a profit]? Why penalize or blame me for making money?" At Pumpipumpe, the founders also see value in profitability, in that it would allow them to further invest in and improve their ideas. "I'm not against growth but for more intelligent producing and consuming," Ochsenbein explained.

At the interface with the market economy, sharing activities also raise questions in relation to private property. Taking Parku as an example, to what extent can private parking spaces be shared publicly? While limited visitor parking is often available in private car parks, the Parku business model would allow any user to open electronic parking gates and access space in otherwise private parking areas. This creates a grey area in how public and private spaces are managed, and one that local authorities have yet to regulate.

Conclusion

This chapter set out to define the opportunity for more solidaristic sharing based on societal and environmental values and participatory decision-making in a democratic society without ignoring the interactions between a sharing economy and the dominant market economy. Drawing on six cases from Switzerland, I considered different shades of "sharing" in relation to these main themes. What emerged from this analysis is the importance of understanding the governance system and institutional setting of particular sharing initiatives. Particularly relevant are the differences among associations, cooperatives, and for-profit enterprises when it comes to maintaining ideals over time and ensuring democratic forms of governance, but also remaining afloat in the context of a wider competitive marketplace. The interface between sharing in the market economy and the solidarity economy remains, from a regulatory point of view, a grey area. Polanyi's work becomes relevant here, as the social embeddedness of all economic activities means being explicit about institutional arrangements, from norms to regulations, and how they shape and are shaped by sharing practices. Sharing in the householding economy, involving livelihood strategies that navigate between a capitalist market economy and a more solidaristic reciprocity economy, requires grappling with very different institutional settings and forms of interdependence. In a market economy, price and scarcity to a large extent define success while in a solidaristic reciprocity economy, people are placed in the center, especially in terms of their societal and environmental well-being.

To further explore the significance of social embeddedness of the sharing economy, I would like to focus on four aspects of how this form of exchange is now evolving. First, the technological developments that have to a great extent facilitated sharing are not showing any signs of slowing down. Car-sharing giant Mobility is not immune to these trends: new initiatives are being piloted that would allow people to share their private vehicles rather than just rely on the existing Mobility fleet. This could have consequences for environmental sustainability, as a centralized stock of vehicles can be maintained in terms of energy efficiency, while private car owners may not be sharing with this objective in mind. Bike sharing will soon follow, as Bluetooth technologies on lock systems will allow for the pooling of private bicycles, as it will a host of other personal items—unlocking homes, garages, and offices.

Second, the changing technology relates directly to how people value ownership and the cultural norms that would need to take root in order to promote more sharing of private or common property. Prevailing habits and norms are extremely resistant to change and a culture of sharing would need to be instilled through political reform, promoting sharing as a value through the school system, for example, or facilitated through public services (see Chapter 7). In Switzerland, this is currently the case with respect to families with children that are familiar with book libraries (*bibliothèques*) but also toy libraries (*ludothèque*), where items can be used on location or borrowed. The sharing of other household items could also be promoted through such venues, with state support.

Third, and related to the two points above, these technological developments and changes in societal norms will place a spotlight on regulatory arrangements around private property, the cornerstone of the capitalist system. The rules and other social arrangements governing the sharing of private goods (and services) are a matter of central concern if more solidaristic forms of sharing are to be promoted in the future. At present, many of the peer-to-peer exchange platforms rely on the reputation of the users, with people able to rate others using a point system—even if these rudimentary systems have their flaws (see, e.g., Ert et al., 2016). Who is liable for property damage or accidents in private settings that are now "shared" will remain a growing area of concern in the future of sharing. Finally, it will become increasingly important for entities in the sharing economy to remain competitive in a rapidly evolving technological landscape and to address the manifold legal issues that will no doubt continue to arise around these activities. In relation to competitiveness and protection from risk, for-profit institutional structures are currently upheld as a favored alternative, particularly in relation to the timely injection of investment funds. While cooperatives can work toward protecting producers and consumers and ensuring ownership and decent wages, as Cohen (2017) suggests in his example of multi-stakeholder cooperatives, the dominant capitalist market remains the overarching system to which sharing activities will likely need to bend to remain competitive in the market. Which leads me to the conclusion that solidaristic forms of sharing, under a multi-purpose cooperative model, for example, would need special support to succeed. One way to deliver this assistance is by establishing strategic partnerships with the public sector (as demonstrated by the Mobility partnership with the Swiss rail system) or more attractive financial arrangements facilitated by the state. Indeed, some forms of protectionism may be necessary to insulate more cohesive forms of sharing from being gobbled up by more capitalist competitors (see also Chapter 10).

If a more socially just and environmentally sound future is to be facilitated by sharing, the SSE provides some guidance on moving forward in terms of making value systems explicit, but institutional arrangements will need to be more thoroughly taken into account. Regardless of what new opportunities are offered through technological innovation, the political and social context needs to be conducive to solidaristic forms of sharing. This entails either building on existing institutions and initiatives, such as cooperative structures and solidaristic sharing already underway, or imagining new ways to further promote sharing at the municipal or state level. Ties could be made between the sharing economy and city-wide initiatives such as efforts to better integrate migrant populations or to reduce carbon emissions. In Switzerland, a small country that boasts an active participative democracy and a rich tradition of sharing services, it may be more practicable to continue to promote sharing on the basis of values concordant with cooperation and reciprocity and supportive of more sustainable forms of consumption. In other contexts, contesting existing norms around individualism and profit-making could prove extremely challenging. And yet, change is already underway, as the so-called sharing economy gains momentum around the world—where, at least in discursive terms, community ideals and a collaborative spirit are endorsed. More attention needs to be placed not on the marketing narrative, but on how sharing initiatives relate to the political context and social values, to distinguish solidaristic sharing from more capitalist interpretations.

Notes

1 The Lima Declaration is at www.ripess.org/wp-content/uploads/2011/07/declaration_lima1997_EN.pdf. The English translation of RIPESS is the Intercontinental Network for the Promotion of Social Solidary Economy.
2 The English translation is the Chamber for the Social and Solidarity Economy (APRES). See www.apres-ge.ch.
3 Couchsurfing is a service that leverages the hospitality of people who are willing to open their home to travelers and provide them with free accommodation. This time-honored tradition is now being facilitated through the Internet, virtually connecting a global community of travelers.
4 Caritas operates on a worldwide basis. For information on Swiss activities, refer to www.caritas.ch/en/what-we-do/switzerland.
5 The sharing economy in Switzerland must be distinguished from examples of how sharing is playing out elsewhere. In Greece, for example, sharing (and bartering) has emerged in reaction to dire economic straits. While inequalities exist in Switzerland, the general population enjoys a high comfort level compared to other countries in Europe and, indeed, the world. Under such circumstances, sharing is not solely motivated by economic necessity.
6 Interview with Sonia Roos, Head of Strategic Projects, Mobility, on July 21, 2015.
7 Interview with Cyrill Mostert, Country Manager, Parku, on July 23, 2015.
8 Interview with Lucas Girardet, Founder of Lausanne Roule and Velopass, on August 19, 2015.
9 Interview with Lisa Ochsenbein, Co-Founder and President of Pumpipumpe, on July 23, 2015.
10 Interview with Dan Acher, Founder and Director, 42 Prod and Tako, on August 8, 2015.
11 A short video showcasing "a day in the life of a neighbourhood exchange box" can be found at: http://happycitylab.com/en/project/exchange-boxes.
12 The American dollar and the Swiss Franc are approximately equal at the time of this writing.
13 For details on the IGG, see http://iggenossenschaftsunternehmen.ch/uber-uns/die-igg-ziele/?lang=en.
14 This lack of familiarity with the social and solidarity economy may be due to a language issue, as the interview was conducted in English and the respondent works in a German-speaking setting.

References

Botsman, R. and Rogers, R. (2010) *What's Mine is Yours: The Rise of Collaborative Consumption*. New York: HarperCollins.
Chambre de l'Économie Sociale et Solidaire (APRES-GE) (2010) *Etude Statistique: Photographie de l'Économie Sociale et Solidaire à Genève (Statistics Study: Snapshot of the Social and Solidarity Economy in Geneva)*. Geneva: APRES-GE (in French).
Cohen, M. (2017). *The Future of Consumer Society: Prospects for Sustainability in the New Economy*. New York: Oxford University Press.

Cretieneau, A.-M. (2010) "Economie sociale et solidaire et développement durable: pensée et actions en conjunction (Social economy and sustainable development: thinking and actions in conjunction)," *Marché et Organisations* 11:31–71 (in French).

Defourny, J. and Develtere, P. (1999) "Origines et contours de l'économie sociale au nord et au sud (Origins and contours of the social economy in the North and South)," in Defourny, J., Develtere, P., and Fonteneau, B. (eds.), *L'économie Sociale au Nord et au Sud (The Social Economy in the North and South)*. Brussels: De Boeck Université (in French), pp. 25–50.

Defourny, J., Develtere, P., and Fonteneau, B. (eds.) (2000) *Social Economy North and South*. Leuven: HIVA and Centre d'Economie Sociale.

Delaye, F. and Vakaridis, M. (2014) "Economie de partage: une révolution se prepare (Sharing economy: a revolution in the making)," *Bilan*, October 8 (in French).

Dubuisson-Quellier, S. (2013) *Ethical Consumption*. Black Point, Nova Scotia: Fernwood Publishing.

Ert, E., Fleischer, A., and Magen, N. (2016) "Trust and reputation in the sharing economy: the role of personal photos in Airbnb," *Tourism Management* 55:62–73.

Fraisse, L. (2003) "Quels projets politiques pour l'économie solidaire? (What political projects for the solidarity economy?)" *Cultures en Mouvement* 62:4 (in French).

Fraisse, L., Guérin, I., and Laville, J.-L. (2007) "Economie solidaire: des initiatives locales à l'action publique: introduction (Solidarity economy: from local initiatives to public action: introduction)," *Revue Tiers Monde* 190:245–253 (in French).

Gansky, L. (2010) *The Mesh: Why the Future of Business Is Sharing*. New York: Portfolio Penguin.

Graeber, D. (2001) *Toward an Anthropological Theory of Value: The False Coin of Our Own Dreams*. New York: Palgrave.

Halperin, R. (1991) "Karl Polanyi's concept of householding: resistance and livelihood in an Appalachian region," *Research in Economic Anthropology* 13:93–116.

Hillenkamp, I. (2013) *L'économie Solidaire en Bolivie: Entre Marché et Démocratie (The Solidarity Economy in Bolivia: Between Market and Democracy)*. Geneva: Editions Karthala (in French).

International Solidarity Globalization Conference (ISGC) (1997) *Lima Declaration*. Lima: ISGC.

Laville, J.-L. (2003) "A new European socioeconomic perspective," *Review of Social Economy* 61(3):389–405.

Laville, J.-L. (2011) "What is the third sector? From the non-profit sector to the social and solidarity economy: theoretical debates and European reality," EMES European Research Network Working Paper 11/01. http://emes.net/publications/working-papers/what-is-the-third-sector-from-the-non-profit-sector-to-the-social-and-solidarity-economy-theoretical-debate-and-european-reality.

Ostrom, E. (2002 [1990]) *Governing the Commons: The Evolution of Institutions for Collective Action*. New York: Cambridge University Press.

Peterson, N. (1993) "Demand sharing: reciprocity and the pressure for generosity among foragers," *American Anthropologist* 95(4):860–874.

Polanyi, K. (1957) "The economy as instituted process," in Polanyi, K., Arensberg, C., and Pearson, H. (eds.), *Trade and Market in the Early Empires*. Glencoe, IL: Free Press, pp. 243–269.

Polanyi, K. (2001 [1944]) *The Great Transformation: The Political and Economic Origins of Our Time*. Boston, MA: Beacon Press.

Rifkin, J. (2014) *The Zero Marginal Cost Society: The Internet of Things, The Collaborative Commons, and the Eclipse of Capitalism*. New York: Palgrave Macmillan.

Sahakian, M. (2016) "The social and solidarity economy: why is it relevant to industrial ecology?" in Druckman, A. and Clift, R. (eds.), *Taking Stock of Industrial Ecology*. Berlin: Springer, pp. 205–227.

Sahakian, M. (2017) "Réciprocité et solidarité: liens et tensions apparentes avec l'économie du partage (Reciprocity and solidarity: commonalities and apparent tensions with the sharing economy)," in Hillenkamp, I. and Saiag, H. (eds.), *Monnaie et Finance: des Pratiques Alternatives? Pour une Socioéconomie Engage (Money and Finance: Alternative Practices? For an Engaged Socioeconomy)*. Paris: Garnier (in French).

Sahakian, M. and Servet, J.-M. (2016) "Separating the wheat from the chaff: sharing versus self-interest in crowdfunding," in Assadi, D. (ed.), *Strategic Approaches to Successful Crowdfunding*. Hershey, PA: IGI Global, pp. 294–312.

Servet, J.-M. (2007) "Le principe de la réciprocité chez Karl Polanyi, contribution à une définition de l'économie solidaire' (The principle of reciprocity in Karl Polanyi, a contribution to the definition of the solidarity economy)," *Revue Tiers Monde* 2(190):255–273 (in French).

Servet, J.-M. (2009) "Toward an alternative economy: reconsidering the market, money and value," in Hann, C. and Hart, K. (eds.), *Market and Society: The Great Transformation Today*. New York: Cambridge University Press, pp. 72–90.

van Griethuysen, P. (2010) "Why are we growth-addicted? The hard way towards degrowth in the involutionary western development path," *Journal of Cleaner Production* 18(6):590–595.

Zobrist, L. and M. Grampp. (2015) "L'économie du partage: partager et gagner de l'argent. Quelle position pour la Suisse?' (The sharing economy: sharing and making money. What is the position of Switzerland?), retrieved March 1, 2016 from www2.deloitte.com/content/dam/Deloitte/ch/Documents/consumer-business/ch-fr-cb-Leconomie-du-partage-partager-et-gagner-de-largent.pdf (in French).

4 Social change at the nexus of consumption and politics

A case study of local food movements

Emily Huddart Kennedy

Local food: the movement that tastes so good

I like local food. It is hard *not* to love a movement that has popularized pickled vegetables and hoppy beer. I appreciate the farmers' market down the street from my house and I enjoy visiting small farms where healthy-looking hippies and hipsters can be spotted among heirloom tomatoes, free-range heritage hens, and rows of kale. And yet, like many other academics, I have been skeptical that the production and consumption of high-priced food catering to relatively elite tastes has much transformative potential (cf., Allen et al., 2003; Guthman, 2008; Johnston, 2008). In contrast, proponents point out that this movement has expanded rapidly, influenced the infrastructure of most industrialized urban areas, and catalyzed debates about the benefits of local food production and consumption (e.g., Desrochers and Shimizu, 2012). Building on these assets, I argue that sustainable consumption researchers should not dismiss the local food movement out of hand, but that we might glean some understanding of how to move beyond consumerism by examining possible shifts in engagement practices in this site of civic action.[1] Specifically, I look within the leadership of the local food movement in state, market, and civic spheres to identify subtle shifts in food-related practices—1) cultivating resistance frames, and 2) questioning convivial approaches to social change—and suggest these shifts may offer hope of a transition beyond consumer society.

Many scholars of sustainable consumption have bemoaned the individualization of efforts to protect the environment (e.g., Maniates, 2001; Szasz, 2007). The local food movement in many ways reflects these critics' worst fears: a movement that at its inception sought to address environmental issues such as soil-nutrient loss now seems to fetishize urban agriculture and has created a "class" of citizenship that reflects consumer-spending choices (Johnston, 2008). Perhaps none of this should come as a surprise since the local food movement grew while governments increasingly came to ideologically pursue economic growth and rely on individuals to "do their bit" for the environment with little to no financial support from the state (Thorsen, 2009). That is, local food enthusiasts have been engaged in politics at a time when the environment, social justice, and community development are intricately bound with individual consumer-spending decisions.

Though this individualization has been extensively observed and analyzed in the food movement (e.g., Allen et al., 2003; Busa and Garder, 2014; Johnston and Baumann, 2010; Lynch and Giles, 2013), these studies sampled food consumers or, in some cases, local farmers. There is comparatively less scholarship analyzing the discourse and practices of those who shape the local food movement and politicize food consumption.

The remainder of the chapter is structured as follows. I begin by presenting some background material on the local food movement in Canada, the theoretical framework of this chapter, and the research project from which the consequent data are derived. The findings are narrowly focused on addressing the question, *what germane political discourse exists in the Canadian local food movement that might incite a shift away from consumer society?* In other words, can a movement created within consumer society offer a way out of consumerism?

The local food movement

It is striking to note similarities that exist across local food movements in geographically, historically, and culturally distinct locations from the United States (Guthman, 2008; Holland and Gómez Correal, 2013) to the United Kingdom (Sonnino and Marsden, 2006) and beyond (Sonnino and Griggs-Trevarthan, 2013). The most compelling explanation for this relative homogeneity is that the local food movements of industrialized, highly developed nations were born during the neoliberal era—a period when diverse spatial and historical differences have been leveled through marketization (Holland and Gómez Correal, 2013). Described in more detail in countless other sources, neoliberalism represents an ideology that has escaped the confines of its stature as a political theory. Moving well past the premise that personal freedom is augmented when the government stops interfering with the market, neoliberalism has been described as being one of the most profound influences on the world today, shaping (most relevant to this chapter) political engagement and cultural norms (Thorsen, 2009). In particular, the neoliberal moment has helped to forge the viewpoint that citizens can enact a better world through their consumption decisions.[2]

The local food movement in Canada was popularized during the early 2000s. Although there were farmers' markets and community gardens long before, these physical spaces supported private-sphere practices—shopping, cooking, eating—rather than the public-sphere practices of identity display, civic engagement and volunteerism, and social entrepreneurship. It is these public-sphere practices (and their transformative potential) that I focus on in this chapter.

By providing a broader frame of reference and situating private consumption choices squarely in the public domain (a move that arguably would have been quite different in an environment less influenced by neoliberal ideology), the local food movement has politicized spaces like farmers' markets, community gardens, and even the kitchen table. This politicization has been supported by the coinciding development of a range of projects and organizations that identify as part of the local food movement, including programs to increase access to healthy fruits and vegetables in low-income communities, urban fruit-gleaning projects (harvesting fruit from trees on public land and distributing it to communities in need), seed libraries, and campaigns to protect farmland from urban and industrial development.

Popular Toronto-based author and icon in the city's local food movement, Wayne Roberts, believes he witnessed the birth of this movement in Canada in 2004 (Elton, 2015). Roberts was chair of the Toronto Food Policy Council for four years, "when suddenly new people started to participate.[3] The meetings went from being sparsely attended to being so popular that the fire marshal had to clear some people from the room. As Roberts indicates, "Food became part of identity, part of place" (Elton, 2015). The movement grew at different paces across the country and across urban and rural locations but was likely fomented by both the growing mistrust of the industrial food system (as outlined in the books *Fast Food Nation* and *The Omnivore's Dilemma*) and the emergence of a generation of young Canadians who were increasingly disaffected with traditional politics and hopeful that their ethical engagement in the market could lead to a more sustainable and equitable world. Other scholars have noted that the success of the local food movement may also be due to changing norms of citizenship, reflecting in particular neoliberal logics wherein people see market-based activity as the most promising pathway to express moral and ethical concerns (Guthman, 2008; Johnston, 2008).

The broad frame that the Canadian local food movement champions is the development of "sustainable, regional food systems in which farmland is spared from urban and industrial sprawl so that ecologically-minded farmers produce food, with consideration for animal, environmental and human health, for a public who knows where their food comes from and is engaged in eating seasonally" (Elton, 2015).[4] The movement comprises a wide range of groups that aspire to support the development of a more sustainable, ethical, and just food system.

Theorizing social change and social stasis

The local food movement—which I conceive as involving all elements of the food system, but primarily consumption and production processes and their associated civic and political engagement practices—includes a wide range of topics studied within the field of sustainable consumption and production (SCP). For example, it involves issues of well-being and quality of life, seeks less ecologically destructive approaches to producing consumer goods, and in the arena of political engagement, pursues policy and technological shifts to support a process of localizing food systems. Yet within food-studies literature, analyses rarely utilize the sustainable consumption lens and within SCP literature, local food politics are often overlooked (see Seyfang, 2009, for an exception). To understand the potential for the local food movement to contribute to debates on how to transition away from consumer society, I turn to scholarship at the nexus of SCP and social practice theories.

Interest in the systematic study of sustainable consumption has developed to the point where numerous theoretical approaches can be identified and distinguished from one another. In this chapter, I refer to recent characterization of the landscape of SCP research developed by Frank Geels and colleagues (see Geels et al., 2015) as a framework to identify promising indicators of a shift beyond consumerism. These authors identify three branches of theorizing sustainable consumption and production that they term the reformist, revolutionary, and reconfiguration positions. Reformist scholarship is rooted in neoclassical economics (rational actor) models and presumes that individual behavior is shaped by preferences. By altering individual preferences, the logic follows, policy programs can also alter individual behavior. Reformist studies of local food consumption and production are prolific (e.g., Conner et al., 2009). From a reformist vantage point, a shift to procuring food from local growers might exemplify a change in production or consumption but not necessarily a *transformation* in support for consumer society.

The revolutionary perspective draws from critical theory and understands sustainable consumption and production to be hampered by a capitalist system within which there is little hope for sustainability. There exists much research on local food consumption *and* local food politics that adopts a revolutionary perspective (e.g., Allen et al., 2003). This perspective largely abandons the individual and their actions, focusing on much broader shifts in political systems rather than the everyday actions needed to change such systems.

The third stance is termed the "reconfiguration" approach. Comprising social practice theories and the multi-level perspective (MLP), theories in this tradition share a focus on taking account of the structuring properties of social context and everyday routines. Here, behaviors secede as *practices* come to the foreground: the sayings and doings of individuals and groups are understood as dynamic and interconnected. As these sayings and doings change, so might social and physical contexts as these are understood to change recursively. The term "reconfiguration" refers to the approach to social change inherent in such theories: social change is understood to depend on *reconfiguring* the social context, including everything from cultural associations, material arrangements, social policy, and techno-social infrastructure. This approach has to date been applied to understanding food consumption in general (Warde et al., 2007; Halkier and Jensen, 2011), but less so to understanding local food consumption specifically (see Sahakian and Wilhite, 2013 for an exception). In this chapter, my aim is to draw on a qualitative dataset and a rich tradition of phenomenologically valid accounts of local food politics to identify shifts in practices that might foster a transition beyond our consumer society.

To clarify, I do not "test" social practice theories here. Rather, I draw on the logic of the reconfiguration perspective to sensitize my analytic approach for identifying subtle changes taking place in how leaders in the food movement understand transforming the food system. I discern several promising avenues that I will discuss in the results section. First, I observe a sense that political engagement may need to look past the consumer as agent of change to broaden the focus to the role of the state. This suggests a change in the political engagement practices that local food leaders are drawing upon to incite social change. Second, I note preliminary challenges to the normative standard of conviviality that is emphasized in food politics. This suggests that the components of political engagement (specifically, the meanings associated with "best" civic engagement practices) are shifting away from envisioning the consumer as the cornerstone of social change. Finally, I observe a willingness to think about who benefits and who loses under the current food system. Such questions seem to necessitate contentious approaches that may involve but will not rely on the consumer. Taken together, these three shifts reflect an emergent awareness that consumer behavior is not the cornerstone of social change, an important recognition for transitioning beyond consumer society.

Analyzing the local food movement in Canada: study design and methods

Between May 2013 and May 2014, with the help of three research assistants, I interviewed fifty-seven leaders in local food movements in three Canadian cities: Edmonton, Toronto, and Victoria. The research team and I also observed advocates and activists in twelve food-related sites in these cities, including protests, city-council meetings, local food-networking events, farmers' markets, community gardens, and working farms. The study was designed with a grounded-theory framework in mind. Data were collected while theory was developed, thus theories and concepts emerging from this research were formed abductively.

Let me briefly review each of the cities that were part of this investigation. First, Edmonton is the most northerly metropolitan city in Canada. Its local politics at the time of data collection were shaped by an extremely profitable oil and gas industry, high real estate values, a business-friendly council keen to obliterate barriers to development, *and* a rapidly growing local food movement. It was easy to locate participants in the city. We used existing local food-related listservs to send out an invitation to contribute to a study about changing the food system. We emphasized that we were interested in respondents who participated on a daily basis or more seldom but that our focus was on those who go beyond personal production or consumption. We selected an initial sample of three government employees (federal, provincial, and municipal), three representatives of civil society (nonprofit organizations and community gardens), and three market-based participants (farmers and a social entrepreneur). From this seed sample of nine individuals we snowballed out to a final Edmonton-based sample of twenty-two respondents, which included four government representatives, nine members of civil society, and nine market-based participants. The semi-structured interview (used in all sites) was designed to elicit information on the individual's path to the local food movement, his or her role in this movement, his or her approach to politics, the ideal food system to which they aspire, and the barriers and opportunities for achieving that objective. Interviews ranged in length from 45 minutes to three hours and were recorded and professionally transcribed.

Second, Toronto is home to the aforementioned food policy council, an exemplary institutional body that uses citizen engagement to develop sustainable and just policy around urban agriculture and local food. Toronto is the most populous city in Canada and at the time of data collection was experiencing tension between residents of the city core and the extensive suburban communities outside the city. Downtown residents favored spending on public transit, downtown schools and public services, and protection of the greenbelt surrounding the city. Suburban residents were largely in favor of lowering municipal spending and taxes and represented a largely ethnic, working-class coalition of fiscal conservatives. The local food movement appeared to be primarily supported by urban Torontonians. With a food policy council established in 1991—Canada's longest-standing food council—and a multifaceted agenda to use urban agriculture to address poverty, urban sprawl, declining social capital, class-based access to nutritious foods, and food waste, sampling in Toronto was straightforward and used the same purposive sampling strategy as described above. Our initial sample included two government representatives (municipal and provincial), four civil society-based participants (non-profit organizations), and four market-based actors (farmers and social entrepreneurs). We used snowball sampling to reach nine additional participants with a final breakdown of four respondents from the state, six from civil society, and nine from the market.

Finally, Victoria is a mid-sized city located on Vancouver Island in the westernmost province of British Columbia. It is a highly desirable location for young families and retired workers from all over Canada—captured in the unfortunate epithet "home of the newlywed and the nearly-dead." Property prices are among the highest in Canada and affordability of land was a contentious issue at the time of data collection. A sense of scarcity was foremost for many participants who spoke of Victoria's vulnerable food system (in the event of an earthquake the city could be cut off from the mainland, which provides at least 75 percent of daily food) and barriers to entry for food production. A bill put forth (and eventually passed) by the provincial government threatened to remove land from the province's Agricultural Land Reserve (ALR) which protects arable land from industrial, residential, and commercial development. Victoria has an active local food scene but it is quite close-knit, making it a more difficult site to access. However, we constructed an initial sample of one state representative, four civil society participants, and three farmers and then snowball sampled to achieve a final sample of three government employees/representatives, seven civil society participants, and six respondents from the market sphere.

Two research assistants and I conducted the data analysis using NVivo 10 qualitative data-management software. We developed themes individually and met to discuss which themes we felt were well supported by the data. In this way, several dozen themes were developed through the data-analysis process. Using matrix coding, we conducted cross-tabulations for these themes to identify differences across site and sector of involvement. This chapter draws primarily on quotations from within the themes "Resistance Frames" and "Questioning Convivial Strategies" and refers to themes developed in other publications from this dataset.

Resistance frames

A few participants spoke about their ideal food system in tones and phrases that differed from the majority of the people interviewed. That is, these respondents imagined a food system that had addressed what they saw as a key failure of the local food movement: the high cost of local food. For those who emphasized the injustice of high costs for consumers and low wages for farmers (a framing centered upon justice and rights), their efforts to envision bringing about such change had little to do with consumers and envisaged a much more active role for the state. For instance, when Sherry, a farmer in Victoria, was asked what she thought about the fact that local food is so expensive, she said:

> That's a good question. Well, there has to be some built-in securities for farmers. Big farmers are subsidized, right? I don't know if a subsidy is an answer. I don't even know how I'd feel about that personally, but if it was … Farmers can't price food low enough so that everyone can eat and eat themselves … But if everyone made a base minimal wage … There are some models in other countries that you're guaranteed an annual income and everyone lives above the low-income cut-off line and everybody can afford to have more choices.

Although the more dominant response among participants was to argue that the price premium simply demands that consumers question their own priorities, Sherry and several others practiced a form of local food politics that makes demands of the state to create a food system that is fair for farmers and eaters.

The following excerpts reaffirm the observation that questioning elitism, costs, and framing food as a right rather than a choice are part of the practice of embedding food-related topics in political engagement. For those participants who have worked toward a more just and sustainable food system, opening more farmers' markets and community gardens is not enough. These individuals express frustration that more local farms sell produce to high-end restaurants that cater to a wealthy clientele; they would rather see local farms supporting local food sovereignty. Sherry, quoted above, makes this point:

> To be honest, I made a lot more money selling to restaurants. But that's just not who local food should go to feed. It should go to feed people here who don't have enough to eat. I argued to death with the restaurant owner about making this stuff affordable and we just didn't see eye-to-eye. Instead of, "we sell it for this much because people will pay this much" it should be "what can people pay?"

Diane made reference to similar themes:

> I actually don't believe in selling my food to restaurants. Even though I worked in them for years and the whole bit, I just don't believe it's a good

thing. The whole notion of producing local food so you can feed tourists …
wait a minute. That is very big in this city. Local is supposed to be for us.
That's my rant.

These two farmers recognize that the financial rewards for food growers are found
in selling to high-end restaurants and marketing nonfood items like cut flowers.
In questioning the value of supporting local food restaurants, these women create
space to challenge the meaning of political engagement in the food movement.
Crucially, they shift from assuming "good" citizens are those who pay more for
local food to reframing food as a right for citizens rather than a consumer
commodity.

The speakers above connected injustice to their vision of political engagement
practices, resulting in an imagined model for transformative change that rejects
consumerism as a path to a more just and sustainable food system. I asked Leora,
who has been involved in the Canadian local food movement for twenty years
and started a food-justice organization in Victoria, to describe her ideal food
system and her answer covers three single-spaced pages of transcript. She explains
that the current fight over the ALR is just a smaller part of a bigger issue over land
rights: "[W]e need to actually have a food-land reserve which includes all the
First Nations and indigenous foods pathways." Leora is aware that the dominant
form of food politics is one that aspires to be positive and pragmatic: "[T]here is
this kind of bright shiny local food and everyone is getting on board with it
without having a deeper understanding of the justice element." She has moved
away from the organizations that promote local food consumption and production
and toward groups that are defining local food politics both regionally and
provincially. In the excerpt below she elaborates how a consumer-focused model
of change can obscure important evaluations of the larger systems that shape food
production and consumption:

> If I'm going down to the farmers' market and buying my organic and therefore
> everything is good … Well the challenge is that a lot of external things
> impact food systems like a living wage and housing prices and all of those
> kinds of things. So how are we working outside of our food systems bubble to
> impact and change structures and political frameworks? That is where the
> conversation needs to keep happening and keep digging but there aren't
> many places we can have those conversations right now.

Alison, an employee of a food access and assistance organization, synthesizes the
two previous excerpts by recognizing the limitations of consumer-based change
tactics, the need for state intervention, and the role of larger systems in shaping
food-related practices:

> I don't know how you make inclusive spaces that really everyone feels okay
> in and everyone can participate in. People talk about it but I actually don't
> think we as a society pay enough attention to class. I think we pay a lot of

attention to other issues and I think we kind of think that class has been erased somehow. I can really only see two ways food insecurity is going to be illuminated. Either you raise people's incomes or you subsidize food, or both. Some combination of the two. I don't really see any other way and to raise incomes sufficiently so that people could buy food at a farmer's market, you're talking about massive increases and the middle class by and large, it's raising social assistance rates and raising minimum wage ... It is immoral that there are people in our society that live this way. That in and of itself is wrong.

Alison approaches the end goal of having greater consumption of healthy, local foods as a moral question. She uses a discourse of rights to assert that there is something wrong with class-based access to good food. While others see overcoming cost-related barriers as a necessary step in localizing the food system, Alison contends that food consumption is intimately tied to politics and distributive notions of justice. Food consumption is not a choice, she articulates, it is a function of socioeconomic inequality.

Interview participants who had been involved in the Canadian local food movement since or before its inception saw food production and consumption as linked to government policy, local land-use decisions, cultural expectations of what politics should look and feel like, the structure of the labor force, webs of power relations, and so forth. They understood that affecting change in one of these arenas is difficult if you do not address the others. For instance, Ernesto, a retired computer scientist who assists in running a farm and food-box program for low-income immigrants in Edmonton said, when asked what ideal food system he aspires to develop:

> We could talk for a while about that ... I want to take the question outside the context of our current system. At the heart of the problem in our agriculture is the monetary system ... So a sustainable system for agricultural supplies has to go back to the roots ... Land was once a communal property that the church was supposed to take care of for the masses. They ended up owning it somehow but in reality, it was a communal property so that every human being had access to grow their own food and eat. So a system that actually will be sustainable has to go back to the very same principle that I'm trying to say here. You as a citizen of this planet, somebody in Africa, China, or Asia or anywhere, the moment you are born into this planet, you should have the same rights to have the same access to the resources that you need. That is not equality in the sense of we are all equal. That is actually your birthright as a citizen of this planet. The access to the resources shouldn't only be for a few. It should be for all humans. But at the center of the problem of that equality is the monetary system.

Ernesto acknowledged that his views are not popular and he feels he has been marginalized from local food politics as a result of voicing his opinions.

That these speakers are trying to have a conversation about how to change social and political structures suggests an evolution of food-related practices, from using local food to shift cultural norms of what connotes "good food" to embedding food-related practices in civic and political engagement. These participants do so by drawing on resistance frames that emphasize rights and envision a role for the state in advancing the common good. The implicit links these speakers make between barriers to a localized food system and social inequality is suggestive of the argument that framing local food as an equity issue may offer a promising path to social change (Gamson, 1992; see also Chapter 6 of this volume). With several respondents raising the idea of a guaranteed annual income and critiquing existing subsidies to industrial farmers, there appears to be some potential for future political engagement at the systemic level.[5] A transition away from consumer society may involve locating and cultivating more spaces for discussions of justice and more sensitivity to a diversity of tastes across social class and ethnicity (Beagan et al., 2015). Frames of social equality and fairness may be productive of movement leaders' capacity to see the food system as shaped by a wider array of political, economic, and cultural practices. However, their ability to utilize these frames in diverse social settings is limited by the ways in which particular topics are viewed as contentious, and the way contention is viewed as undesirable and ineffective for mobilizing support.

Questioning convivial strategies

As Leora indicates in her reference to a "bright shiny local food," the local food movement is largely a site of convivial and collaborative practices. The few individuals who thought about food as a system were hesitant to discuss an issue like the guaranteed annual income. Leora speaks to a (strategic) tendency to avoid publicly invoking systemic challenges like inequality out of an awareness that such narratives are important but off-limits:

> If I start spewing off around power and oppression, I'm going to get shut down immediately. We need people who can speak truth to power and we need that to happen but there is a time for that. Right now you can be written off as a marginal freak and we have so much work to do that we need to figure out how to speak those messages in a way that people can actually start to understand.

Leora's comments reflect her skills in intuiting that civic action is shaped by cultural taboos against discourse that may be offensive to elites and focused on problems that cannot be easily solved (Bellah et al., 2008). At the same time, she questions whether that convivial approach will yield transformative social change.

Instead of speaking directly about injustice, participants tended to focus on incremental, market-based policy prescriptions or building physical infrastructure for urban agriculture (e.g., new farmers' markets, specialty grocers, community gardens). Paul, who had been a city councilor in Victoria and believes strongly in the need for a local food system explains: "[T]here wasn't a lot of political resistance against [having a downtown public market] where I have seen a tremendous amount of political resistance around spending money on a living wage or whatnot. Those run a much more significant resistance." Leora, quoted above, thinks about ways to incite that necessary conversation about a living wage:

> We could talk about why the food banks are so heavily utilized right now is because, well the rent is this much and this is this much and I'm on long-term disability because I have chronic this, and that leaves me $100 to feed my family a month. So even if we could keep these messages. Maybe those are the kinds of things that make people think.

Leora also notes that the appeal to relatively elite consumers is a fairly unique feature of local food movements in Canada. As a student, she participated in an exchange to Chile in the early 1990s where she deepened her knowledge of urban agriculture. She returned to Victoria with the aim to start community gardens in low-income neighborhoods as a food-security strategy as she had witnessed in Santiago, but found that, "engaging with people was different. In the South, the community garden was much more of a necessity in terms of food security … whereas we first found traction for community gardens in much more affluent neighborhoods in Victoria." She attributed part of this difference to the fact that the Canadian local food movement was beginning to resonate with a particular (high) cultural class and attributed the resistance from low-income communities to patterns of labor-force engagement (i.e., a reliance on shift work).

Above, Leora ascribed the convivial nature of Victoria's local food movement to the socioeconomic make-up of its supporters—mostly high-income individuals not concerned with food security. She casts doubt as to whether such feel-good, friendly politics can advance social justice. Another interesting example of questioning convivial strategies in the eat-local movement comes from Dana, a 50-year-old community organizer in Edmonton. Below, she voices some hesitation with using convivial and incremental approaches to bringing about a better food system. After playing a leading role in a year-long campaign to protect arable land from residential development and losing the campaign (what she calls "the food action"), Dana reflects on the participation choices that her group made. The local government at the time invited representatives of organizations both opposed to and in favor of the development to voluntarily participate in a time-consuming public deliberation process (see Beckie et al., 2013 for more details). Early on, one cohort in the group in which Dana was involved wanted to pursue direct action and resistance activities, targeted at the state and corporate (development) spheres through tactics that fit the contentious model of civic action. Others felt the group should participate in the official deliberation process and promote individual, consumer-based reforms. Ultimately, the group decided to support the latter course and Dana has spent considerable time mulling over that decision:

For the food action, we decided not to go the polarizing route and we worked with [City] Council instead. I'm not sure that was the right decision. We've thought about that a lot. I think the issue for us, that some councilors and other people have told us, is the developers knew from day one that they had the Council votes [to rezone the agricultural land for development] ... So I think there are times to polarize. I wish we were in a different place, but I think given the context and the citizens are awake now and there's lots of groups talking about the election ... We didn't get the land, but I think people are awake and we do have a fairly good relationship with the city [government].

Dana's comments illuminate evidence-based reflections on the limitations of pursuing change by calling on individual consumers to reform their eating habits.

Conclusion

Critics of the local food movement are not difficult to find: traditional farmers who question the tenacity of a new generation of urban farmers, rural dwellers who cannot stomach the sight of five carrots sold for $5, people weary of hipsters, and scholars skeptical of the touted win–win scenarios supposedly on offer (e.g., Busa and Garder, 2014; Lynch and Giles, 2013). In this chapter, I have not sought to defend or refute such statements. Rather, my aim has been to look within the discourse of leaders in the Canadian local food movement to locate kernels of possibility in the practices and meanings these leaders describe that might inform a transformation beyond consumer society.

I begin this conclusion by returning to the central question guiding this chapter: what germane political narrative exists in the Canadian local food movement that might incite a shift away from consumer society? I contend that the discourse and practices that appear most hopeful are those that encourage reflection on the role of the state in advancing the common good and in this way shift attention away from the consumer; those that question the normative standard that politics should be fun and friendly; and those that imagine or practice more contentious politics that cannot be conducted solely in the marketplace. Taken together, these emergent ways of approaching civic engagement challenge the accepted wisdom that we can change the world by altering our consumption choices. Several leaders I spoke with seem to understand food consumption very much in a "reconfigurationist" way—that is, not as a *behavior* that might generate revenue for farmers or feed people, but as a *practice* that has a place in civic and political life. These individuals are using the question of class-based access to local food as an entry point to discuss and challenge dominant market-based ideologies, potentially remaking societal connections to the neoliberal state.

This emphasis on embedding normative notions of food within political engagement practices is central to the reconfigurationist approach. While a reformist stance focuses on individual behavior as the axis along which social change will unfold and the "revolutionary" position might concentrate entirely on altering the broad system of capitalism, most of the food advocates I quote here understand food consumption as a moment of many socially structured practices and are beginning to imagine ways of making food part of political engagement to address barriers to a more just and environmentally sustainable food system. These obstacles may be political (e.g., subsidy programs), economic (e.g., income inequality), or cultural (e.g., the privileging of particular tastes; a gap in food skills). By inadvertently rejecting a reformist approach to social change, some local food advocates are beginning to work on *reconfiguring* the social context.

It also merits commenting on some signs of progress in the local food movement, in particular a shift to try to influence policy at local, provincial, and federal levels. Such strategies present advantages over approaches to change that rely on individual shopping choices. As systems theorist John Sterman (2014) writes: "The leverage points for action on overconsumption do not lie within business organizations, but in the beliefs, goals and values of the public, and in public policies that would both enact and reinforce those values." In the case of ending subsidies and promoting a guaranteed annual income—two potential developments raised by the participants cited in this chapter—there are no known active projects to implement policy change. However, in the province of Ontario, the local food movement has been working alongside environmental organizations and health-advocacy groups to demand the government ban neonicotinoids (a class of insecticide linked to the collapse of bee colonies and human-health issues). Untangling causal linkages is nearly impossible, but the efforts of local food advocates in petitioning elected representatives and promoting awareness may have contributed to this policy change. At the local level, the work of food advocates in establishing food-policy councils across Canada has helped the movement to tackle barriers to urban agriculture and represents a platform to pursue a more just and sustainable local food system.

These policy developments are taking place within a movement whose engine has (largely) been the consumer society. The local food movement is immersed in a time and place that eschews contentious politics yet it is finding and creating spaces to have political discussions (Holland and Gómez Correal, 2013; Lorenzen, 2014) and it is becoming an important site for people interested in collective action. Leaders such as the farmers interviewed for this project who seek a more systemic solution to underpaid local farmers and overpriced food and the state representative who is looking for spaces to discuss social inequality have been involved with the movement for over a decade and are now pursuing radical changes, whether or not these changes taste good.

Of note, opportunities to discuss topics like social justice and inequality may be difficult to find in public arenas like farmers' markets and town-hall meetings. I witnessed, in private spaces, participants arguing for the need to fight perverse government subsidies that privilege industrial food actors over local food alternatives, lobby for a living wage, and confront corrupt politicians who curry favors to the development industry and oil and gas companies. In public settings many of these same individuals, and others, stressed the deliciousness of local food and the simplicity of "voting with your fork." This may be because they sensed that such messages would be more likely to resonate with the public and the media—an intuition quite possibly correct (see Kennedy, 2016 for a more in-depth discussion).

There are significant limitations to these findings. First, the goal of this research was not to understand the discourse and practices of leaders who had been involved with the local food movement in Canada since its inception. Thus the final sample included only a handful of individuals who had worked in local food politics for over a decade. These participants explained that theirs are marginal and often unpopular views in the local food movement, where the success of the movement (as evidenced by increasing levels of consumption and production of local food) is understood as contingent upon its feel-good approach to politics. Future research should purposively seek such respondents to examine how widespread the initial findings reported here might be. Second, because of the small sample size, I was not able to examine differences across city or sector of involvement. To better understand the connection between local food consumption/production and politics, future work should focus on identifying similarities and differences in how civic, market, and state representatives approach systemic change to the food system. Finally, the opportunities for observation in this study did not reveal any instances of participants voicing calls for substantial policy changes or acute concerns for justice and sustainability. Subsequent research could more specifically focus on how these topics are avoided in public spaces and seek contexts where such issues are raised and discussed head-on.

To conclude, I return to the reconfigurationist theoretical position. My approach to understanding whether local food movements can help foster a shift to a post-consumer society is influenced by the idea that social action is first and foremost a social practice. Social practices are entangled in structures and systems like neoliberal ideologies and cultural norms and in this way, practices constitute actors. That is, social practices that ostensibly have little to do with food—local or otherwise—establish the identity and actions of participants of the local food movement. I argue that sustainable consumption scholars should not dismiss local food movements as potential conduits to move beyond consumer society and use the reconfigurationist lens to illuminate evidence to support this position.

There are two reasons why sustainable consumption scholars ought to maintain an interest in local food movements. First, local food is increasingly becoming imbued with meanings that are relevant to social change—the speakers quoted in this chapter stressed that local food is part of much-needed discourse on rights to nutritious, culturally appropriate foods, land rights, and the right to livelihoods. That is, food in this site is more than a commodity. Second, a minority of participants are beginning to cultivate a systemic approach to food politics that decenters the individual and brings practices to the foreground, along with an attendant focus on the social, cultural, political, and economic structures that shape those practices. In short, as a site that has realized the limitations of consumer-driven socioecological transformation, the local food movement represents a natural ally for those working to facilitate a shift to a post-consumer society. To sharpen the potential that I believe is inherent in this movement, scholars and practitioners should seek to identify and support the development of spaces where systemic and contentious views on food politics can be discussed, debated, and used as fodder for future action.

Notes

1 Civic action, defined by Lichterman and Eliasoph (2014), refers not only to activities taking place in the civic sphere, and thus allows for a broader and more phenomenologically valid lens through which to understand social change: "considering 'civic' as a particular kind of action rather than a kind of sector-specific actor, a researcher can notice civic action in complex organizations that may include noncivic action as well."
2 There are engaging and informative discussions of the relative drawbacks and merits of the so-called "citizen-consumer" that are beyond the scope of this chapter. See, for instance, Johnston (2008), Maniates (2001), Szasz (2007), and Willis and Schor (2012).
3 Food policy councils, or food councils, are becoming more prevalent in North America and beyond. In brief, these are typically groups of citizens representing various facets of a local food system (e.g., farmers; volunteers from food banks, community gardens, farm-to-school programs, and more; entrepreneurs; farmers' market managers; and food-studies scholars). The council is usually sanctioned by a local government. Their primary goal is to analyze the functioning of the local food system and provide ideas and recommendations for how to use advocacy and policy to make improvements.
4 See also www.thecanadianencyclopedia.ca.
5 Community Food Centres Canada, an umbrella organization that works to localize food systems, among other goals, has recently begun focusing on gathering political support for a guaranteed annual income. This proposal has an interesting history in Canada: in the 1970s in Dauphin, Manitoba, the provincial and federal governments collaborated in an experiment to provide residents with a minimum annual income, which functioned as a negative income tax. That is, based on the previous year's tax return, any residents whose income fell below the regional threshold for their household size would have their income topped up to that threshold. The impact of this experiment (called the MINCOME project) has not been robustly evaluated but existing evidence suggests significant reductions in mental health problems, hospitalizations, accidents, and high school dropouts (Forget, 2011).

References

Allen, P., FitzSimmons, M., Goodman, M., and Warner, K. (2003) "Shifting plates in the agrifood landscape: the tectonics of alternative agrifood initiatives in California," *Journal of Rural Studies* 19(1):61–75.

Beagan, B., Chapman, G., Johnston, J., McPhail, D., Power, E., and Vallianatos, H. (2015) *Acquired Tastes: Why Families Eat the Way They Do*. Vancouver: UBC Press.

Beckie, M., Hanson, L., and Schrader, D. (2013) "Farms or freeways? Citizen engagement and municipal governance in Edmonton's food and agriculture strategy development," *Journal of Agriculture, Food Systems, and Community Development* 4(1):15–31.

Bellah, R., Madsen, R., Sullivan, W., Swidler, A., and Tipton, S. (2008) *Habits of the Heart: Individualism and Commitment in American Life*. Berkeley, CA: University of California Press.

Busa, J. and Garder, R. (2014) "Champions of the movement or fair-weather heroes? Individualization and the (a)politics of local food," *Antipode* 47(2):323–341.

Conner, D., Montri, A., Montri, D., and Hamm, M. (2009) "Consumer demand for local produce at extended season farmers' markets: guiding farmer marketing strategies," *Renewable Agriculture and Food Systems* 24(4):251–259.

Desrochers, P. and Shimizu, H. (2012) *The Locavore's Dilemma: In Praise of the 10,000-Mile Diet*. New York: Public Affairs.

Elton, S. (2015) "Local food movement," in *The Canadian Encyclopedia*. Accessed June 18, 2015 from www.thecanadianencyclopedia.ca.

Forget, E. (2011) "The town with no poverty: the health effects of a Canadian guaranteed annual income field experiment," *Canadian Public Policy* 37(3):283–305.

Gamson, W. (1992) *Talking Politics*. New York: Cambridge University Press.

Geels, F., McMeekin, A., Mylan, J., and Southerton, D. (2015) "A critical appraisal of sustainable consumption and production research: the reformist, revolutionary, and reconfiguration positions," *Global Environmental Change* 34:1–12.

Guthman, J. (2008) "Bringing good food to others: investigating the subjects of alternative food practice," *Cultural Geographies* 15(4):431–437.

Holland, D. and Gómez Correal, D. (2013) "Assessing the transformative significance of movements and activism: lessons from A *Postcapitalist Politics*," *Outlines: Critical Practice Studies* 14(2):130–159.

Johnston, J. (2008) "The citizen-consumer hybrid: ideological tensions and the case of Whole Foods Market," *Theory and Society* 37(3):229–270.

Johnston, J. and Baumann, S. (2010) *Foodies: Democracy and Distinction in the Gourmet Foodscape*. New York: Routledge.

Kennedy, E. (2016) "Environmental evaporation: the invisibility of environmental concern in food system change," *Environmental Sociology* 2(1):18–28.

Lichterman, P. and Eliasoph, N. (2014) "Civic action," *American Journal of Sociology* 120(3):798–863.

Lorenzen, J. (2014) "Convincing people to go green: managing strategic action by minimising political talk," *Environmental Politics* 23(3):454–472.

Lynch, M. and Giles, A. (2013) "Let them eat organic cake," *Food, Culture & Society* 16(3):479–493.

Maniates, M. (2001) "Individualization: plant a tree, buy a bike, save the world?" *Global Environmental Change* 1(3):31–52.

Sahakian, M. and Wilhite, H. (2013) "Making practice theory practicable: towards more sustainable forms of consumption," *Journal of Consumer Culture* 14(1):25–44.

Seyfang, G. (2009) *The New Economics of Sustainable Consumption: Seeds of Change*. New York: Palgrave MacMillan.

Sonnino, R. and Marsden, T. (2006) "Beyond the divide: rethinking relationships between alternative and conventional food networks in Europe," *Journal of Economic Geography* 6(2):181–199.

Sonnino, R. and Griggs-Trevarthen, C. (2013) "A resilient social economy? Insights from the community food sector in the UK," *Entrepreneurship and Regional Development* 25(3–4):272–292.

Sterman, J. (2014) "Stumbling towards sustainability: why organizational learning and radical innovation are necessary to build a more sustainable world—but not sufficient," in R. Henderson, R. Gulati, and M. Tushman (eds.), *Leading Sustainable Change: An Organizational Perspective*. New York: Oxford University Press, pp. 51–80.

Szasz, A. (2007) *Shopping Our Way to Safety: How We Changed from Protecting the Environment to Protecting Ourselves*. Minneapolis: University of Minnesota Press.

Thorsen, D. (2009) "What is neoliberalism? The neoliberal challenge," University of Oslo Working Paper. Accessed June 10, 2015 from http://folk.uio.no/daget/neoliberalism2.pdf.

Warde, A., Wright, D., and Gayo-Cal, M. (2007) "Understanding cultural omnivorousness or the myth of the cultural omnivore," *Cultural Sociology* 1(2):143–164.

Willis, M. and Schor, J. (2012) "Does changing a light bulb lead to changing the world? Political action and the conscious consumer," *The Annals of the American Academy of Political and Social Science* 644(1):160–190.

5 Institutionalization processes in transformative social innovation

Capture dynamics in the social solidarity economy and basic income initiatives

Tom Bauler, Bonno Pel, and Julia Backhaus

Introduction

Researchers, policy actors, and practitioners have begun to acutely apprehend the current combination of deeply rooted crises concerning the economy, ecology, and other domains. Scholars argue that structural, multi-dimensional, and sustainability-oriented transitions are needed to address persistent and systemic challenges (Grin et al., 2010; Jackson, 2010), or what have been called "wicked problems" (Brown et al., 2010). In many places around the world relatively structured experiments—sometimes organized by citizens (e.g., transition towns), sometimes with scientific impetus (e.g., Resilience Alliance), and sometimes induced by public authorities (e.g., municipal decarbonization strategies)—aim to manage, to govern, or to guide communities or certain economic sectors into transition.

Complementary to these planned activities in governed transitions are a wider, less readily discernible, and wilder bet on what have been termed transformative social innovations (TSIs) as an avenue toward sustainability (Avelino et al., in review; Pel at al., 2016; Moore and Westley, 2011). According to Frances Westley (2013) "social innovation is any initiative, product, process, program, project or platform that challenges and over time contributes to changing the defining routines, resources and authority flows of beliefs of the broader social system in which it is introduced; successful social innovations have durability, scale and transformative impact." Emphasis is on the systemic nature of these efforts. Drawing on the work of Alex Haxeltine and his colleagues (2015), TSIs can be conceptualized as social innovations that strive toward "challenging, altering or replacing dominant institutions" in a given social context where "transformative" implies an irreversible, persistent adjustment in societal values, imaginaries, and behaviors. Important to note is that TSIs cannot be restricted to specific types of social innovation, but rather are processes that co-evolve with and co-produce societal transformation.

An increasing number of national, regional, and local governments are adopting social innovation (SI) as a leading policy concept and the trend is especially notable in Europe. Particularly with the support of the European Commission, which provides the institutional context and spatial frame for this chapter's empirical focus on transnational initiatives, SI is promoted with the objective that "if encouraged and valued, social innovation can bring immediate solutions to the pressing social issues citizens are confronted with" (Hubert, 2010). The Bureau of European Policy Advisors (BEPA) has defined SI as "innovations that are social both in their ends and in their means" and emphasized that these projects can provide a lever to "empower people" and to "drive societal change." BEPA further notes that "at a time of major budgetary constraints, social innovation is an effective way of responding to social challenges, by mobilizing people's creativity to develop solutions and make better use of scarce resources" (Hubert, 2010).[1] The notion of SI has inspired businesses, entrepreneurs, and civil society actors to pursue initiatives that question and redefine existing boundaries of market, state, civil society, producer, consumer, and distributor. Through these processes, proponents assume that SI can help to remedy market or state failures. These developments have prompted policy makers to seek better understanding of how these activities are working out on the ground and have requested analyses of their associated policy principles and procedures, actualized initiatives, and proto-businesses and how they could be institutionally anchored.

This chapter explores a particular dimension of that growing interest, namely the governance of TSIs and focuses specifically on the challenges that emerge during institutionalization processes. We highlight the tensions that emerge when TSIs (by definition SIs that intend to alter, challenge, or change dominant institutions) are interacting with institutions that they want to transform, and often quite radically so. This chapter examines the perspectives of TSI actors and how they anticipate, avoid, refuse, welcome, or accept the governance intentions of TSI initiatives and the networks advanced by public and market authorities. The chapter ultimately grapples with the question of how we should think about alternative practices at the micro-level as experiments that could shed useful light on heterodox macroeconomic perspectives for social change.

In particular, our present-day interconnected worlds continue to encourage mainstream commitments to economic growth, economies of scale, and consumerist lifestyles. Such a condition, from the standpoint of supporting social change, implies a discernible need to maintain a viable as well as governable set of alternatives, critical approaches, and practices that form the field of TSI. Borrowing from the field of ecology and the defense of biodiversity, social scientists have argued for a conservationist position on governance alternatives and critical approaches and practices, by which they mean protecting them from attempts to aggregate under the "big tent" of mainstream innovation policies. For example, Clive Spash (2013) has called for safeguarding a culture of heterodox thinking and alternative practice in ecological economics. His analysis suggests that ecological economists subscribe, on the one hand, to strong pragmatism (embracing notions of weak sustainability and methodological classicism) in the tradition of John Dewey or, on the other hand, regard themselves as deep "social ecological economists" committed to principles such as value and methodological pluralism. Similarly, in the emergent field of TSI, efforts to draw attention to adaptive pragmatism does not easily comport with questions pertaining to the current dynamics of mainstream social change.

Belgian philosopher Isabelle Stengers (2015) and other scholars who have reflected on the interface of policy, science, and practice urge adoption of a definitive and stable self-positioning regarding the value of alternatives as a necessary starting point. They argue that ontological and epistemological transparency is a prerequisite for thinking and working at the nexus between humans and nature. Consistent with this perspective, we contend that adoption of a parallel approach with respect to alternative ideas and practices for social change enables us to broaden our view of "TSI ecosystems" that display intriguing forms of diversity and resilience.

This chapter is also grounded in insights of scholars like Adrian Smith (2006) who argue that multi-actor quests for a governance of alternatives might not be adequately addressed by mainstream understanding of innovation. In particular, in the field of socioecological transitions, the rapidly growing body of knowledge on transition management and transition governance does not necessarily apply to TSI even if both approaches have a shared comprehension of the systemic qualities of both crises and opportunities for remediation. A partial explanation might be that the principles of transitions governance are based on mechanistic notions of steering and "cockpit-ism" more generally (Hajer et al., 2015). Additionally, since transitions by definition involve considerable creative destruction, we should not be surprised when they prompt resistance from vested interests (Meadowcroft, 2009) (see also Chapter 10). Apart from the overt sabotage of transformation attempts (Hess, 2014; Geels, 2014), transitions studies have brought forward ample accounts of half-hearted innovation or "greenwashing." In the case of TSI, governance dynamics are expected to arise from diverse actor operations, dispersed over various societal subsystems, some of them deliberately centered on opposing, ignoring, or excluding incumbent actors and, in particular, public authorities and businesses. In the emergent network and platform economies to which TSI is often linked, such diversity and dispersal is expected as actors differ in their understandings of systemic problems, solutions, and desirable states (Smith and Stirling, 2010). The institutionalization of TSI can be a winding and bumpy road. Obstacles arise from the tendency for relevant activities to be captured by incumbent actors and institutional logics that blunt sharp edges and disruptive features and thus jeopardize the transformative potential of SI.

Regarding TSI, which often looks to sail at a distance from the institutional mainland, a particularly problematic situation revolves around TSI's resistance to such capture. We thus focus in our subsequent discussion on proximity and detachment when TSI initiatives are seeking to challenge, alter, or replace dominant institutions. In the subsequent discussion, we argue that a key question for TSI governance is how to manage vulnerability to capture and how to avoid this threat. Our empirical analyses focus on the "grey zone" between, on the one hand, transformative social innovation and, on the other hand, captured social innovation to address our central question: How do these conflicting processes underlying social innovation interact and interlink during the institutionalization processes? The discussion explores confrontations between the diverse institutional logics and societal ambitions that characterize activities associated with social innovation.[2] We approach the dynamics of capture with two framings in mind. First, we acknowledge that capture is a multifaceted and fundamentally ambiguous phenomenon with many faces. Second, we treat capture as a dynamic process in which moments of domesticating capture and radicalizing transformation alternate and evoke each other (Pel, 2016).

This chapter is organized as follows. First, we situate our understanding of the capture dynamics in TSI institutionalization processes in the wider literature on transition governance. The chapter then provides a brief methodological account of our empirical sources and explores how the dynamics of capture and transformation manifest in two cases of international networks working to promote particular TSI initiatives. The first case focuses on members of the Réseau Intercontinental de Promotion de l'Economie Sociale et Solidaire (Intercontinental Network for the Promotion of Social Solidary Economy and generally known by its French acronym RIPESS) who are seeking to avoid shallow institutionalization of their transformative ideals. Our second case is the Basic Income Earth Network (BIEN) which has, at least to date, been a less notable target for capture. The work of this latter social innovation is, somewhat paradoxically, devoted to institutionalizing its transformative proposals and the case demonstrates an effort to achieve self-initiated domestication while simultaneously holding to explicit radicalization of its final goal. The conclusion describes the wider implications for TSI governance that emerge from the RIPESS and BIEN cases.

A dynamic perspective on capture and transformation

The progression of TSIs is shaped by fundamentally diverse forces. Taken as individual practices and local phenomena, these innovation processes tend to co-evolve over time, sometimes collaboratively and sometimes in conflict with each other. The inherent dynamics—and the underlying developments on which they rely—support and enable wider processes of social change. In this section, we argue that these activities can be fruitfully analyzed by concentrating on the forces at work during specific periods of transformation and capture with respect to dominant institutions. We consider these processes to be exemplars of the institutional dynamics of TSI in general. The question arises whether these undercurrents are reducible to standardized patterns or pathways that could provide guidance for maneuvering in the grey zones that TSI actors encounter. If such regularities could be identified, they could also help us to understand how alternative practices aggregate into social change.

From a theoretical perspective, the transformation and capture outcomes of institutionalizing innovations are conceptualized as niche-regime interplay combined with changing "landscape" developments (see also Chapter 10). Geels and Schot (2007) distinguish particular transition pathways as typical evolutionary outcomes of such interactions. Their work shows the extent to which transition-oriented analyses of institutionalization might be unworkable. Unless there are exceptional system-feedback mechanisms at work in the niche-regime interplay, processes of system reproduction are maintained. Extensive discussions and analyses are currently crystallizing around questions of scaling (up, out, deep) without considering that in transition approaches social innovation is just one dimension of the sociotechnical systems at play. Nevertheless, there are also in the transition literature abundant examples of how the social dimension is central. "Niches," in particular, often have crucial social characteristics and these features potentially subordinate their "technical" aspects to secondary consideration. For example, among energy cooperatives innovative human interactions are key components of a larger energy transition. Other instances are alternative currency collectives that have attained critical mass and competences to become viable alternatives or sharing collaborations and informal service-provisioning schemes that challenge incumbent actors and structures in mobility, housing, and agriculture.

Situated and dynamic studies of the institutionalization of TSI reveal that transformative impulses are channeled, encapsulated, domesticated, and eventually stifled by the very institutional structures and participants that the TSI actors are targeting for change. Prior studies point, for example, to sustainable houses being stripped from their underlying social sustainability principles (Jensen et al., 2012), sharing projects becoming commoditized into crypto-businesses that merely mimic the communicative rational sharing philosophy (see Chapters 2 and 3), renewable energy activists turning themselves into defenders of sector interests (Geels, 2014), and citizen-empowerment programs acting as Trojan horses for neoliberal ideology (Swyngedouw, 2005). We can regard such unfortunate side effects of institutionalization as mere consequences of incumbent actors who exert their natural tendencies toward keeping systems stable by absorbing or abducting the most disruptive innovations. The ensuing transformation and capture processes are then normal results of the interactions between dominant and subordinate actors, the entanglement of hegemonic and counter-hegemonic discourses, and the existing institutional/constitutional backgrounds (Jasanoff, 2004, 2015). When these interactions are sharpened at the level of actors, institutions, and politics, they help to further unravel the subtlety of the relevant capture and resistance dynamics. This is the significant and slippery grey zone between transformative or captured social innovations that makes it extremely difficult to identify clearly demarcated pathways.

A further argument in favor of observing transformation-capture dynamics is linked to the origins of much of the theorizing about TSI. Indeed, the broad area of SI, although notoriously difficult to define and delineate (cf. Lévesque and Lajeunesse-Crevier, 2005; Moulaert et al., 2013; Howaldt et al., 2015), can be delimited as processes in which new social practices, roles, and relations are brought forward, and in which social changes occur along the dimensions of "knowing, doing, organising and framing" (Haxeltine et al., 2015). As such, SI is connected to several other innovation processes pertaining to governance (Voß, 2007), grassroots innovation (Seyfang and Haxeltine, 2012), public innovation (Bekkers et al., 2013), and institutional innovation (Hargrave and van de Ven, 2006). These overlaps help to understand why some authors situate SI precisely in the aforementioned grey zone between transformation and capture and typically consider it to entail the repositioning of multiple actors, as well as the fading of boundaries among different institutional logics (Nicholls and Murdoch, 2012; Avelino and Wittmayer, 2016).

In summary, TSI is collectively shaped by a multitude of actors pursuing their particular interests, ambitions, and action programs and one of the main challenges that they face entails determining whether to avoid or acquiesce to their own capture and transformation. The wider governance challenge regarding TSI entails the creation of ample opportunities for these processes to unfold. It is thus important to be attentive to those moments in which innovation activities are channeled through diverse institutional logics and captured by actors seeking leverage that might be useful for their own potentially divergent programs of action. Moreover, this framework highlights nuanced differences between, on the one hand, malevolent seizure and, on the other hand, regular appropriation and domestication of novelties.

Tracing divergent translations in transformative social innovation networks

This dynamic perspective on TSI institutionalization—and the typical grey zones between transformation and capture—builds on the sociology of translations as developed by Michel Callon, Bruno Latour, John Law, Wiebe Bijker, and others (see, e.g., Bijker and Law, 1992; Latour, 2005). This focus on framings, adaptations, appropriations, and twists of innovations is not new (Smith, 2007; Smith and Raven, 2012; Jørgensen, 2012; Hoffman and Loeber, 2016), but it allows the capture dynamics of TSI processes to become observable by enhancing attention devoted to the relations between actors and entities. It is about reconstructing the actors involved with a certain TSI, their particular interests in it, and the problem perceptions into which it is playing. Our approach (see Pel, 2016) in particular stresses the elements of strategic behavior, deceit, and latent programs

The chapter draws on empirical material collected from two extensive case studies that we conducted as part of a larger project on TSI in Europe and Latin America.[3] We traced TSI institutionalization processes through data on the RIPESS and BIEN networks. Both networks promote modes of TSI that involve radical changes in economic production and consumption and in economic/social relations. In the first instance, RIPESS seeks to empower civil society actors, alter prevailing relations between governance actors and "institutional logics," and better meet social needs than is done by present arrangements. A striking feature of RIPESS is that it is generally considered a radical movement aimed at fostering broad societal changes in market economies. As indicated by Poirier (2013), RIPESS strives for structural and global change in the dominant economic system.

This transformative character is put forward in the RIPESS declaration which was developed at a conference in Lima and that led to establishment of the network in 1997. BIEN similarly advocates a drastically altered and fundamentally more inclusive and fair economic order. In addition to its focus on production and consumption, the network strives to ameliorate social insecurity. Its key idea is that freedom is guaranteed best by a system in which every individual is assured an unconditional basic income. This basic income would allow people to make authentic choices in their activities and contribute to a more equitable distribution of wealth as well as to more satisfying labor conditions.

We draw in the following discussion on these two case studies to provide contrasting illustrations and to argue that vulnerability to capture is both unavoidable and multi-dimensional. The BIEN case exemplifies the somewhat counterintuitive experience that the complete avoidance of capture is not always an ideal scenario for TSI processes. In this sense, TSI is understood to rely on constantly reconfiguring relations among various actors who typically adapt and translate attempts at social innovation rather than simply adopt or reject them. TSI agency is thus highly dispersed and constantly evolving.

The two case studies are built on extensive investigation of two national initiatives associated with each case study (Belgium and Romania in the case of RIPESS and Netherlands and Germany for BIEN) and their respective transnational networks. Through literature reviews, media analyses, and interviews with network representatives and other actors, we gathered data on the contents of TSI, the actors involved with the two case studies, and the institutional logics that they address and through which innovations are translated. The case studies are also instructive because they chart development of the respective social innovations over time.

Contrasting evidence on capture and transformation dynamics

We can develop an understanding of the targeted capture dynamics by contrasting the RIPESS and BIEN cases. The members of the former social innovation network typically seek to circumvent shallow institutionalization of their transformative ideals while representatives of the latter face the challenge of having their proposals institutionalized at all. In the following subsections, we contrast the cases on the basis of a few characteristics. After a description of their organizational features and aims as transnational networks of transformative social innovation, we discuss their impacts and the processes of capture that they have confronted during attempts to institutionalize their ambitions. Finally, we briefly describe how these transformative and capturing translations can be put into perspective one against the other.

Two transnational networks for transformed economies

RIPESS was founded in 1997 as a transnational network to promote the social solidarity economy (SSE). Organizers constituted it as a network-of-networks (or an intercontinental network) to unite a great array of alternative, socially innovative economic practices including social entrepreneurship, informal economies, cooperatives, producer-consumer alliances, food-sovereignty initiatives, micro-credit schemes, grassroots projects supported by corporate social responsibility programs, social inclusion ventures, and work-insertion practices. Some of these undertakings have a long history within the social economy, but the Latin/Francophone initiators have explicitly and consistently stressed the more transformative nature of the SSE. The very RIPESS acronym, containing both the "social" and "solidarity" economy, expresses an ambition to unify these alternatives. This network-based alignment of diverse local endeavors was a reaction to the diagnosis that the neoliberal way of globalization needed a visible counterweight and, in isolation, the various expressions could hardly amount to a challenge of the Thatcherite doctrine that "There Is No Alternative." The RIPESS network therefore maps various extant SSE practices, provides a discussion space to connect them, and articulates shared messages and scientific analyses of SSE potentials. It enhances the exposure of alternative economic ideas and offers a more unified banner behind which proponents can march. The shared transformative goal of RIPESS is to serve as an "ecology of social innovations" and to develop (and show the viability of) an alternative economy that is more humane, sustainable, and respectful toward traditions and social ties.

BIEN was established initially in Belgium in 1986 as the Basic Income European Network. At the time, it connected people and organizations in northwestern Europe (and the occasional North or Latin American) that had been mainly contemplating the concept in academic settings. According to the BIEN website, the network agreed to "serve as a link between individuals and groups committed to or interested in basic income, and fosters informed discussion on this topic" by means of a regular newsletter and biennial conferences. BIEN continues to maintain an online platform that features information on the network's history and all its national and regional affiliates as well as background on the concept, news, and reflections on current basic income-related developments and an archive of relevant publications. What started as a mainly European academic undertaking with a focus on oral and written exchange about general philosophical underpinnings, economic feasibility, and social implications of basic income has evolved into a global network with twenty-three national and two regional affiliates. This organizational capacity gives BIEN a presence in virtually every corner of the world and strong capabilities to focus on political advocacy, program feasibility, and implementation strategy. In 2004, the network acknowledged its expansion and, keeping its acronym intact, became the Basic Income Earth Network.

Context-sensitive translations of transformative ideals

The efforts of RIPESS to advocate for an alternative, social, and solidarity-based economy are somewhat paradoxical. That is to say, in many global regions such practices already have a respectable period of existence and in some places have even become fairly well-established parts of the institutional landscape. Prominent examples are the cooperatives and the informal economies that exist on a worldwide basis. Likewise, the institutionalization of practices of work insertion, social entrepreneurship, and ethical banking is evidence of significant achievement toward the transformative ambitions of SSE—to the point that one is tempted to forget that they were initially started as social innovations.

RIPESS members and the founders of SSE initiatives are typically involved in efforts to translate operative principles in ways that work in particular contexts. They seek to develop them into practices that meet social, economic, and ecological needs that are locally experienced so that other actors can join, support, or create their own favorable conditions. The Belgian work-insertion enterprises are prominent examples in which SSE ideals have been translated through both state and market logics. These initiatives for employing marginalized individuals in not-for-profit production practices—for instance in recycling companies—could easily be supported and subsidized by a social welfare system confronted with high structural unemployment and various other challenges of social inclusion and sustainable development. They could also be translated via prevailing market logic as the inefficient waste-and-disposal economy that has created underexploited commercial opportunities for subsidized work.

The implementation of SSE initiatives has typically involved translation in accordance with the logics of market, state, and civil society—but not equally or to the same degree. Differences in depth and spread pertain even across Europe. For instance, the Belgian work-insertion companies display all three types of rationality, but individual initiatives have different emphases and balances. More generally, Western European countries typically produce SSE practices that are tightly knit into the policies of the welfare state, while in Eastern Europe, for instance, they have emerged mainly out of the absence of institutional support. Similarly, entrepreneurial and community-based schemes typically emerge in contexts where welfare states and third-sector organizations are weak or nonexistent (cf., Sahakaian and Dunand, 2015).

Comparable context-sensitivity is apparent in the BIEN case. Combined reforms of national tax, labor, and welfare policies are perhaps the only way to implement a full, universal, and unconditional basic income. Various financing and operational models have been formulated and they serve as blueprints for the large number of social problems that could be addressed with one strategy. An increasing group of unemployed people could be adequately secured in financial terms and growing social inequities and economic inequalities could be addressed through redistribution. In post-industrial, individualized societies, basic income would provide the basis for individual self-fulfillment without a work requirement but with opportunities to allocate time and energy to meaningful activities. And finally, the bloated, complicated, inefficient, and de-humanizing bureaucracy associated with the administration of current social welfare benefits would, once and for all, be replaced by a lean and straightforward system.

However, precisely because implementation of a basic income suggests such a seemingly simple, yet radical and comprehensive reform of long-standing arrangements with unknown consequences for the life choices of individuals, the labor market, and the economy in general, it is usually ignored or quickly brushed aside by established political parties. BIEN members, in public appearances and publications, regularly point out how well a basic income aligns with institutionalized rights to individual freedom. They also point out how much better it might achieve this shared principle than our current system aimed at full employment, with its unjust and unrealistic requirement for everyone to "earn a living." Instances of experimental, partial, or intended implementation are heralded, celebrated, and studied, including past programs in Canada, India, and Namibia. Forthcoming experiments are pending in the Netherlands and a pilot program was recently launched in Finland. On top of these initiatives, the Alaska Permanent Fund has been dispensing annual dividends since 1982 and the Brazilian *Bolza Família* is a step-wise introduction of a basic income consolidated in national policy. Drawing on this experience, the BIEN network weaves a narrative that explains how and why a basic income is a logical, if not necessary, next step in social welfare reform. The basic income movement, of which BIEN, along with its most prominent and active individual members and national and regional affiliates, is the mainspring has increasingly succeeded in spreading the word widely about this century-old and yet (at least until a few decades ago) hardly known concept.

Capture processes

Different SSE practices have become institutionalized in various regions across the globe. In that sense, there has already been considerable transformative impact—even if only a very small part is attributable to RIPESS and its work as a network pulling together proponents of different ideological stripes. Importantly, the different alternative economies under the SSE banner have proven very amenable to translation by numerous actors and institutional logics. For instance, the work-insertion social enterprises can typically be translated in terms of "niche markets," employment and activation strategies, social inclusion trajectories, and vehicles for community development. As institutionally hybrid organizations (Defourny and Nyssens, 2013) these multiple sources of attractiveness are built in.

This particularly high malleability and transferability of SSE principles and practices is treated with a large dose of skepticism within the RIPESS network itself. Members acknowledge that SSE ideas have been widely translated, but this has typically occurred in diluted form (Laville, 2013). Advocates of a solidarity-based economy widely deplore the diffusion of cooperatives and their commercial success as social enterprises is seen to increasingly relapse into regular businesses and work-insertion facilitators become little more than employment machines. To a large extent, these SSE practices have developed into the integrated safety valves of the dominant economic system. The prominence of discourses on micro-credit, social business, and social innovation are seen as signs that these practices have been subjected to perverting translations of SSE principles (Poirier, 2013; Laville, 2013). The very concept of a *solidarity* economy was therefore brought forward as a way to reinvigorate and radicalize the institutionalized and diluted initiatives of the *social* economy.

The capture dynamics that BIEN has encountered show further interesting evolutions. In particular, the theorized transformative potential of basic income dwarfs its actual transformative impact. Given its radicalness, basic income is, from a comparative perspective, less amenable to capture either in partial terms or by aberrant translation. Whenever attempts are made to connect experiments—such as through more lenient administration of social benefits or temporary payments to certain individuals or groups—to the idea of basic income, guardians of the concept's purity point out that one or several defining criteria (universality, unconditionality, and, for some, sufficiency) are not adequately satisfied. When all other arguments have failed, strident proponents seeking to avoid capture have highlighted the temporal limitation of various experiments.

Next to "hardline" advocates of basic income, there are other actors in the broader movement that have been more readily inclined to translate the implementation of tax-exempt expenditures as an example of basic income "by stealth." Equally, some commentators have identified efforts to achieve a more flexible administration of social security as basic income-inspired experimentation. Occasional political interest in testing basic income programs has been interpreted as proof that the concept has arrived in mainstream policy making. Furthermore, advocates strategically exploit whatever democratically anchored instruments might be available—national referenda, citizen initiatives, petitions—to compel policy to take note of, publically discuss, and thereby oppose, appreciate, appropriate, but in any case, translate the concept.

Interplay between transformation and capture

RIPESS aims to unite a variety of local initiatives around the world, but the network embodies significant internal tensions regarding the precise principles and practices to promote. It seeks to reconcile two different conceptions of alternative economies (social and solidarity-based economy) that are similar but also somewhat antagonistic—the latter being an explicit and oftentimes polemically positioned radicalization of the first. The network initially emerged as a response to earlier institutionalization processes to forestall the steering of uncontrolled capture in the name of a weakened notion of an alternative economy. Apart from this historical legacy and generally shared objectives toward radicalization, RIPESS members are quite aware that their common mission for a more humane and social economy also involves a requirement to accept quite divergent translations. RIPESS members are overtly conscious that they navigate between ideological advocacy and practical action, between localism and globalism, between market conformity and alternative commercial practices, between insertion into policy processes and refusal to cooperate with administrations, and between Western post-materialist social movements and pursuit of distributional justice in the developing world. There is thus also within the network a continual internal debate in which radicalizing and domesticating translations mutually inform one another. Finally, there is the striking simultaneity of RIPESS, on the one hand, pragmatically lobbying national and European-level public authorities on behalf of social economy enterprises and, on the other hand, more ideological and strategic advocacy by proponents of a solidarity-based economy directed toward the United Nations and the World Bank.

The notion of a basic income, by comparison, is defined more rigidly but its precise configuration nevertheless prompts debate. For example, some advocates support a basic income that is sufficient to live on and to ensure social participation. This level of payment entails a quite substantial monthly sum, while other proponents are readily prepared to accept, for reasons of pragmatism and with the aim that benefits will expand over time, an initially effective amount and individually symbolic entitlement. So far, BIEN as the umbrella network has deliberately confined its activities to advocating in support of three criteria: universality, unconditionality, and absence of a work requirement. In recent years, the attraction of more politically minded members has led to calls to include a fourth principle that would ask for sufficiently high payments to cover basic costs of living. Such a shift implies further radicalization of the already quite progressive proposition that basic income represents. At the same time, such a step would make it exceedingly difficult for basic income to be captured and translated by public authorities into a form of complementary social benefit. BIEN members appear to understand that the concept resonates differently in various economic and social situations. More generally, up- and down-swings of public and political attention for the concept coincide with the peaks and valleys of macroeconomic cycles. Although the notion of a basic income fits in well with already institutionalized ideals like personal freedom and social security, it is diametrically opposed to others, such as the Keynesian commitment to full employment. Serious political considerations and wide public debates on basic income hence become more salient when systemic failures of current social welfare and employment institutions become all too apparent.

Conclusion: confronting capture dynamics

We posed the following question in the introduction to this chapter: How do processes of transformation and capture of social innovation interact and interlink during institutionalization processes? Presenting them as contrasting cases, the accounts of the RIPESS and BIEN networks allow for some general observations regarding TSI. In particular, we discuss how actors navigate the grey zones created by capture and transformation dynamics and the conditions of vulnerability that are created by the capture of transformative potentials.

A first observation is that TSI networks are aiming for transformative societal changes, but encounter different degrees of compatibility with dominant institutions. The RIPESS and BIEN case studies show how the principles of "challenging, altering or replacing dominant institutions" are interpreted, implemented, and even discussed very differently within the circles of TSI actors. The SSE banner is uniting a very broad group of socially innovative practices and many of them modestly challenge dominant institutions while reproducing them or providing them with ameliorative patches. Consistent with Emily Huddart Kennedy's observation in Chapter 4 with respect to the Canadian local food movement, there are social innovation initiatives that may appear transformative, but also fully capable of accommodating dominant institutions. Likewise, the various economic alternatives at the heart of RIPESS are potentially transformative vehicles, but still fit in well with dominant commitments to market diversification and customary governmental policies. Indeed, this compatibility accounts for significant institutionalization of a number of SSE principles and practices. For instance, cooperatives and work-insertion companies have become regular parts of the contemporary economic landscape in many European countries. By contrast, proponents of a universal, unconditional, individual, and sufficient basic income appear to harbor more extreme ambitions toward radical replacement of dominant institutions. As its unqualified implementation tends to prompt palpable fears of adverse side effects, administrative complexities, and economic shocks, it is not difficult to understand why institutionalization of basic income principles has to date been quite limited. Still, even this exceedingly radical social innovation has made its way into mainstream political discourses and agendas and continues to appeal to commonly held intuition about fairness, freedom, and sustainable social security. This contrasting position with respect to institutional reality might well be linked to the initial ground on which each of the two networks build. BIEN was created on the foundations of a philosophical concept—economic equality—and is part of a larger strategy and sequence of events that are deemed necessary to trigger social change. RIPESS, however, emerged from a coalition of practices and their actors who were seeking at the time a vehicle to improve their visibility and effectiveness in policy circles. Arguably, an emphasis on practice appears to be less prone to tests of radical purity than relatively abstract concepts.

Second, the degree of vulnerability to capture or translation into less transformative forms is a key problem for SSE practitioners and a subset of the basic income advocates. Some of the watered down and co-opted SSE practices are exemplar illustrations of how dominant policy actors embrace social innovations. In some Western European countries, work-insertion companies within the SSE have been extensively promoted as part of institutional responses to the economic crises. SSE activities are appearing and instrumentalized as safety valves for the economic mainstream and, in the end, might even help to keep the dominant economic order in place. Viewed dynamically, such vulnerability to capture appears to support the emergence of SSE as a mode of counter reaction. Basic income advocates can be divided into, on the one hand, those members of the network who relentlessly fight capture of the concept and, on the other hand, their counterparts that regard basic income-inspired experimentation as a sort of silver lining.

Finally, these processes of transformation and capture of social innovation are highly dispersed and nonaligned. Various attempts to radicalize and domesticate translations develop in parallel, in different cities, regions, and countries. We also see, especially with regard to RIPESS, that transnational networks are seeking to unite these various and dispersed local initiatives. They actively seek to weld "ecologies" of social innovation into coherent frameworks and to encourage interaction among different translations of a transformative social concept. Crucially, both RIPESS and BIEN support their members by providing them with examples of good practices elsewhere in the world—with concrete examples of translations that might work in their particular context as well. As expressed by RIPESS, this crucially reinforces the message that alternative economies can be, and have already been, institutionalized and that "There Is An Alternative," albeit elsewhere and applied in particular national settings.

The above observations substantiate our theoretical understanding that TSI typically evolves in a grey zone between transformation and capture. Our methodology of contrasting case studies usefully highlights the distinct variations that are needed to ground our intuitions about generic insights on institutionalization dynamics. This approach is additionally useful as a way to gain insight on how vulnerability to capture is managed by TSI actors. From our observations, this susceptibility also depends on the degree of reversibility of capture, or partial translation. We have seen that capture can be renegotiated or, in contrast, actively embraced by TSI actors themselves. Because capture is potentially temporary and rescindable, it is a phenomenon that easily allows for observation of actors' agency, reflexivity, and learning. One practical implication of our analysis is that avoidance of capture is not always the most obvious and effective strategy for proponents of TSIs to follow during institutionalization. It is desirable to resist capture under certain circumstances but other conditions may suggest more nuanced approaches that encourage, for instance, impermanent and reversible radicalization.

Notes

1 It merits noting that BEPA is the internal European Commission think tank established by former Commission president José Manuel Barroso.
2 Our assessments are conceptually grounded in the results of an earlier theoretical exploration that included the insights gained during a workshop sponsored by the TRANSIT (TRANsformative Social Innovation Theory) project. See www.transitsocialinnovation.eu/downloads.
3 All project-related materials including methodological guidelines, extensive individual case-study reports, and analytical/comparative work are accessible at www.transitsocialinnovation.eu.

References

Avelino, F. and Wittmayer, J. (2016) "Shifting power relations in sustainability transitions: a multi-actor perspective," *Journal of Environmental Policy and Planning* 18(5): 628–649.
Avelino, F., Wittmayer, J., Pel, B., Weaver, P., Dumitru, A., Haxeltine, A., Kemp, R., Jorgensen, M., Bauler, T., Ruijsink, S., and O'Riordan, T. (2016, in review)

"Transformative social innovation and (dis)empowerment," *Technological Forecasting and Social Change*.

Bekkers, V., Tummers, L., Stuijfzand, B., and Voorberg, W. (2013) Social innovation in the public sector: an integrative framework. LIPSE Working Papers. Rotterdam: Erasmus University. http://lipse.org/userfiles/uploads/Working%20paper%201%20Bekkers%20et%20al.pdf.

Bijker, W. and Law, J. (1994) *Shaping Technology/Building Society: Studies in Sociotechnical Change*. Cambridge, MA: MIT Press.

Brown, V., Harris, J, and Russell, J. (2010) *Tackling Wicked Problems through the Transdisciplinary Imagination*. London: Earthscan.

Defourny, J. and Nyssens, M. (2013) "Social innovation, social economy and social enterprise: what can the European debate tell us?" in F. Moulaert, D. MacCallum, A. Mehmood, and A. Hamdouch (eds), *The International Handbook on Social Innovation; Collective Action, Social Learning and Transdisciplinary Research*. Northampton, MA: Edward Elgar, pp. 40–52.

Geels, F. and Schot, J. (2007) "Typology of sociotechnical transition pathways," *Research Policy* 36(3):399–417.

Geels, F. (2014) "Regime resistance against low-carbon transitions: introducing politics and power into the multi-level perspective," *Theory, Culture, and Society* 31(5):21–40.

Grin, J., Rotmans, J., and Schot, J. (2010) *Transitions to Sustainable Development: New Directions in the Study of Long Term Transformative Change*. New York: Routledge.

Hajer, M., Nilsson, M., Raworth, K., Bakker, P., Berkhout, F., de Boer, Y., and Kok, M. (2015) "Beyond cockpit-ism: Four insights to enhance the transformative potential of the sustainable development goals," *Sustainability* 7(2):1651–1660.

Hargreaves, T. and Van de Ven, A. (2006) "A collective action model of institutional innovation," *Academy of Management Review* 31(4):864–888.

Haxeltine, A., Kemp, R., Dumitru, A., Avelino. F., Pel, B., and Wittmayer, J. (2015) *A First Prototype of TSI Theory, Project on Transformative Transition Theory (TRANSIT)*. Rotterdam: Dutch Research Institute for Transitions, Erasmus University Rotterdam.

Hess, D. (2014) "Sustainability transitions: a political coalition perspective," *Research Policy* 43(2):278–283.

Hoffman, J. and Loeber, A. (2016) "Exploring the micro-politics in transitions from a practice perspective: the case of greenhouse innovation in the Netherlands,' *Journal of Environmental Policy and Planning* 18(5):692–711.

Howaldt, J., Kopp, R., and Schwarz, M. (2015) *On the Theory of Social Innovations: Tarde's Neglected Contribution to the Development of a Sociological Innovation Theory*. Weinheim: Beltz Juventa. http://nbn-resolving.de/urn:nbn:de:0168-ssoar-419633.

Hubert, A. (2010). Empowering people, driving change: Social innovation in the European Union. Brussels: Bureau of European Policy Advisors. http://ec.europa.eu/bepa/pdf/publications_pdf/social_innovation.pdf.

Jackson, T. (2010) *Prosperity without Growth: Economics for a Finite Planet*. London: Earthscan.

Jasanoff, S. (ed.). (2004) *States of Knowledge: The Co-production of Science and the Social Order*. New York: Routledge.

Jasanoff, S. (ed.) (2015) *Dreamscapes of Modernity: Sociotechnical Imaginaries and the Fabrication of Power*. Chicago: University of Chicago Press.

Jensen, J., Jørgensen, M., Elle, M., and Lauridsen, E. (2012) "Has social sustainability left the building? The recent conceptualization of 'sustainability' in Danish buildings," *Sustainability: Science, Practice, and Policy* 8(1):94–105.

Jørgensen, U. (2012) "Mapping and navigating transitions—the multi-level perspective compared with arenas of development," *Research Policy* 41(6):996–1010.

Latour, B. (2005) *Reassembling the Social: An Introduction to Actor-Network Theory.* New York: Oxford University Press.

Laville, J.-L. (2013) "Economie sociale et solidaire, capitalisme et changement démocratique," in D. Hiez and E. Lavillunière (eds), *Vers une Theorie de l'economie Sociale et Solidaire (Towards a Theory of the Social and Solidarity Economy).* Larcier: Bruxelles, pp. 17–32 (in French).

Lévesque, B. and Lajeunesse-Crevier, F. (2005) *Innovations et Transformations Sociales dans le Développement Économique et le Développement Social: Approches Théoriques et Politiques Publiques (Social Innovations and Transformations in Economic and Social Development: Theoretical Approaches and Public Policy).* Montréal: Centre de Recherche sur les Innovations Sociales. http://crises.uqam.ca/upload/files/publications/etudes-theoriques/CRISES_ET0507.pdf (in French).

Meadowcroft, J. (2009) "What about the politics? Sustainable development, transition management, and long term energy transitions," *Policy Sciences* 42(4):323–340.

Moore, M. and Westley, F. (2011) "Surmountable chasms: the role of cross-scale interactions in social innovation," *Ecology and Society* 16(1):5.

Moulaert, F., MacCallum, D., Mehmood, A., and Hamdouch, A. (eds.) (2013) *The International Handbook on Social Innovation: Collective Action, Social Learning, and Transdisciplinary Research.* Northampton, MA: Edward Elgar.

Nicholls, A. and Murdock, A. (eds.) (2012) *Social Innovation: Blurring Boundaries to Reconfigure Markets.* New York: Palgrave Macmillan.

Pel, B. (2016) "Trojan horses in transition: a dialectical perspective on innovation 'capture,'" *Journal of Environmental Policy and Planning* 18(5):673–691. www.tandfonline.com/doi/full/10.1080/1523908X.2015.1090903.

Pel, B., Wallenborn, G., and Bauler, T. (2016) "Emergent transformation games: exploring social innovation agency and activation through the case of the Belgian electricity blackout threat," *Ecology and Society* 21(2):17.

Poirier, M. (2013). "Origins and definitions of solidarity economy and related concepts," in Jayasooria, D. (ed.), *Developments in Solidarity Economy in Asia.* Chamonix: Les Rencontres du Mont-Blanc, pp. 71–89.

Sahakian, M. and Dunand, C. (2015) "The social and solidarity economy towards greater 'sustainability': learning across contexts and cultures, from Geneva to Manila," *Community Development Journal* 50(3):403–417.

Seyfang, G. and Haxeltine, A. (2012) "Growing grassroots innovations: exploring the role of community-based initiatives in governing sustainable energy transitions," *Environment and Planning C (Government and Policy)* 30(3):381–400.

Smith, A. (2006) "Green niches in sustainable development: the case of organic food in the UK," *Environment and Planning C (Government and Policy)* 24(3):439–458.

Smith, A. (2007) "Translating sustainabilities between green niches and socio-technical regimes," *Technology Analysis and Strategic Management* 19(4):427–450.

Smith, A. and Stirling, A. (2010) "The politics of social-ecological resilience and sustainable socio-technical transitions," *Ecology and Society* 15(1):11.

Smith, A. and Raven, R. (2012) "What is protective space? Reconsidering niches in transitions to sustainability," *Research Policy* 41(6):1025–1036.

Spash, C. (2013) "The shallow or the deep ecological economics movement?" *Ecological Economics* 93(1):351–362.

Stengers, I. (2015) *In Catastrophic Times. Resisting the Coming Barbarism*, Andrew Goffey, trans. London: Open Humanities Press and Meson Press. http://openhumanitiespress. org/books/download/Stengers_2015_In-Catastrophic-Times.pdf.

Stirling, A. (2011) "Pluralising progress: from integrative transitions to transformative diversity," *Environmental Innovation and Societal Transitions* 1(1):82–88.

Swyngedouw, E. (2005) "Governance innovation and the citizen: the Janus face of governance-beyond-the-state," *Urban Studies* 42(11):1991–2006.

Van Parijs, P. (1995) *Real Freedom for All*. New York: Oxford University Press.

Voß, J.-P., Smith, A., and Grin, J. (2009) "Designing long-term policy: rethinking transition management," *Policy Sciences* 42(4):275–302.

Westley, F. (2013) The history of social innovation. Keynote address at NESTA Conference on Social Frontiers: The Next Edge of Social Science Research, November 14–15, London.

6 Consumption and social change

Sustainable lifestyles in times of economic crisis

Tally Katz-Gerro, Predrag Cvetičanin, and Adrian Leguina

Introduction

Studies of the economic crisis that started in 2007, and has shaped social life in many countries during the intervening years, tend to emphasize issues at the macro-level and to focus on the antecedents, effects, and consequences of the unfolding event (Alimen and Bayraktaroglu, 2011; Shiller 2012). Research has, for example, emphasized the changing production structure and its influence on various sectors of the economy and declining economic growth rates. Less prevalent have been investigations detailing the effect of the crisis on the daily lives of individuals, the way it has changed lifestyles, and the manner in which people have adjusted their consumption patterns to new economic situations (but see Ang, 2000; Alimen and Bayraktaroglu, 2011; Faganel, 2011; Prothero and McDonagh, 2014). The few studies that have explored these issues conclude that protracted economic strain has changed household-consumption practices and reshaped social perceptions of necessity and luxury. However, did this change have any effect on sustainable consumption practices? Did it encourage the disavowal of behaviors associated with consumerism or enhance awareness of the risks of excess and saturation? Did it prompt people to seek a new balance between consumption and production behaviors?

This chapter discusses sustainable lifestyles from the point of view of individuals and households living under conditions of economic crisis in four countries located in southeastern Europe (Serbia, Bosnia-Herzegovina, Croatia, and Slovenia). Residents of these countries are experiencing a growing mismatch between, on the one hand, their economic and social resources and, on the other hand, their material and social needs. This situation has led to circumstances where, by necessity, they have had to respond by either changing their resources or their needs. Lifestyle changes in times of crisis exemplify the embeddedness of the economy in social structures and the need to interpret consumption practices as strongly interwoven with social and cultural contexts (see Chapter 7). Given this linkage between lifestyle practices and the economic context, we investigate whether and how strategies for coping with economic crises have consequences for sustainable consumption practices.

While the main discussion of sustainable lifestyles usually focuses on the motivations, understandings, and preferences of individuals in Western countries, who by and large live in affluent advanced societies, this chapter will consider sustainable lifestyles in the context of economic crisis and societal transition. This context is characterized by the combined effects of post-socialist transformations and global upheaval: privatization processes, high rates of unemployment, insecure labor markets, decline of social security systems, economic recession, inactive and partially inactive households, and growing importance of informal social networks and precarious living.

Economic crisis and sustainable consumption

The economic crisis discussed here is the result of a combination of factors including the progressive financialization of the economy, the growth of financial market speculation, and the considerable increase in private debt, along with a rise in poverty and a reduction in the labor market's distributive capacity (Stiglitz, 2009; see also Chapter 8). The turmoil that first unfolded in several countries beginning in 2007, and spread contagiously to large parts of the world during the following year, has affected the daily lives of many people (Schneider et al., 2010) and had far-reaching effects on the fabric of social relations and individual spending habits. These impacts are evident from indicators of economic development, such as inequality and poverty, as well as from measures of the level of consumption in areas such as food, housing, and transportation. Some of these responses, including a decline in the use of personal automobiles, could have positive long-lasting effects on the ability of societies to reduce their level of energy and material throughput (Goodwin and van Dender, 2013).

Researchers have analyzed the economic crisis across Europe with regard to its financial and economic consequences (Stiglitz, 2009), regulatory implications (Greta and Lewandowski, 2015), and political dimensions (Bosco and Verney, 2012). However, studies have also considered its effect on consumer values, perceptions, and practices, which are related to future consumption growth and behavior (Ludvigson, 2004; Cohen, 2013; Biswas and Roy, 2015; Vitell, 2015).

Given that the restructuring of consumption is one of the ways to ameliorate dilemmas associated with global ecological unsustainability, the opportunity to change consumption patterns inadvertently offered by the economic crisis can lead to more extensive, long-term sociocultural transformation. The hegemonic discourse about economic growth and technological development could be usefully complemented by significant changes in social practices. Historical experience suggests that culturally embedded routines are often significantly transfigured under conditions of limited resources and escalating social inequality and precariousness. Moreover, individual and collective lifestyles are socially, materially, and culturally embedded. Assuming that the reshaping of consumption provides one possible strategy to mitigate problems of global ecological and social sustainability, there is important value in exploring the sociocultural transformations that might underlie such interventions. Examples of outcomes of behavioral change due to the ongoing economic crisis might be withdrawal and indifference or proactive rearrangement of lifestyles. Accordingly, the recent economic downturn is an opportunity to explore what happens when rapid, externally induced changes involving forced downshifting occur, making current consumption volumes and styles financially nonviable.

The connection between limited economic resources and a change of lifestyle is not linear. A lack of financial capacity restricts consumption in various ways. Individuals who must rearrange their practices due to a lack of money may eventually adopt a change in values. For example, Luis Alonso and his colleagues (2015) reported that Spaniards tended to blame the crisis on past excesses and called for a return to frugality. Other evidence reported by Orru and Lilleoja (2015) suggests that for many adversely affected people, the resultant turmoil created an urgent need to alter buying habits, leading in some cases to support for environmentally friendly products in poorer countries. Research has shown that in some instances, the goal of a higher standard of living is replaced by an alternative set of aspirations, which include satisfying basic needs and managing uncertainty and vulnerability (see, e.g., Ion, 2014). For example, work in Slovenia by Armand Faganel (2011) found a shift from individualistic consumerism toward more consideration of the community and family, as well as the challenging of conventional consumption norms.

Consumers typically adapt themselves to a new economic situation by spending less, favoring less expensive substitutes, postponing the purchase of durable items, repairing more, and engaging in self-provisioning (Brown, 2013). One response entails a change in expenditure habits, in terms of spending less overall, but also cutting back on the purchase of certain categories of consumer goods (e.g., food, clothes, personal care, technological products) and in how purchasing decisions are made (e.g., special offers, price comparison). Sociologist Giorgio Gosetti (2012) shows that in Italy, one out of three families has cut its spending on food during the past several years, while one out of four households has reduced its purchases of medicines and toiletries. For the other categories of goods monitored (clothes, home furnishings, and technological products), the percentage of respondents declaring that they had curtailed their spending exceeded 60 percent. Interestingly, this study also found that over preceding years there had been an increase across all categories of consumer goods in terms of the percentage of people that had been making fairly drastic cuts in spending. Regarding whether changes in consumption patterns had affected different socioeconomic cohorts, Gosetti finds that the majority of individuals that indicated making expenditure cuts belonged to lower income groups, had less education, and lived in areas that traditionally have had economic difficulties. However, between 2009 and 2011, a very large and increasing proportion of the population in Italy stated that the crisis had prompted changes in modes of shopping, a figure that reached 71 percent in 2011. Gosetti concludes that in Italy there has been a change in households' spending habits caused by the weakening of their purchasing power, but there are few signs of a cultural shift in attitudes toward consumption.

While changes in consumer behavior as a result of economic contraction are not always accompanied by changes in cultural values, in some cases a fiscal crisis does have an effect on the discourse on consumption (Alonso et al., 2015) as well as on the practices and perceptions of consumers and a redefinition of needs. This shift may lead to the emergence of a new moral narrative on consumerism and the risks of excess and saturation. Several scholars have analyzed the dynamics of crisis-induced consumption patterns, focusing on changes in values and attitudes in different countries (Faganel, 2011) and on the discursive context in which these adjustments are framed (Alonso et al., 2015). Triin Vihalemm and her collaborators (2016) studied media treatment of consumption and the crisis in Estonia and indicate that conversations on how to spend money more wisely, buy cheaper goods, and limit consumption were discussed in the national media as the main solutions for individual economic problems (see also Kaytaz and Gul, 2014). To some extent, the norm of downshifting contradicted the norm of being active and sought by the labor market. Vihalemm et al. (2016) further report that the media did discuss values, with 10 percent of texts including a shift in values as a way out of the crisis. Media accounts also criticized the pre-crisis consumer culture and presented some new alternatives. However, in general, the storylines described the period of upheaval as a temporary situation. Alonso and his colleagues (2015) also studied the discourse associated with the crisis, focusing on the way Spaniards moralize about consumption. Consumers described how members of the middle and upper classes in the country expressed a desire for frugality not because they had a critical view of consumerism but rather as an intention to return to morality and self-control, as well as a penchant to revert to the neoliberal logic of self-management and the work ethic. Rather than associating the economic crisis with a significant lifestyle change where the long-term goal included the curbing of consumption or a new politics of consumption, the respondents viewed it as a temporary situation in which freedom and choice were turned into rules and norms to restrain spending. They did not think that there was any space for suggesting that there might be a limit on the needs that a consumer society constructs. There was furthermore no articulation of a discourse based on basic necessities, but rather an emphasis on the need for savings, austerity, and protecting oneself from the perils of the market.

How does coping with the economic crisis correlate with demographics? Nazli Alimen and Gül Bayraktaroglu (2011) describe seven types of adjustments: cautious spending, simplicity in purchases and distribution, adjustments in products, quest for low prices, financial anxiety, adjustments in promotions, and awareness. They also established correlations between these responses and participants' occupation, income level, gender, age, and marital status.

People in different socioeconomic classes perceived the economic crisis differently. Those in superordinate positions attributed it to irrational spending while simultaneously relieving themselves of any responsibility for the situation. For others, the economic crisis was simply their existential condition. They criticized counterparts for their excessive consumption without personally considering the possibility of developing alternative forms of consumption or questioning the sustainability of the current model. In this case, the economic crisis did not challenge the predominant model of consumerism.

In sum, the association between economic conditions and consumer culture has proved to be a fascinating area for analyzing social changes currently taking place and, in particular, for understanding the complexity of sustainable consumption patterns and whether changes triggered by the economic crisis have induced people to reflect on and confront their lifestyles and consumption habits. In broader terms, the prevailing situation has created a salient moment to consider the extent to which there is a public propensity to interrogate the relationship between economic growth and societal development.

This discussion prompts us to pose several research questions. First, how has the economic crisis changed consumption practices in four southeastern European countries—Serbia, Bosnia-Herzegovina, Croatia, and Slovenia? Second, can we identify significant areas in which the strategies of coping with the turmoil could be conceptualized as more or less sustainable? Third, are these new lifestyles focused on consumption or production? Finally, can we identify specific groups based on socioeconomic class, educational level, or urban residency that are particularly disposed to making sustainable changes in their lifestyle?

Social context of countries

The data for this chapter come from a study entitled "Life Strategies and Survival Strategies of Households and Individuals in South-East European Societies in Times of Crisis" (2014–2016) conducted within the SCOPES program of the Swiss National Science Foundation.[1] The project was carried out by researchers based in the Department of Sociology, University of Zurich; the Centre for Empirical Cultural Studies of South-East Europe (Serbia); the regional branch of the Institute of Social Sciences, "Ivo Pilar," in Split (Croatia); the Department of Sociology, University of Maribor (Slovenia); and the Economic Institute in Sarajevo (Bosnia-Herzegovina). The goal of this initiative was to identify, to describe, and to classify changes in the social practices of households in Serbia, Bosnia-Herzegovina, Croatia, and Slovenia (former members of the Yugoslav federation) brought about by the current world economic crisis.

Appendix Table 6.A1 summarizes the economic and demographic characteristics of the four countries. Slovenia is the smallest among them (both in terms of territory and population), but is the most advanced in terms of economic status. It seceded from the Yugoslav federation in 1991 and was mostly unaffected by the ensuing civil wars. In 2004, Slovenia was granted membership in the North Atlantic Treaty Organization (NATO) and the European Union (EU) and in 2007 was the first country of the former Communist bloc to join the Eurozone. The Slovenian economy is well developed and, based on its per capita gross domestic product (GDP), is the second richest Slavic country after the Czech Republic. In 2004–2006, Slovenia recorded an average annual economic growth rate of nearly 5 percent and in 2007 grew by almost 7 percent. However, the global economic crisis that began that year reduced the Slovenian GDP per capita by 8 percent, making this one of the largest economic declines recorded in the EU during this period (exceeded only by that of the Baltic countries and Finland). At the end of 2015, the total Slovenian national debt was estimated at €32 billion or 83.2 percent of the country's nominal GDP and its official unemployment rate was 9 percent.

Croatia also declared its independence from Yugoslavia in 1991, but this intention led to a war of independence that lasted until 1995. The conflict had severe consequences for the Croatian economy and society in general. The national economy revolves mostly around the service sector, with tourism making up as much as 20 percent of Croatian GDP. Approximately eleven million tourists visit Croatia each year (mostly residing in the coastal regions) which led to a 2014 estimate of the annual income from tourist activities of €7.4 billion. General government gross debt at the end of 2015 was almost €38 billion (86.7 percent of the nominal GDP) and the unemployment rate was 16.3 percent. Croatian membership in NATO was finalized in 2009, and was followed by the country becoming a member of the EU in 2013.

According to estimates based on the 2013 census, 48.4 percent of the population of Bosnia-Herzegovina are Bosniaks, 32.7 percent are Serbs, 14.6 percent are Croats, and 4.3 percent are other. It is this ethnic diversity that architects of the war misused and which led to the worst atrocities of the Yugoslav hostilities taking place on the territory of Bosnia-Herzegovina. The war lasted from 1992 until 1995, leaving over 100,000 casualties and displacing more than 1.8 million persons. The fighting also had a devastating effect on the economy of Bosnia-Herzegovina, which experienced a decline in GDP of approximately 60 percent during this period, accompanied by extensive destruction of economic infrastructure. The war ended with the Dayton Peace Accord in 1995, an agreement that set the foundations for several very complex legal and political arrangements. The parliament of Bosnia-Herzegovina consists of two houses (House of Peoples and House of Representatives) and a three-person presidency comprising representatives of the country's largest ethnic groups. However, the power of the central government is extremely limited, with actual decision-making power invested in two autonomous entities: the Federation of Bosnia-Herzegovina and the Republic of Srpska. The former jurisdiction is itself especially complex and consists of as many as ten federal units called cantons. The economic problems in Bosnia-Herzegovina are closely connected to the high unemployment rate (42.9 percent in 2015) and large trade deficit.

Of the six former Yugoslav republics, Serbia is the largest in terms of both territory and population. During the 1990s, it was directly or indirectly involved in all of the wars on the territory of the former Yugoslavia, trying to prevent the dissolution of the country by force. In 1999, NATO intervened in the Kosovo crisis and this led to ruin of the national economy. Once the regime of Slobodan Milosevic lost power in October 2000, Serbia underwent a process of rapid transition and today has EU candidate status. The current economic crisis has taken its toll on the economy of Serbia as well. A period of economic growth that lasted for eight years (with an average of 4.5 percent per year) was followed by a slide into recession in 2009, at which time the country recorded a growth of −3 percent and again in 2012 with −1.5 percent. The government's methods of trying to combat the effects of the economic crisis led to a doubling of public debt, from a pre-crisis level of 29.2 percent to 63.8 percent of nominal GDP. General government debt in 2014 stood at €23.2 billion, accounting for 72.3 percent of the nominal GDP. A high unemployment rate remains one of the country's most acute problems, standing at 17.9 percent in 2015.

Overall, we are focused here on four post-socialist and post-conflict societies with differing levels of economic development and each of them has a vulnerable economy that is still recovering from war and the severing of mutual economic bonds. Given these pre-existing circumstances, the 2007 crisis had a particularly devastating effect on the region. Once we add the fact that the informal economy plays a significant role in the daily life of these societies, it becomes clear that the countries offer fertile ground for the study of household-coping strategies and lifestyle changes during periods of extreme disruption.

Data and variables

The data analyzed here are derived from surveys of probability samples of 3,906 respondents in total (national proportional samples of 1,000 respondents in Serbia and Croatia, 1,002 respondents in Bosnia-Herzegovina, and 904 respondents in Slovenia), carried out between January and March 2015.[2] The instrument included sixty-five questions organized into seven batteries: 1) sociodemographic data on household composition and membership; 2) indicators of households' economic, social, political, and cultural capital; 3) questions on values, attitudes, value orientations, and trust; 4) questions on household participation in the formal economy (work or benefits received), activities pursuant to the household economy (production for household consumption), engagement with the social economy (dependence upon interpersonal networks—favors and help from friends, relatives, symbolic kin, neighbors), and participation in the cash or black economy (additional monetized activities); 5) questions on the influence of the economic crisis on households' economic situation; 6) questions on internal household dynamics; and 7) questions on material and cultural consumption and the digital practices of household members.

Analysis

The analysis reported here is based on three groups of questions used to reconstruct the production and consumption lifestyles and strategies of households:

1   *The influence of the crisis on households*: the views of respondents on how the economic situation in the household was five years ago compared to the period of data collection (the beginning of 2015); their views on whether overall household income from all of activities in which household members were involved was sufficient for a "normal" life; and data on household

practices during the last five years, ranging from investing in a business and purchasing real estate to borrowing money and selling arable land.

2   *Household production capacities and practices*: main sources of household income, additional economic activities in the household; household production of food and other goods; the percentage of food that the household produces itself; the percentage of food brought by parents or relatives living in the country and percentage of food bought in stores.

3   *Household consumption during time of crisis*: whether household members were forced to reduce their own consumption ranging from reducing meat in their diet, limiting going to the hairdresser, and getting a pedicure or manicure to recreational activities such as time spent on vacation in the five years prior to the survey; frequency of eating out with friends during the three months prior to the survey; and frequency of purchasing clothes in shopping malls, small local stores, or flea markets.[3]

We categorized the lifestyle strategies using multiple correspondence analysis (MCA) (Lebart et al., 1984; Greenacre, 2007; Le Roux et al., 2008; Le Roux and Rouanet, 2010)[4] and then examined them in association with other variables including geographic place of residence (village, town, city); number of household members; educational and occupational profiles of members of the household;[5] average monthly household income from all sources per household member, and the number of regular incomes on which the household relies (see Table 6.A2).

We present the results of the analyses first by describing the perceived influence of the economic crisis on households in Serbia, Bosnia-Herzegovina, Croatia, and Slovenia. We next identify two basic dimensions that structure the lifestyles and household strategies in these countries. Finally, we create five clusters in each country and indicate their characteristics, especially in terms of the extent of the sustainability of their conditions and lifestyles under conditions of economic crisis.

The influence of the economic crisis on households in southeastern Europe

The economic crisis has clearly had an impact on the lifestyles of households in the countries of southeastern Europe that were part of this study. Table 6.1 presents a self-assessment of the economic situation of households five years ago and today scored on a scale of one (completely unsatisfactory economic situation) to ten (completely satisfactory economic situation). As the table illustrates, most respondents rated the prevailing state of the economy as worse than it was five years prior to the survey. The gap between the current and the past situation is greater in the relatively more economically developed countries of Slovenia and Croatia than in Bosnia-Herzegovina and Serbia.

Table 6.2 presents results in response to the question about whether total household income was sufficient to get by scored on a scale ranging from one (not sufficient at all) to ten (quite sufficient). The average answer in all of the countries except for Slovenia was below five.

The respondents were also asked to indicate whether they engaged in activities that typically occur in times of crisis. We differentiated between proactive activities such as investing in a business or saving money and reactive activities such as borrowing cash or selling a car, residence, or arable land. Table 6.3 details the percentage of respondents engaged in each of these activities. It is notable that some households did manage to make investments (mostly by buying a new car), to save money, and to reduce debt during the most severe part of the economic crisis. Of the reactive practices, the most widespread were those that relate to spending savings and borrowing money.

Table 6.1 Self-assessment of the economic situation of the household five years ago and now

Country	Bosnia		Croatia		Serbia		Slovenia	
	Mean	SD	Mean	SD	Mean	SD	Mean	SD
Five years ago	5.18	2.309	6.19	2.089	5.49	2.148	6.68	1.898
Now	4.03	2.205	4.50	2.385	4.13	2.245	4.73	2.286

Table 6.2 Is the household's total income sufficient to get by?

Bosnia		Croatia		Serbia		Slovenia	
Mean	SD	Mean	SD	Mean	SD	Mean	SD
4.14	2.319	4.69	2.614	4.16	2.382	5.56	2.758

Table 6.3 Activities carried out in the last five years (in percent)

Crisis-related Activity	Bosnia	Croatia	Serbia	Slovenia
Invested in a business	7.6	7.2	8.3	5.3
Bought real estate	4.4	5.1	5.4	7.5
Bought a car	13.9	16.8	14.4	34.8
Saved money	10.2	14.5	8.3	20.4
Reduced debt	10.2	16.0	12.6	16.7
Terminated some of the household members' education	2.2	1.3	3.4	5.4
Been forced to spend some savings	11.6	25.8	26.2	28.5
Been forced to borrow money	16.5	26.3	34.4	16.9
Been forced to sell gold, silverware, or jewelry	4.1	12.4	5.0	4.8
Been forced to sell a car	3.2	6.5	5.6	6.8
Been forced to sell real estate (house, apartment)	1.7	1.0	1.1	1.4
Been forced to sell arable land	1.2	3.4	3.9	2.6

The sustainability dimensions of the economic crisis are perhaps most noticeable in answers to questions on household-consumption practices in the years prior to the survey (2010–2015), depicted in Table 6.4. Approximately one-third of the sample from Bosnia-Herzegovina and Serbia and one-fourth of the sample from Croatia and Slovenia were forced to change their dietary habits. More than half of the sample from Croatia and Serbia, as well as more than 40 percent of the sample from Bosnia-Herzegovina and Slovenia, had to reduce purchases of clothes, footwear, and appliances and limit dining out in restaurants and travel. Finally, with the exception of Slovenia, residents of all countries significantly curtailed their cultural consumption by limiting recreational and leisure activities.

Our goal here was to identify the main dimensions that structure and frame particular lifestyle configurations. Determining these factors allowed us to create specific clusters of production and consumption activities. Table 6.A2 depicts the eigenvalues and variances explained by the first five axes. Tables 6.A3 and 6.A4 illustrate the active variables and supplementary variables, their map codes, and their percentage in the sample.

The analyses show that in all four countries two basic dimensions structure lifestyle and household strategies: 1) whether the household is treated as a *production or consumption unit*, and 2) whether the household has a *proactive or*

Table 6.4 Reduction of consumption in the last five years (in percent)

Reduction in Goods and Activities	Bosnia	Croatia	Serbia	Slovenia
Reduced meat in diet	32.5	27.7	33.1	22.4
Reduced fruit and vegetables in diet	28.1	22.6	24.5	12.6
Reduced purchases of hygiene products and cosmetics	26.0	22.4	28.7	22.5
Reduced purchases of clothing and footwear	41.6	52.8	52.3	43.6
Reduced purchases of household appliances	44.8	51.3	59.2	33.4
Limited hairdresser, pedicure, manicure	38.9	44.8	42.5	32.8
Reduced using own car	29.0	31.5	29.8	21.8
Reduced dining out	43.8	53.1	52.7	41.6
Reduced tourist travel	46.7	52.1	55.7	40.3
Reduced summer vacations	45.7	47.3	55.1	37.5
Reduced consumption of cultural goods and programs	40.7	44.0	45.7	26.5
Reduced recreational activities	35.5	35.7	48.8	21.6
Reduced hobbies and leisure activities	32.9	26.4	33.5	17.8

reactive approach to the economic crisis. Since the resultant figures for all of the countries are almost identical (with a different distribution of these dimensions for Slovenia[6]), from this point onward we will discuss only the results of these two dimensions for Serbia.

The basic axis that emerges in the analyses represents the household as a consumption unit or as a production unit. This axis in Serbia accounts for 53.9 percent of the variance (60.9 percent in Croatia and 46.5 percent in Bosnia-Herzegovina). On the left-hand side of Figure 6.1, and especially in the upper left-hand quadrant, one finds indicators of a high degree of personal food production and of various household goods (e.g., fruits and vegetables, fowl, livestock, preserves, jams, milk, cheese, clothes, furniture) and agriculture as a source of income. On the opposite side of the figure, especially in the lower right-hand quadrant, are indicators of the absence of any household production and data that point to the fact that almost all food in the household is store-bought.

Along the other basic axis (proactive vs. reactive approach), in the upper right-hand quadrant, we see indicators of excessive consumption—frequent vacations, recurrent outings to restaurants, purchases of clothes at shopping malls, absence of any decrease in consumption, proactive practices during a period of crisis (e.g., investing in a business, buying real estate or a car, saving money, paying down of debt) and, interestingly, a significant percentage of food brought back from parents or relatives living in the country. By contrast, in the

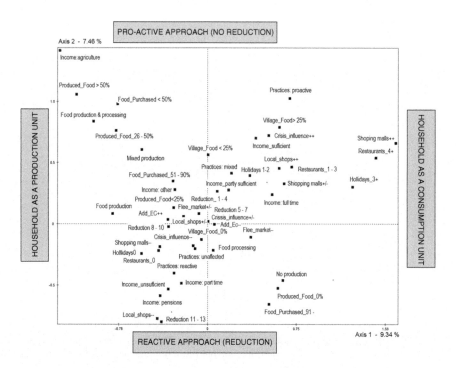

Figure 6.1 Lifestyles and household strategies in Serbia (A)

bottom left-hand quadrant, there are indicators of a reduction in consumption in the form of not going on any holidays or eating out and not buying clothes and footwear, even at flea markets.

Figures 6.2 and 6.3 show the projected supplementary variables, which indicate the sociodemographic profile of the different lifestyle dimensions. Figure 6.2 depicts the link with the occupational profile of the household, regular income of the household, and income per household member. Figure 6.3 illustrates the educational profile of the household, the number of household members, and the location of their permanent residence.

In Figure 6.2, we observe a strong class division along the first axis. On the left-hand side of the figure one finds indicators of all members of the household belonging to the working class; households that either do not have any regular income or have only one regular income (Regular income 0 or Regular income 1); and an average monthly income per household member of less than €200. On the opposite side of the figure, there are indicators of upper-class occupations such as experts, managers, or politicians; multiple regular incomes in the household; and an average monthly income exceeding €400 per household member in Serbia and Bosnia, €550 per household member in Croatia, and more than €1,000 per household member in Slovenia.

Figure 6.2 Lifestyles and household strategies in Serbia (B) (with supplementary variables projected: average monthly household income per household member, number of regular incomes, and household occupational profile)

Figure 6.3 Lifestyles and household strategies in Serbia (C) (with supplementary variables projected: household educational profile, place of residence, and number of household members)

As expected, we find that the production orientation is more evident in rural parts of the country. Under these circumstances having a higher number of household members is an important resource, and such a situation is more typical of households with an elementary educational level. By contrast, a consumer orientation is characteristic of people living in cities, relatively smaller households, and households whose members are more highly educated.

Results of the cluster analysis

Our next set of analyses uses hierarchical cluster analysis (Le Roux and Rouanet, 2004) to determine whether there are distinct groups within each country that are defined according to the two dimensions of differentiation and that represent transformations of specific values along them.[7] To capture potential differences across countries, analyses were not restricted to produce similar numbers of groups. Nevertheless, the results suggest that a five-cluster solution is optimal for each country.[8]

We defined the five groups of clusters using the basic lifestyle dimensions discussed above and treated the household either as a production or consumption unit with a proactive relationship (without a reduction in consumption) or a reactive relationship (based on a reduction in consumption). Combining these dimensions leads to emergence of four groups of clusters—productive proactive, productive reactive, consumer proactive, and consumer reactive—along with a fifth group made up of clusters with mixed characteristics (see Figure 6.1, Table 6.5,[9] and Figures 6.5–6.8).

The characteristics that describe a proactive response to the economic crisis and treat the household as a production unit (in Serbia and Bosnia it is Clusters 4 and 5, in Slovenia it is Cluster 5, and in Croatia it is Cluster 3) generally comprise agricultural workers and working-class individuals with an elementary school education and relatively low income. They are able to meet their own needs to a large extent and spend very little money. They rarely take vacations or go to restaurants, and when they do not make their own clothes, they buy them either in local stores or at flea markets. Their proactive strategy could be defined as *self-provisioning*.

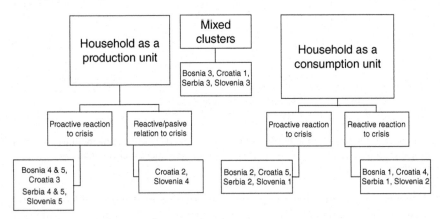

Figure 6.4 Typology of household strategies (reactions to the crisis)

Table 6.5 Cluster distribution per country

Cluster labels/Country	Bosnia	Croatia	Serbia	Slovenia
Household production proactive	No. 4–11%	No. 3–14.6%	No. 4–14.0%	No. 5–8.4%
Household production proactive	No. 5–20.2%		No. 5–13.4%	
Household production reactive		No. 2–20.0%		No. 4–19.8%
Mixed clusters	No. 3–20.8%	No. 1–20.7%	No. 3–19.7%	No. 3–26.3%
Household consumption proactive	No. 2–15.0%	No. 5–18.1%	No. 2–21.4%	No. 1–21.1%
Household consumption reactive	No. 1–33.1%	No. 4–26.6%	No. 1–31.5%	No. 2–24.3%

Cluster 2 in Croatia and Cluster 4 in Slovenia exhibit a passive response to the crisis, although the households are treated as production units. This group is largely made up of pensioners with working-class occupations, less education, lower incomes, and who live in the country and produce very little. What is most characteristic about these households is that during the period of the economic crisis they did not invest, buy, or manage to save; nor did they spend, borrow, or sell property that they had previously acquired. They simply waited for the economic crisis to pass. This group's strategy is best described as *passive endurance of the crisis*.

The third group of clusters comprises households that are considered consumption units and responded to the crisis through a drastic reduction in consumption (Cluster 1 in Bosnia and Serbia, Cluster 4 in Croatia, and Cluster 2 in Slovenia). They did not produce any of the food that they consumed and did not have the ability to obtain even some food from parents or relatives in rural areas. These are households that live in the city, have a high-school education and middle-class jobs, but insufficient income. Their basic strategy is *consumption reduction*.

The fourth group is made up of Cluster 2 in Serbia and Bosnia, Cluster 5 in Croatia, and Cluster 1 in Slovenia. These households are sustained by two or more incomes from full-time employment. Their members have the highest level of education, upper-class professions (experts and managers), and they live in cities. This group considers the household a consumption unit and has demonstrated a proactive approach to the economic crisis (including investments, shopping, increased consumption, decrease in debt), accompanied by the absence of a reduction in consumption. This is the only group in all four countries that continues to regularly go on holidays, eat out at restaurants, shop for clothing in specialized stores and shopping malls, has not changed its dietary habits, and has not altered its level of cultural consumption. Their strategy is *proactive, without a reduction in consumption*.

Finally, the fifth group of clusters that we describe as mixed clusters (Cluster 3 in Bosnia, Serbia, and Slovenia and Cluster 1 in Croatia) exists on a single monthly income from full-time jobs and supplements this income with a low level of food production accompanied by a low level of consumption. They generally buy their clothes and footwear in local stores, usually do not travel during the summer holidays, and very infrequently go out to restaurants. Their strategy combines elements of a low level of production and a moderate level of consumption, and so is described as a *mixed strategy*.

When analyzing the differences among the clusters in their perceived economic situation in 2010 and in 2015 (Table 6.6[10]), we note that in all four societies only members of the *proactive without a reduction in consumption* cluster indicated that the crisis did not significantly change their economic situation. In Croatia and Bosnia-Herzegovina, the most drastic perceived economic change in response to the crisis occurred among small farmers who self-satisfy most of their needs and whose strategy we define as *self-provisioning* (in Bosnia this is Cluster 5 and in Croatia it is Cluster 3). By contrast, in Slovenia and Serbia the economic crisis

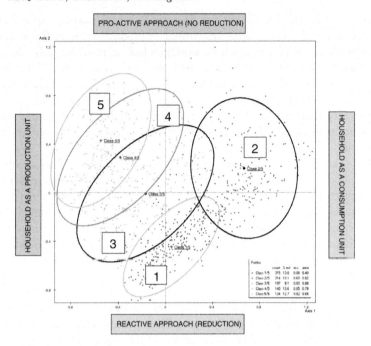

Figure 6.5 Distribution of clusters in the maps of lifestyles (Serbia)

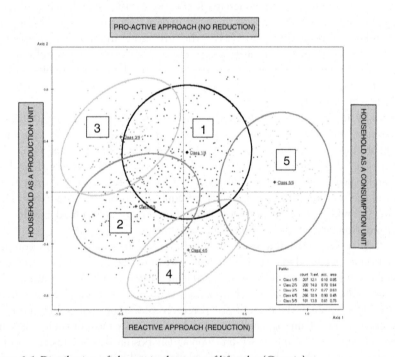

Figure 6.6 Distribution of clusters in the maps of lifestyles (Croatia)

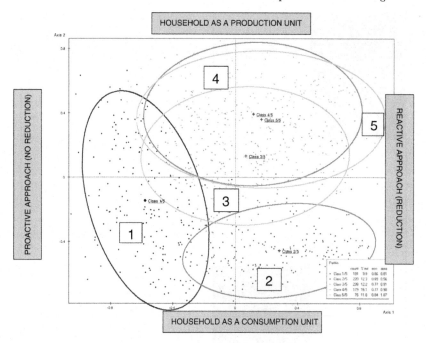

Figure 6.7 Distribution of clusters in the maps of lifestyles (Slovenia)

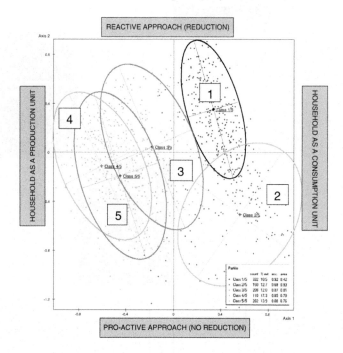

Figure 6.8 Distribution of clusters in the maps of lifestyles (Bosnia)

Table 6.6 Self-assessment of the household's economic situation five years ago and now

Bosnia	Cluster 1		Cluster 2		Cluster 3		Cluster 4		Cluster 5	
	Mean	SD	Mean	SD	Mean	SD	Mean	SD	Mean	SD
5 years ago	4.26	2.565	5.78	2.222	5.33	2.203	5.16	2.060	5.54	1.952
Now	3.34	2.095	6.02	2.203	4.03	2.017	3.80	1.947	3.84	1.853

Croatia	Cluster 1		Cluster 2		Cluster 3		Cluster 4		Cluster 5	
	Mean	SD	Mean	SD	Mean	SD	Mean	SD	Mean	SD
5 years ago	6.63	1.812	5.63	2.147	6.11	1.958	5.78	2.250	7.00	1.822
Now	4.65	1.974	3.63	2.142	3.87	2.011	3.70	2.167	6.97	1.898

Serbia	Cluster 1		Cluster 2		Cluster 3		Cluster 4		Cluster 5	
	Mean	SD	Mean	SD	Mean	SD	Mean	SD	Mean	SD
5 years ago	5.15	2.340	6.25	1.813	5.20	2.184	5.42	2.036	5.58	1.936
Now	3.30	1.975	5.61	1.932	3.62	2.085	4.30	2.256	4.30	2.320

Slovenia	Cluster 1		Cluster 2		Cluster 3		Cluster 4		Cluster 5	
	Mean	SD	Mean	SD	Mean	SD	Mean	SD	Mean	SD
5 years ago	7.42	1.766	6.36	2.019	6.55	1.780	6.59	1.914	6.33	1.716
Now	6.52	2.049	3.95	1.983	4.38	2.176	4.49	2.048	4.17	2.241

had the strongest impact on the *consumption reduction* group—vocational employees with a high-school education who live in cities, are not involved in any kind of production, do not receive any help from others living in rural areas, and have a regular but insufficient income (in Serbia this is Cluster 1 and in Slovenia it is Cluster 2).

On the one hand, in the highest ratings of the extent to which the overall income of their households is sufficient for a normal life (Table 6.7[11]), members of the most educated and wealthiest group of people with a proactive response to the crisis also stand out. On the other hand, in Slovenia and Serbia the groups that indicated the most drastic change in position as a result of the economic crisis usually claimed that their income was not sufficient for a normal life, but in Bosnia and Croatia this role was taken over by groups that we define as mixed clusters (in Bosnia it is Cluster 3 and in Croatia it is Cluster 4).

Table 6.7 Is household's total income sufficient to get by?

Bosnia									
Cluster 1		Cluster 2		Cluster 3		Cluster 4		Cluster 5	
Mean	SD	Mean	SD	Mean	SD	Mean	SD	Mean	SD
3.26	2.045	6.75	2.154	3.09	2.121	3.92	2.010	4.03	1.943

Croatia									
Cluster 1		Cluster 2		Cluster 3		Cluster 4		Cluster 5	
Mean	SD	Mean	SD	Mean	SD	Mean	SD	Mean	SD
5.05	1.998	3.65	2.389	4.42	2.529	3.52	2.286	7.38	1.872

Serbia									
Cluster 1		Cluster 2		Cluster 3		Cluster 4		Cluster 5	
Mean	SD	Mean	SD	Mean	SD	Mean	SD	Mean	SD
3.13	1.958	5.81	2.154	3.69	2.143	4.49	2.349	4.40	2.501

Slovenia									
Cluster 1		Cluster 2		Cluster 3		Cluster 4		Cluster 5	
Mean	SD	Mean	SD	Mean	SD	Mean	SD	Mean	SD
7.56	2.444	4.30	2.457	5.36	2.638	5.40	2.437	5.14	2.741

Conclusion

Our three main aims in this chapter have been to identify the strategies that households in four southeastern European societies have adopted to cope with the economic crisis, to evaluate the degree to which these strategies strike a new balance between consumption and production and move toward sustainable lifestyles, and to identify specific groups that are particularly disposed to changes consistent with a sustainable lifestyle based on socioeconomic class, educational level, and geographic status.

Our results show that in Serbia, Bosnia-Herzegovina, Croatia, and Slovenia there was a significant reduction in spending with more than 25 percent of the sample changing dietary habits (as evident in decreases in the amount of meat intake, the volume of fresh fruit and vegetables consumed, and reductions in the purchase of hygiene products and cosmetics). Similarly, more than 40 percent of respondents in Bosnia-Herzegovina and Slovenia (and more than 50 percent of the sample from Serbia and Croatia) curtailed purchases of clothing and footwear, dined out less, and went on fewer trips and vacations. In addition, with the exception of Slovenia, more than 40 percent of the remaining sample spent less on cultural and recreational activities. More than half of the respondents in this study turned to the informal economy, including behaviors that could be considered more environmentally sustainable, such as self-provisioning and small-scale food production in plots located on the periphery of the city, cultivating produce in smaller gardens in neighboring villages, or bringing food from parents or relatives living in the country. The second most frequent behavior, which was demonstrated by approximately 10 percent of the sample in the four countries, occurred in the realm of the gray economy (small repairs around the neighborhood, cleaning and maintaining other people's houses, sewing, taking care of children or the elderly).

Despite significant differences among the four societies in terms of their economic development and structure, only groups with considerable capital (households with numerous sources of regular income from full-time jobs, members with managerial and expert positions, and high levels of education) remained relatively unaffected by the economic crisis. All other households experienced significant changes in lifestyles evident in both their production and consumption behavior, some of it with consequences for environmental sustainability. The division between sustainable and unsustainable lifestyles clearly replicates the class distinctions in these societies.

Our central finding is the identification of five strategies in which households have engaged to manage the vicissitudes of the economic crisis. Interventions vary depending on whether the household operates as a production or consumption unit, and whether it adopts a proactive or reactive approach. Some aspects of the proactive approach have significant implications for sustainable practices, in particular those that have to do with changes in production behavior such as self-provisioning. This behavior is typical of farmers or industrial workers who live in outlying villages. The proactive approach characterized by a change in consumption behavior is more prevalent among capital-rich households whose members work in managerial and professional occupations and it emphasizes investments in economic activities.

Two groups adopted reactive strategies. The first group comprising households that exhibit passive endurance of the economic crisis, mostly elderly individuals and single-person households, experience the adverse effects of the prevailing situation without much attempt to mitigate them. The second group consists of households that curtail consumption (sometimes drastically), withdraw savings or borrow money, or sell resources such as arable land, cars, or property. This reactive strategy has notable implications for sustainability as it involves reducing, selling, and reusing.

Finally, we identified mixed strategies, prevalent among middle-class households that live in cities. They combine a reliance on reduction in consumption and participation in the informal economy, usually by providing intellectual services such as tutoring and accounting assistance that is readily tradable through personal networks.

What makes these four countries of southeastern Europe different from other European nations and renders them interesting exceptions to study is that during the past twenty-five years they have been exposed to the effects of three social processes that have caused tectonic changes: 1) the violent dissolution of the country of which they were previously constituent parts; 2) the post-socialist transformation that transpired; and 3) the effects of the post-2007 economic crisis. What also sets them apart from other socialist nations is that elsewhere in Eastern Europe the transition was largely completed by 2007. By contrast, in the four countries of the former Yugoslav federation that we studied (aside from Slovenia), this process had only just begun to have positive results and these developments were annulled by the effects of the economic crisis. Continuing with the same analogy that has often been used to describe transition processes, this experience was like a ship hitting an iceberg in the middle of the sea while the vessel was in the midst of being rebuilt.

If the civil wars devastated the economic infrastructure, severed mutual economic ties, and destroyed previous internal markets, the post-socialist transformation led to (at the same time) a rise in unemployment and the disappearance of basic welfare functions that were a staple of socialism. Furthermore, the policy of austerity during the period of economic crisis only exacerbated these tendencies. This situation led to the rise of an informal economy and greater reliance on the household and extended families to provide certain functions, especially those aimed at self-provisioning and services that had once come from the welfare state.

The economic crisis has brought about shortages and recessions that influence consumers' plans and expectations regarding wages, employment opportunities, products, services, and prices. Some of these effects have resulted in changes in behavior that challenge culturally embedded social practices. In turn, some of these new routines have had consequences for environmental sustainability—the postponement of purchases of durable goods, the rescaling of consumer needs, the pooling of consumption (by sharing and bartering for resources), the development of self-provisioning arrangements, and the general shift from a consumption to a production orientation.

The main question that remains open given our findings is whether lifestyle changes that occur in times of crisis are potential turning points leading to the adoption of more sustainable practices in post-crisis times. Can we envision a framework that regards constraints as opportunities and survival as an inducement for lifestyle change? Are these new behaviors temporary or permanent? An additional component of the research described here relates to the interviews conducted with household members in the four countries. Using qualitative analysis, future work could aim to tap the deeper layers of the changes we describe here and assess the extent to which they are indeed long term and embedded in cultural practices. Such an analysis would identify the social construction of consumption in the context of the economic crisis; the articulation of new norms of consumption and their relation to sustainability, resource conservation, and conditions of life for the future generations; and the feasibility of reverting to pre-crisis patterns of consumption.

Notes

1 SCOPES is the acronym for the program on Scientific Co-operation Between Eastern Europe and Switzerland.
2 In addition to the survey, the mixed-methods research design included 120 semi-structured interviews with the survey respondents (thirty in each of the four countries) and 100 semi-structured group interviews (twenty-five in each of the four countries) including household members of particularly vulnerable groups: the Roma, social care recipients, small farmers, pensioners, households relying on remittances, and single mothers.
3 Descriptive statistics of these variables are provided in Table 6.A2.
4 This approach was designed by a group of French mathematicians and statisticians working around J.-P. Benzecri. The basic tenet of this school, known as geometric data analysis (GDA), is that it will not suffice to make a priori assumptions on the nature of the analyzed data (e.g., their division into independent and dependent variables). The idea is to let the data "speak for themselves." Thus, MCA is conceived of as an inductive, exploratory technique whose basic task is to identify hidden structures within the given data. In that sense it is similar to factor analysis—especially the extraction method which is also known as principle component analysis. However, by introducing so-called "supplementary" variables, MCA can also be used for explanatory purposes. In the data analysis based on MCA, two types of variables are employed: "active" variables whose mutual relations constitute maps and "passive" (or "supplementary") variables which can be projected over them, without any changes within the maps themselves, but with an indication of the relations with the active variables. MCA represents its results in two ways: the so-called "clouds of modalities," which highlight the spatial relations between the variables or the so-called "clouds of individuals" where one can see the position of the individual on these maps based on certain characteristics (e.g., gender, age, education, profession). Simply put, MCA works by grouping in space the responses from various participants which frequently occur together, and separating those responses which are infrequent (in space, i.e., on the maps). In the case that, for example, we were to remain in the sphere of our research (see Figure 6.1, upper right-hand quadrant), all of the respondents who cited that they

most often shop in shopping malls, cited that they ate out in restaurants more than four times in the last twelve months prior to the survey, and went on holiday more than three times over the past five years, then these three indicators would appear as the same point in space. The fewer the respondents who cite all of these factors together, the further these three points will be spread out in the figure. The responses which never occur together are the furthest possible from one another on the figure. In our analysis we used specific MCA (Le Roux and Rouanet, 2010), with the "missing" variables as passive categories.

5 Since our unit of analysis is the household, we use educational and occupational profiles of households rather than respondents, calculated based on the education and occupation of three adult members of the household in larger households or all adult members in smaller households.

6 In Slovenia the order of the dimensions is different. The first axis to emerge is the one whose poles represent the proactive vs. reactive approach (47.34 percent of the variance), while the second axis is related to the concept of the household as a production or consumption unit (23.58 percent of the variance).

7 Technically speaking, the process detects the existence of clusters (sub-clouds of points in our MCA) where members of the same cluster are as close as possible, whereas those from a different one are as separate as possible.

8 We decided to inspect the dendograms and level indices obtained from the SPAD statistical software (Le Roux and Rouanet, 2004).

9 The first column shows the cluster labels, while in the table we find the percentage of households which belong to certain clusters in each of the countries. It should be noted that in Bosnia-Herzegovina and in Croatia, two clusters each belong to the group of clusters which we marked "Household production proactive."

10 Black shading indicates the clusters evaluating the household economic situation as greatly deteriorated at the time of the survey compared to a period of time five years ago, while, on the other hand, gray shading indicates clusters where the difference in the evaluation of the economic situation in the household at the time of the survey and five years ago was the smallest. Or, for example, in the case of cluster 2 in Bosnia-Herzegovina whose economic circumstances at the time of the survey were assessed better than prior to the economic crisis.

11 In this table black shading indicates the lowest grade (arithmetic mean) in response to the question of whether the total household income is sufficient to get by (i.e., the worst economic situation of households which belong to these clusters), while gray shading indicates the highest grade (arithmetic mean) in response to this question (i.e., the best economic situation of the households in these clusters).

References

Alimen, N. and Bayraktaroglu, G. (2011) "Consumption adjustments of Turkish consumers during the global financial crisis," *Ege Akademik Bakis* 11(2):193–203.

Alonso, L., Fernández-Rodríguez, C., and Ibáñez-Rojo, R. (2015) "From consumerism to guilt: economic crisis and discourses about consumption in Spain," *Journal of Consumer Culture* 15(1):66–85.

Ang, S. (2000) "Personality influences on consumption: insights from the Asian economic crisis," *Journal of International Consumer Marketing* 13(1):5–20.

Biswas, A. and Roy, M. (2015) "Green products: an exploratory study on the consumer behavior in emerging economies of the East," *Journal of Cleaner Production* 87(1):463–468.

Bosco, A. and Verney, S. (2012) "Electoral epidemic: the political cost of economic crisis in Southern Europe, 2010–11," *South European Society and Politics* 17(2):129–154.

Brown, M. (2013) The transmission of banking crises to households: lessons from the 2008–2011 crises in the ECA region. Policy Research Working Paper 6528. Washington, DC: World Bank.

Cohen, M. (2013) "Collective dissonance and the transition to post-consumerism," *Futures* 52(1):42–51.

Faganel, A. (2011) "Recognized values and consumption patterns of post-crisis consumers," *Managing Global Transitions* 9(2):151–170.

Goodwin, P. and van Dender, K. (2013) "'Peak car': themes and issues," *Transport Reviews* 33(3):243–254.

Gosetti, G. (2012) "Work and spending habits: an exploration inside the social issues of crisis," *Italian Sociological Review* 2(3):176–190.

Greenacre, M. (2007) *Correspondence Analysis in Practice*, 2nd ed. Boca Raton, FL: Chapman and Hall/CRC.

Greta, M. and Lewandowski, K. (2015) "The impact of the global financial and economic crisis convergence process in OECD countries," *Comparative Economic Research* 18(1):81–96.

Ion, I. (2014) "Households' adjustment to the economic crisis and the impact on the retail sector in Romania," *Revista de Management Comparat International* 15(2):174–189.

Kaytaz, M. and Gul, M. (2014) "Consumer response to economic crisis and lessons for marketers: the Turkish experience," *Journal of Business Research* 67(1):2701–2706.

Lebart, L., Morineau, A., and Warwick, K. (1984) *Multivariate Descriptive Statistical Analysis: Correspondence Analysis and Related Techniques for Large Matrices*. New York: Wiley.

Le Roux, B. and Rouanet, H. (2004) *Geometric Data Analysis: From Correspondence Analysis to Structured Data Analysis*. Berlin: Springer.

Le Roux, B. and Rouanet, H. (2010) *Multiple Correspondence Analysis*. Thousand Oaks, CA: Sage.

Le Roux, B., Rouanet, H., Savage, M., and Warde, A. (2008) "Class and cultural division in the UK," *Sociology* 42(6):1049–1071.

Ludvigson, S. (2004) "Consumer confidence and consumer spending," *Journal of Economic Perspectives* 18(2):29–50.

Orru, K. and Lilleoja, L. (2015) "Contextual drivers of environmental values cross-culturally: evidence from Europe between 2004 and 2012," *Studies of Transition States and Societies* 7(3):38–51.

Prothero, A. and McDonagh, P. (2014) "Consuming austerity: visual representations," in Schouten, J., Martin, D., and Belk, R. (eds.), *Consumer Culture Theory*. Bingley: Emerald Group Publishing Limited, pp. 133–153.

Schneider, F., Kallis, G., and Martinez-Alier, J. (2010) "Crisis or opportunity? Economic degrowth for social equity and ecological sustainability," *Journal of Cleaner Production* 18(6):511–518.

Shiller, R. (2012) *The Subprime Solution: How Today's Global Financial Crisis Happened, and What To Do About It*. Princeton, NJ: Princeton University Press.

Stiglitz, J. (2009) "The global crisis, social protection and jobs," *International Labour Review* 148(1–2):1–13.

Vihalemm, T., Keller, M., and Pihu, K. (2016) "Consumers during the 2008–2011 economic crisis in Estonia: mainstream and grass roots media discourses," *Italian Sociological Review* 6(1):57–86.

Vitell, S. (2015) "A case for consumer social responsibility (CnSR): including a selected review of consumer ethics/social responsibility research," *Journal of Business Ethics* 130(4):767–774.

Appendix

Table 6.A1 Country characteristics (in 2015)

Country	Slovenia	Croatia	Bosnia	Serbia
Area (in km²)	20,273	56,594	51,197	77,474
Population	2,062,874	4,232,919	3,809,027	7,132,578
GDP (in billions of USD)*	$65.521	$91.096	$37.966	$100.18
GDP per capita	$31,872	$21,169	$9,980	$14,047

*Calculated in purchasing power parity.

Table 6.A2 Eigenvalues and raw and modified inertia for the first five axes in MCA

Bosnia–Axes	1	2	3	4	5
Eigenvalues (λ)	0.211	0.186	0.139	0.118	0.105
Raw inertia	8.7%	7.7%	5.7%	4.9%	4.3%
Modified inertia	46.53%	31.12%	10.7%	5.15%	2.65%
Croatia–Axes	1	2	3	4	5
Eigenvalues (λ)	0.231	0.159	0.129	0.118	0.100
Raw inertia	9.4%	6.4%	5.2%	4.8%	4.1%
Modified inertia	60.98%	19.34%	8.87%	5.86%	2.57%
Serbia–Axes	1	2	3	4	5
Eigenvalues (λ)	0.225	0.177	0.142	0.109	0.093
Raw inertia	9.4%	7.4%	5.9%	4.06%	3.9%
Modified inertia	53.91%	28.28%	12.19%	3.9%	1.52%
Slovenia–Axes	1	2	3	4	5
Eigenvalues (λ)	0.195	0.157	0.131	0.120	0.103
Raw inertia	8.3%	6.7%	5.6%	5.1%	4.4%
Modified inertia	47.34%	23.58%	11.91%	8.26%	3.77%

Table 6.A3 Distribution of indicators (active variables) (in percent)

Modalities and map codes	Bosnia %	Croatia %	Serbia %	Slovenia %
1) Is household's income sufficient to get by				
I: insufficient	41.6	36.7	43.5	26.2
I: partly sufficient	42.0	37.0	38.2	35.2
I: sufficient	16.4	26.3	18.3	38.6
2) How household has been affected by the economic crisis				
CA: negatively	36.9	48.9	43.9	54.3
CA: unaffected	55.8	43.1	46.1	40.1
CA: positively	6.1	7.1	9.9	5.6
Missing	—	0.9	0.1	0.4
3) Household practices influenced by economic crisis				
Practices: reactive	21.3	25.7	34.4	15.3
Practices: mixed	4.3	33.3	16.0	26.5
Practices: unaffected	58.4	17.8	35.2	30.8
Practices: proactive	16.0	19.5	14.2	27.4
Missing	—	3.7	0.2	—
4) Household sources of income				
I: full-time jobs	41.3	51.1	42.8	47.3
I: part-time and seasonal jobs	7.4	—	6.2	—
I: pensions	35.6	32.8	30.4	36.8
I: other sources	10.1	8.5	15.5	8.8
I: mixed sources	—	7.2	4.7	7.0
Missing	5.6	0.4	0.7	0.9
5) Household's additional economic activities				
No additional economic activities	90.0	90.9	85.2	87.4
Additional economic activities	10.0	9.1	14.8	12.6
6) Type of household production				
Food production	21.9	8.3	3.1	11.1
Food processing	—	10.0	19.3	7.0
Food production and processing	8.2	24.3	23.6	—
Mixed production	13.2	6.4	8.6	30.3
No production	56.8	51.0	45.4	51.7
7) Percent of food household produces itself				
Produced food 0	49.4	48.0	53.1	41.6
Produced food < 25%	21.4	27.0	18.5	30.9
Produced food 26–50%	19.6	15.4	15.1	19.0
Produced food > 50%	9.7	9.6	13.3	8.5
8) Percent of food household brings from the countryside				
Village food 0%	81.2	69.0	83.6	66.9
Village food < 20%	8.6	20.4	9.4	24.3
Village food > 21%	10.2	10.6	7.0	8.7

Modalities and map codes	Bosnia %	Croatia %	Serbia %	Slovenia %
9) Percent of food household has to buy				
Purchased food < 50%	20.6	22.8	24.5	20.4
Purchased food 51–75%	16.1	—	—	18.0
Purchased food 76–90%	17.8	38.2	25.5	26.8
Purchased food 91–100%	45.6	39.0	50.0	34.8
Missing	—	—	—	0.6
10) Reduction in goods and activities				
Reduction 0	40.8	28.2	23.3	36.9
Reduction 1–4/Reduction 1–5	21.6	21.8	23.4	27.0
Reduction 5–7/Reduction 5–10	17.6	17.5	19.5	23.8
Reduction 8–10	—	18.9	14.7	—
Reduction 11–13	20.1	13,6	19.1	12.3
11) Number of summer holidays in the last five years				
Holidays 0	64.7	51.5	58.8	22.9
Holidays 1–2 / Holidays 1–3	21.8	13.2	20.7	26.1
Holidays 3+	—	—	20.5	—
Holidays 4+	13.6	10.5	—	—
Holidays 5+	—	22.8	—	28.1
Holidays 6+	—	—	—	22.9
12) Dining out with friends (three months before survey)				
Dinner never	76.1	73.5	68.6	50.7
Dinner 1–3	18.0	21.3	23.2	35.0
Dinner 4+	5.9	5.2	8.2	14.4
13) How often they buy clothes in shopping malls				
Shopping malls (–) (never)	38.8	21.0	67.7	18.3
Shopping malls (+/–) (sometimes)	54.5	63.1	25.9	63.9
Shopping malls (++) (often)	6.7	15.9	6.4	17.8
14) How often they buy clothes in local shops				
Local shops (–) (never)	26.4	22.4	16.8	29.1
Local shops (+/–) (sometimes)	66.1	71.1	57.7	64.3
Local shops (++) (often)	7.5	6.5	25.5	6.6
15) How often they buy clothes in the flea market				
Flea market (–) (never)	33.8	54.9	35.4	71.6
Flea market (+/–) (sometimes)	57.1	41.3	50.8	21.5
Flea market (++) (often)	9.1	3.8	13.8	0.9

Table 6.A4 Distribution of indicators (supplementary variables) (in percent)

Modalities and map codes	Bosnia %	Croatia %	Serbia %	Slovenia %
1) Permanent place of residence (type)				
Village	45.5	45.1	37.5	62.2
Town	22.7	12.4	15.6	21.1
City	31.2	42.4	46.9	16.5
Missing	0.6	0.1	—	0.2
2) Total number of household members				
1 member	19.3	22.2	18.3	23.6
2 members	28.5	28.7	28.9	32.0
3 members	18.9	20.9	20.4	20.4
4 members	20.4	15.5	18.5	17.8
5 members	8.6	7.3	8.0	4.8
6+ members	4.4	5.4	5.9	1.5
3) Educational profile of the household members				
Household education profile 1 (elementary school)	16.2	11.3	12.5	8.8
Household education profile 2 (high school)	26.3	33.4	6.9	32.1
Household education profile 3 (higher education)	5.8	10.0	38.9	13.6
Household education profile 4 (mixed elementary and high school)	34.1	26.9	10.1	18.9
Household education profile 5 (at least 1 member with higher education)	17.6	19.3	31.6	26.5
4) Occupational profile of the household members				
Household occupational profile 1 (working-class occupations)	50.7	37.9	40.1	36.2

Modalities and map codes	Bosnia %	Croatia %	Serbia %	Slovenia %
Household occupational profile 2 (middle-class occupations)	10.8	13.2	17.5	16.0
Household occupational profile 3 (upper-class occupations)	6.0	9.5	9.8	10.0
Household occupational profile 4 (mixed: working and middle class occupations.)	19.3	24.8	16.4	21.6
Household occupational profile 5 (at least 1 member with upper class occupation)	13.3	14.6	16.2	16.3
5) Income per household member				
I: < €100 / I: < €150	23.8	22.2	22.5	—
I: €101–200 / I: €151–250	26.9	20.8	32.3	5.5
I: €201–300 / I: €251–350	8.9	22.4	15.3	—
I: €301–400 / €351–550	4.9	15.4	5.7	19.5
I: €400+ / €401–600	4.1	—	3.4	21.5
I: €550+ / €601–800	—	6.8	—	24.9
I: €801–1000	—	—	—	11.9
I: €1000+	—	—	—	8.4
Missing	31.4	12.4	20.8	8.3
(6) Number of incomes household relies on				
Regular income 0	14.7	12.4	14.6	6.3
Regular income 1	54.1	40.6	42.8	37.5
Regular income 2	26.9	38.0	35.2	48.2
Regular income 3	4.1	9.0	7.4	8.0
Missing	0.2	—	—	—

Part III

Post-consumerist transitions

7 When "gestures of change" demand policy support

Social change and the structural underpinnings of consumer culture in the United States

Cindy Isenhour

Introduction: on consumer culture and the nature of change

This chapter begins from three assumptions. First, it assumes that readers are already well aware of the ecological crises of modernity—the depletion of natural resources, dangerous greenhouse-gas concentrations, biodiversity loss—the list is woefully long (e.g., Rockström et al., 2009; Kolbert, 2014). Second, I presume that readers recognize that these "environmental" issues are poorly named as they are, in fact, symptoms of problems that are fundamentally social and economic in nature (Nader, 1981; Castree et al., 2014). Finally, given that nearly all of our "environmental" problems can be linked to historical and contemporary levels of human consumption (e.g., materials extraction, land conversion, fossil-fuel combustion), the chapter also draws upon a now broad consensus that global consumption patterns must be addressed if we hope to ensure the fulfillment of basic needs for all humans and future generations (IPCC, 2014; Reichel et al., 2014).

Many environmentally progressive nations have come to similar conclusions and are working in earnest to reduce impacts on the biosphere through investments in more efficient technologies. In many cases, these programs of ecological modernization have resulted in considerable gains—helping to improve the energy, materials, and carbon efficiency of economic activity (IEA, 2015; Jackson et al., 2016) (see also Chapter 9). Yet despite improvements, global energy demand, materials use, and emissions continue to grow (e.g., Jenkins et al., 2011; Reichel et al., 2014; WMO, 2015). Efficiency gains have been offset at the international level by overall expansion in total consumption and macro-level rebound effects (Barker and Rubin, 2007; Peters et al., 2012; Barrett et al., 2013). While technological optimists argue that innovation can simultaneously enable the expansion of consumer expenditures and a reduction of energy and materials use, empirical observations and modeled scenarios raise significant doubts about whether such a transition can be achieved in time and if the resulting gains can outpace economic growth indefinitely (Jackson, 2009, 2015; Dietz et al., 2013). Recognizing the very real possibility that technological shifts may not be sufficient to avoid resource depletion and dangerous climate change, many scientists now argue that we need something more than technological improvements. What we require, these experts argue, is culture change.

As an environmental and economic anthropologist, trained to utilize a comparative and deeply historical perspective to explore the interaction of environment, economy, and culture, the recent focus on changing the culture of consumption is at once refreshing and highly concerning. The focus on consumer culture is certainly welcome, drawing our collective attention to the material embodiments of a historical anomaly, a highly consumptive global economic system. On the one hand, this emphasis highlights the energy and emissions embodied in international trade, unsustainable levels of materials throughput, and severe global inequalities in access to resources. On the other hand, I fear that if we are not careful, contemporary interest in the culture of consumption has the potential to severely limit our efforts. I briefly outline these concerns as a matter of introduction before turning to an overview of the chapter's primary arguments.

Culture is an amorphous and ill-defined term that can take on drastically divergent meanings as it moves through social, political, and economic spaces. It can, at once, connote individual levels of class-based capital, ideological boundaries among communities with diverse backgrounds, and unconscious patterns of shared behaviors. Even anthropologists, the traditional keepers of the culture concept, have suggested ditching the term altogether due to: 1) its potential to misrepresent and homogenize the interests of highly heterogeneous groups; 2) the widespread misconception that culture is limited to the traditional ideological realm without consideration of the historical, material, and political processes at the root of cultural construction; and 3) its potential to bind "authentic" or "traditional" cultures in time and space (e.g., Abu-Lughod, 1991; Gupta and Ferguson, 1992).

Most important to recognize, given the recent emphasis on changing the culture of consumption, is that culture is not created in a vacuum and involves much more than traditional beliefs, attitudes, and values. It is, essentially, a product of history, context, and geography—but one that also responds to and shapes the present. Looking through time and across cultures, anthropological theory therefore understands culture not as a thing but as a process deeply influenced by the material and structural elements of society, the strong ideational pull of past human experiences, and encounters with new natural, economic, political, or intellectual environments (e.g., Bourdieu, 1977; Giddens, 1979). Empirical, cross-cultural studies of culture change have moved anthropological theory beyond linear and deterministic frames of change once linked to technological innovation (e.g., Morgan, 1985), energy capture (e.g., White, 2010), ideology (e.g., Weber and Kalberg, 2001), or environmental endowments (e.g., Diamond, 1999) as independent drivers of change. Instead, we have come to recognize that changes can be spurred by shifts in environmental conditions, modes of production, technologies, or ideologies—but that sustained culture change eventually requires a transition in both the structural and the ideological elements of society.

Unfortunately, popular calls to change the culture of consumption are usually conceptually limited to an understanding of culture in the ideological realm, as a set of shared values, beliefs, and attitudes. Imagined as such, strategies for influencing culture change among popular environmental groups are all too often limited to discussions about improved information and education, providing "the right incentives" for behavior modification, or reframing well-being in an effort to encourage more sustainable individual choices and behaviors. Having researched sustainability policy and practice in several different international contexts (Isenhour, 2010; Isenhour and Feng, 2014), and having participated in a variety of interdisciplinary sustainability science initiatives and community/ university partnerships (Isenhour and Blackmer, 2015), my experiences suggest that strategies designed to encourage culture change through education and individual behavioral modification remain absolutely pervasive but are rarely successful over the long term.

These education and awareness strategies, while well-intentioned, neglect widespread insights from studies of consumer behavior which suggest that the focus on individual choices is not working well to address consumption, a genuinely social act ingrained in the most basic social and economic structures of society. If culture is more than our ideas and values, then does it not make sense that culture change would require more than an ideological shift? The first argument of this chapter suggests that if history can serve as a guide, we should assume that significant change, of the sort required given the urgency of addressing climate change and rapid environmental deterioration, requires a shift not only in ideology and worldview (culture narrowly defined), but also in our social and economic organization, a task that will require both civil action and governmental intervention. Imagine, for example, where the environmental or civil rights movements in the United States would be without the policies that institutionalized their ideals and helped to restructure social and economic organization—the National Environmental Policy Act or the Civil Rights Act. These policies were essential as we restructured our social relations and terms of exchange in light of new understandings and the common interest.

In the pages to come, I draw on the work of political economist and economic historian Karl Polanyi (1957) and his conceptualization of the "double movement" in capitalist democracies to suggest that the time is growing ripe for decades of environmental education and consciousness raising to be matched by complementary policy interventions that can shift social and economic relations. That said, this chapter is focused on the United States and harbors no false illusions that policy approaches are easy in the current political climate. But we must recognize that progress has become unlikely due to the prevailing emphasis on voluntary, market-based actions—a strategy entirely consistent with the neoliberal devolution of responsibility onto market actors (Halkier, 2001; Hobson, 2002). While private consumption behaviors and lifestyle shifts that "gesture" toward change in the market are necessary and important, there is greater potential to build policy legitimacy by encouraging a new era of citizen activism focused not on individual well-being and sustainability in the customary sense of these terms, but on the collective social and economic structures that script for ongoing consumption growth, environmental degradation, and growing wealth disparities.

The argument to follow proceeds in three sections. First, I lay the foundation for the assertion that sustained culture change will require social movement and policy support with a brief historical analysis of the rise of "consumer culture" in the United States. While far from comprehensive, the discussion is meant to demonstrate that, like nearly all culture change in democratic societies, its contemporary variant arose: 1) from the formation of particular social and economic structures; 2) in ways that were ideologically consistent with pre-existing cultural values; and 3) with the support of public policy able to institutionalize a shift in the structure of social and economic organization. Second, drawing on Polanyi's concept of the double movement in capitalist democracies, the chapter asserts that the dominance of neoliberalism in the United States has interrupted the necessary pairing of social and policy movement. Building on this point, I argue that, in a neoliberal era, social movements can more effectively inspire policy legitimacy by drawing on already deeply seated democratic values—justice, democracy, and equal opportunity.

The emergence of consumer capitalism

It is instructive, when thinking about culture change, to analyze historical examples. How, for example, did contemporary consumer culture emerge and what lessons can we gather as we think about adapting to a future very different from that imagined by its architects? While consumer culture has been defined in myriad and contradictory ways, I adapt Slater's (1997), and later Arnould and Thompson's (2007), definition to refer to a social arrangement in which the meaning of life and individual identity, and their relationship to material resources, are mediated by market-based consumption. Consumer culture should not be automatically conflated with materialism or consumerism, which carry a negative connotation as a "cultural orientation in which the possession and use of an increasing number and variety of goods and services is the principal cultural aspiration and the surest perceived route to personal happiness" (Ekins, 1991) or a "particularly pernicious ideology which is not conducive to promoting human wellbeing" (Schor, 2008). While it is certainly true that contemporary consumer culture in the United States is contributing to overconsumption of natural resources and global atmospheric pollution and may be responsible for diminished perceptions of well-being, it remains, nonetheless, instructive to understand the historical construction and rationality of all cultural forms (Trentmann, 2012). This is particularly true if we acknowledge that cultural systems are typically seen as highly rational within the historical context from which they emerged (by at least some segments of society), but can appear, over time, increasingly maladaptive given new understandings, present circumstances, and projections for the future. As historian Lawrence Glickman (1999) observed, "Consumption is woven into the fabric of American life—it is bound up with national unity as well as fragmentation; democracy as well as inequality; conformity but also protest; work and play." Indeed, understanding the logic and rational roots of contemporary consumer capitalism is essential to fully comprehend contemporary American culture, as well as the possibilities for change.

Most historical analyses of the emergence of consumer culture begin with the transition to capitalist economies, when post-feudal resource consolidation left a large portion of the populace without access to productive resources and little choice but to abandon subsistence production in favor of wage labor. This trend helped to fuel urbanization and population growth. When combined with the Enlightenment's technological optimism, these trends resulted in a period of rapid productivity gains and accumulation. Scholars from multiple disciplines and time periods have outlined in great detail how the structure of the capitalist system, centered on accumulation and profits gained through the capture of surplus labor, contributed to the formation of social hierarchy and class differentiation through consumption (e.g., Adorno and Horkheimer, 2000; Blim, 2000; Hornborg, 2001). But with the Industrial Revolution and technologically aided production growth, the owners of capital soon discovered that their investments would require sustained market demand and an expanded consumer base. Drawing on the writings of the Frankfurt School, Richards (1991) has argued that the Industrial Revolution, "the final unification of the capitalist system ... required the creation of a compatible cultural form."

As economist John Kenneth Galbraith (1958) argued, the "culture industry," comprising retail, communication, and advertising professionals, arose in the late nineteenth and early twentieth centuries to help production create the desires it seeks to satisfy. But the genius of early advertising was not that it forged a brand new cultural system, but rather that it drew upon three different threads of already existing and firmly rooted democratic ideologies to establish the appeal of consumer capitalism (Strasser et al., 1998). First, admen used a number of metaphors to compare consumers with citizens and purchasing with voting. These descriptions were built on the idea of a free and sovereign consumer engaged in a form of civic responsibility (Sassatelli, 2007; Davidson, 2012; Trentmann, 2012). Second, advertisers drew on the idea that consumption provides a tool for building democracy and supporting equal access (Leach, 1993). The American "Democracy of Goods" provided low-cost mass-produced goods, enabling people of all means to live a life of luxury and to participate in the public realm of consumerism. But as historian William Leach (1993) wrote, this conceptualization of democracy and equal access emphasized individual pleasure, freedom, and self-fulfillment over communal well-being. As an increasing number of consumers gained access to goods, identities became increasingly tied to consumption, rather than the products of an individual's labors, enabling an acceleration of product replacement and disposal (Strasser, 1999; MacBride, 2012). Finally, Charles McGovern (1998) argued that advertisers were effective in tying consumerism and products to American nationality. Not only did this rhetoric assert that vigorous consumption was patriotic, helping the country toward economic recovery and prosperity following the Great Depression and World War II, but consumption was also presented as the "distinct heritage and privilege of living in the United States." Thus consumerism became tied to a sense of freedom, personal responsibility, and patriotism. McGovern proceeds further to observe that "American people fitfully but firmly came to equate the consumer with the citizen, a consumer standard of living with democracy, and the full participation in such an economy of spending and accumulation with being an American." The genius of these marketers as they sought to engineer culture change was that they framed consumption not in the language of radical change, but in already comfortably embedded and culturally consistent logics. Indeed, it can be argued that the appeal to these ideologies fulfilled an essential precondition, necessary in the first instance to open up the very possibility of acceptance for a cultural shift, an important point to which I will return in the penultimate section.

But most relevant to the argument here is that the shift toward consumer capitalism involved a new social and economic structure, an ideational move consistent with already deeply rooted cultural logics and, importantly, the support of state policies. Recognizing the significance of consumption to the revenue base, the government of the United States also became an active partner in the institutionalization of consumer culture in the country (Edsforth, 1987). The New Deal, for example, was based on the Keynesian assumption that under-consumption was the basic cause of the Great Depression. Therefore, recovery hinged on public efforts to increase purchasing power and to drive the economy. Historian Lizabeth Cohen (1998) has argued that "empowering the consumer seemed to many New Dealers a way of enhancing the public's stake in society and the economy while still preserving the free enterprise system ... and without having to confront more directly existing bastions of power such as American business." In the end, the legacy of this period was not only a new focus on the consumer, but also the idea that economic growth and expansion, built on the backs on strong purchasing power and consumer confidence, was the key to improving standards of living, democracy, and equality for all Americans. From the establishment of the Federal National Mortgage Association (Fannie Mae) in 1938 to the American Recovery and Reinvestment Act of 2009, public policy has long supported consumer culture through stimulus and the extension of credit. In the United States, the shift to consumer culture was thus expressly institutionalized by a wide array of public policies.

All this is not to say that citizens and consumers have been passive recipients of a capitalist and state-imposed culture of consumption or that culture is a *tabula rasa* inscribed solely by the capitalist economy. Scholars have also noted strong historical and contemporary opposition to consumer culture on various grounds and from diverse sectors of society. Political scientist Michele Micheletti (2003) traces the antecedents of boycotts and consumer activism which have occasionally played important roles in social change including, for instance, proscriptions against slave-produced goods during the nineteenth century and the Swadeshi movement for self-determination in India during the first decade of the twentieth century. Despite the achievements of these cases, many commentators have noted the generally short-lived success of consumer movements and cooperatives (Furlough and Strikwerda, 1999). Even strong and effectively organized consumer movements have ultimately had little power relative to those who benefited the most from the reproduction of consumer capitalism. As Erik Olin Wright, George

Ritzer, and several other scholars observed in their remarks to the colloquium on consumption and social change sponsored by the Sustainable Consumption Research and Action Initiative in 2014 and 2015 (see Preface), those who stand to gain through increased consumption and environmental exploitation in consumer capitalism use their influence to structure the "rules of the game" and ensure the maintenance of that advantage. Sociologist Jean Baudrillard (1981) also urged us to recognize consumption as a "mechanism of power." While many consumers and citizens have expressed dissatisfaction with the "culture of consumption," and despite decades of consumer activism, the proliferation of ecolabels and green goods, technical improvements, efficiency gains, and widespread environmental education campaigns have not yet facilitated development of sustainable societies, or the cultural shift necessary to avoid resource depletion and dangerous climate change.

Those engaged in trying to create a more sustainable consumer culture, while participating in an important gesture of change, are in a structurally disadvantageous position, with relatively little power to prevent the environmental or social damages inflicted by unregulated markets. Altering the social and economic structures that underlie contemporary consumer culture would require a significant and sustained social movement—and the power of the state. However, I argue in the next section that despite widespread environmental knowledge and concern about everything from unsustainable food systems to climate change, this essential pairing of social movement and policy support has been disrupted by neoliberal ideology, presenting a significant barrier to efforts to transition contemporary consumer culture (including ideology, economic organization, and public policy) into a more sustainable form.

Capitalism, Karl Polanyi, and the double movement in the neoliberal era

Since the era of Ronald Reagan and Margaret Thatcher, the movement to liberalize markets has enjoyed considerable strength. Large segments of the economic landscape, including major industries and the finance sector, have been deregulated, tax systems made more regressive, and social programs weakened or dismantled in the name of economic growth and free trade (Harvey, 2005; Block and Somers, 2014; see also Chapter 8). Through these processes, a new era of liberalization has shifted responsibility for public welfare away from the state (viewed as political, overly bureaucratic, and potentially corrupt) and toward voluntary market actors, including individuals increasingly regarded as consumers entitled to free choice rather than citizens with rights guaranteed by the state (Cohen, 1998). Proponents of neoliberal ideology see market regulation and social, economic, and environmental protections as "heavy handed" and unnecessary in a system where people are imagined as free to consume in ways consistent with their personal concerns. Contemporary efforts to "place consumers at the heart of policy making" and to change the culture of consumption "one consumer at a time" are thus entirely consistent with market liberalization (Hilton, 2001). They shift responsibility for environmental health and societal well-being onto voluntary, market-based actors while significantly eroding the possibility of policies that can restructure the "rules of the game" to prioritize long-term social, economic, and environmental sustainability over short-term economic gain.

Economic historian and political economist Karl Polanyi (1957) provides important insight into processes of change in capitalist democracies. Drawing on cross-cultural and historical comparisons of economic systems, Polanyi's studies of economic form led him to argue that economic exchanges, spanning culture and history, have typically been "embedded" in society. By this he meant that our relations of exchange, the terms of trade, and even the products we consider subject to exchange are governed by highly variable social and cultural logics, norms, and morals.

In capitalist economies dominated by market exchange, Polanyi observed what he referred to as a "double movement." In the first movement, those who stand to benefit the most from capitalist exchange encourage the state to disembed market transactions from the societal structures that govern behavior, subjecting them instead to a seemingly apolitical and neutral monetary logic. Free-market liberals have effectively argued that supply and demand can regulate the market based on an objective rationality, independent of the constraints of potentially corrupt or overly bureaucratic regulations. In response to this movement, and the interests of the capitalist class, the state supports the conditions for free trade by investing in infrastructure and removing regulatory barriers. Once accomplished, from the neoliberal perspective, there are few aspects of society that cannot be integrated into the market and governed according to the "laws" of supply and demand. This is accomplished by transforming nature and human beings into commodities—land, labor, air, water—all of which can be bought and sold in the market like any other good (Block, 2003).

The subsequent, second movement that Polayni observed occurs in reaction to the first, when the democratic state is confronted with the need to protect the citizenry from the effects of a deregulated market, disembedded from societal norms and morals. When citizens rally against child labor, unsanitary conditions, environmental degradation, or extreme poverty and a growing wealth divide, democratic states typically intervene through legislation and regulation to restructure social and economic systems.

For Polanyi, understanding this double movement—the separation of economic exchange from societal institutions and society's subsequent efforts to reinsert the economy into the moral codes of society—is key to comprehending the political economy of capitalist economies. In the case of consumption, we find examples scattered throughout the last several centuries in which the state worked to facilitate trade but later responded to social pressure and intervened, most notably, as historian Gary Cross (2001) writes, to "safeguard the private rights of parents and the innocence of the young," or to constrain unfair or manipulative trade. Specific initiatives have ranged from reform of tariffs and the regulation of consumer products containing toxic chemicals to prohibitions on marketing to minors.

But not all capitalist democracies have responded to the need to protect the citizenry in the same ways. Many historians and scholars of consumption have observed that some countries have been much more open to the concept of a free market than others. Similarly, operating on different models of the relationship between the citizen and the state, nations also display significant variability in their willingness to intervene in the market, as historian Gunnar Trumbull (2006) observes in his comparison of French and German consumer protection policy. Likewise, Victoria de Grazia's (2005) study of consumer culture in the United States and Europe during the twentieth century reveals significant differences between notions of a sovereign consumer and a social citizen. As consumer ideology was adopted in Europe, it was often mediated and informed by historical notions of social rights and shared values. As a result, European "citizen-consumers" took a much more ambivalent stance toward the promises of American consumer culture and the free market, in favor of a more politicized and active role for both the consumer and the state. These findings are echoed by other empirical comparisons, including Tom O'Dell's (1997) and Rita Erikson's (1997) analyses of the relationship between consumer culture and the state in the United States and Scandinavia. A more recent study (Pew Research Center, 2011) suggests that Europeans are much more likely than Americans to prioritize state actions to ensure "nobody is in need" over "freedom to pursue life's goals without interference."

Neoliberal ideology has been particularly strong over the last several decades in the United States, leaving little room (or willingness) for the government to intervene in the market. Yet this is not to say that the relationship between the citizen, market, and state is static, even within a particular national context. Certainly, the diverse configuration of these relationships is not limited to a comparison of nations, but can also be examined within a country, over time, opening up a greater understanding of past changes and possibilities for the future (Trentmann, 2004).

The experience of the United States has long lent credibility to Polanyi's concept of the double movement, illustrating how strong free-market ideology has translated into the commodification of a wide assortment of unexpected "goods" —from carbon to the human genome—and the remarkable accumulation of material possessions in just a few generations. Conversely, governance in the United States is also premised on democracy and a history of public engagement and activism. While Polanyi's insights are certainly still useful, it is also clear that recent decades have brought a shift which has strengthened the first movement relative to the second. I argue that the focus on the culture of consumption (again narrowly defined) has helped to contribute to the relative disempowerment of the second movement.

Many scholars have observed that the shift toward consumer responsibility has had a profoundly individualizing effect which has worked to atrophy participation in public collective action. De Grazia (2005), for example, persuasively argues that while creating a wide but inauthentic sense of community among loyal users, in actuality consumer culture produces consumers who are "atomized" in an "intensely private depoliticized world." When individuals concerned about the environmental and social damage wrought by the capitalist system turn toward private solutions in frustration (as in many grassroots yet highly insular self-sufficiency movements) or toward participation in the market realm (through "green" consumption)—discontent, anxiety, and outrage do not even make it to deaf ears. If consumer actions become overly intimate and limited to the personal realm, they become "silent routines" (Halkier, 1999) not legible to public representatives and policy leaders. Through the strengthening of market-based activism, corporations have come to understand consumer discontent, and to understand it well; wrapping resistance into new opportunities to create niche products and alternative forms of consumption (Gladwell, 2000).

The shift toward consumer responsibility also places a considerable burden on consumers themselves, who are now held responsible for ensuring environmental and social welfare. But even conscientious individuals who are acutely aware of the ills of consumption face significant barriers when attempting to channel their concern through their purchasing decisions—despite the pervasive illusion of free choice (e.g., Princen et al., 2002; Jackson, 2004). These barriers range from the mundane (availability, price, and quality) to the complex and unimaginable (social and economic ostracism). Social barriers have proven to be particularly salient in many studies, indicating that while we often talk about consumption as a matter of individual choice, it is fundamentally a social act best regulated through collective rather than individual measures (Matti, 2009; Middlemiss, 2011; Isenhour, 2012). Thus many researchers argue that social change requires a turn toward "environmental citizenship" and have observed that sustainable behaviors are more likely to be adopted when drawing upon collective strategies that can overcome problems associated with free riding or accusations of unequal access (Thøgersen and Olander, 2006; Hobson, 2013; Kennedy and Bateman, 2015). Consumption decisions are also significantly influenced by reference groups and social comparison (Welsch and Kühling, 2009), making it much more likely that individuals will modify their behaviors if others around them have acted similarly under a uniform policy or when the most dangerous products have been removed through policies of choice editing.

Cross (2001) asserts that efforts to constrain consumerism have largely failed in the free market due to the "narrowing of consumer rights to a public policy that fosters market consumption rather than articulating consumer interests." Indeed, if responsibility for long-term environmental and social welfare becomes overly individualized, there is, as political scientist Michael Maniates (2002) cogently observes, "little room to ponder institutions, the nature and exercise of political power, or ways of collectively changing … society."

All this said, it is important not to devalue the efforts of the many engaged and concerned consumers who have gone to great lengths to modify their lifestyles and to leave a smaller footprint. Sociologist Roberta Sassatelli (2007) has argued that while these "gestures of change" are important to build policy legitimacy, individuals are much more powerful when active in the civic realm (see also Gabriel and Lang, 2005; Johnston, 2008). In the United States, strong and growing consumer-based lifestyle and sharing movements have emerged over the last decade. Indeed, expansion of organic food sales, community-supported agriculture initiatives, and fair-trade products is testament to considerable concern. I suggest here that if this awareness were channeled toward the public realm, it could provide increased policy legitimacy for programs designed to shift the structural roots of contemporary consumption patterns, thus creating greater potential for Polanyi's second movement.

Restoring the second movement: connecting inequality and environmental degradation

In this section, I argue that, just as the admen of the twentieth century built upon powerful American values to solidify a culture of consumption, efforts to create legitimacy for the second movement—for policies that can once again alter the structural underpinnings of consumer society—are more likely to be successful if they begin with extant cultural values. However, rather than continuing to focus on the now tired appeals to individual responsibility, freedom, and choice that reproduce neoliberal commitments, I suggest that an entreaty to democratic values centered on equal opportunity and justice may help citizens and policy makers to focus on the social and economic structures that script for environmental degradation, overconsumption, and inequality. I suggest that consumption be re-embedded in values rooted as deeply as neoliberalism's connection to freedom. Here I echo anthropologist Richard Wilk (2010) who contends that we must "reframe the issues so that they appeal to powerful values like justice and fairness" and planner Julian Agyeman's (2003) poignant calls for "just sustainability."

The strength of free-market ideology, after all, lies in its claim to serve common interests. As Polanyi astutely observed, "If the movement for laissez-faire simply argued that expanding markets would create more profit opportunities for certain firms, their arguments would have little resonance" (see also Block, 2008). Rather, classical political economists like Adam Smith and David Ricardo framed the benefits of self-regulating markets in universal terms, a prosperous economy and freedom from state intrusion *for all*. But there are significant and widening empirical cracks in the ideology. Recent Wall Street protests, anti-free trade movements, new economy mobilizations, populist "Main Street" politics, and public indignation over corporate greed signal significant outrage about growing inequalities and doubts about the capacity of free markets to deliver comprehensive benefits and ensure compliance with appropriate standards of environmental security. Recent polling data suggest that a large majority of Americans perceive that the country's economic system is unfair and therefore support policies like a higher minimum wage to regulate the market in the interest of equal opportunity (Pew Research Center, 2016). Not only are we witnessing a growing wealth divide and the erosion of the American middle class, but also issues like climate change have brought increased attention to an acutely uneven global society in which those least culpable for atmospheric pollution and environmental degradation are often those with the least access to the resources and political capital necessary for adaptation. Stories of endangered islands, glacier-dependent communities, and eroding Arctic coastlines have raised awareness of environmental injustices on an international scale. We have also understood for quite some time that environmental inequalities are perpetuated by capitalist firms compelled, by design, to seek out low-cost production opportunities to remain competitive. This "race to the bottom" requires that environmental and social costs are externalized to future generations and producer communities without the political power or economic capital to insist on stronger safeguards. Calls for social protection focused on inequality could be more effectively linked to environmental movements given that contemporary forms of ecological destruction, growing inequalities, and overconsumption are all fundamentally linked to the very structure of our economy and social relations. While environmental degradation and social inequality are both perpetuated by unregulated capitalist markets, the links between sustainability and social justice movements remain underdeveloped and poorly articulated (Berthe and Elie, 2015).[1]

Indeed, environmental organizations in the United States have long relied on appeals to individual rationality and self-interest to encourage pro-environmental behaviors (e.g., less stuff, more fun; good for the pocketbook; protect your family, buy organic), based on a prevalent assumption that humans are more likely to act in the common interest when consistent with personal gain (Isenhour, 2012). This assumption has, of course, been heavily critiqued by empirical research suggesting that concerns about equity and justice have more resonance than is commonly assumed (Thaler, 2000; Henrich et al., 2001; Sigmund et al., 2002). There is also evidence to indicate that people who are motivated to act out of concern for collective well-being (linked, for example, to an awareness of environmental inequalities, global injustice, and concern for future generations) are more likely to participate in the civic realm and to undertake sustained behavioral shifts than those impelled exclusively by ecologically oriented risk perceptions. My research with Scandinavian households, for example, indicates that individuals who are concerned mainly with personal environmental risks were significantly less likely to engage in actions in the civic realm (e.g., advocacy work, communication with politicians, community-level collaborations). By contrast, respondents who were primarily apprehensive about displaced environmental risks in developing nations and on future generations were significantly more prone to take actions beyond the market, namely in the civic realm through activism and political engagement (Isenhour, 2012). Several studies in other international contexts mirror these findings, suggesting that awareness and concern for collective well-being and environmental justice may be more salient for encouraging both behavioral change and citizen involvement among a wider range of individuals than is currently assumed (Lorenzoni and Pidgeon, 2006; Zwick et al., 2007; Lorenzoni and Hulme, 2009).

Certainly, people who benefit most from the capitalist mode of accumulation will leverage powerful tools to obstruct policy and regulations designed to restrain the market and address total consumption. Sociologist Frances Fox Piven's (2008) concept of "interdependent power" provides insight into how counter-movements can make gains, given that they often comprise the individuals in most need of protection (Block, 2008). She argues that due to the functionally dependent nature of contemporary society, many different groups, often with quite diverse interests, have the collective capacity to exercise interdependent power by "collectively refusing to follow the standard institutional routines" (Piven, 2008). Piven further contends that this is particularly likely when there is an "ideological opening that makes a particular injustice appear remediable through political action." I suggest here that both growing discontent with inequalities and climate change have the potential to draw together and make explicit the links between overconsumption, growing wealth divides, and unregulated consumer capitalism that requires sustained growth and externalizes costs onto society's most vulnerable populations and future generations. And because those types of systemic and structural problems cannot possibly be ameliorated by buying rainforest crunch cereal, chocolate made without palm oil, or fair-trade coffee, they have the potential to motivate political activism and a stronger collective demand for our governments to safeguard collective welfare.

Conclusion

If culture change is necessary to protect long-term socioenvironmental health, then we must recognize that, from the very start, this process will involve much more than ideological and value shifts. Such changes are essential, but ultimately insufficient without complementary adjustments in the social and economic structures that underlie our shared beliefs and behaviors. This chapter argues that to achieve a shift in the contemporary culture of consumption, it will be necessary for us to supplement social movements with policies that can challenge free market fundamentalism to alter the social and economic relations at the very root of consumer capitalism.

In his comments delivered at the aforementioned colloquium on consumption and social change, sociologist Erik Olin Wright argued that "smashing" capitalism is unlikely, and I agree. However, there is great appeal in the suggestion that change might be achieved by complementary and simultaneous attempts to erode unregulated consumer capitalism through alternative grassroots movements that can re-embed social and economic exchange in shared moral logics and through efforts to "tame" unregulated consumer capitalism with policies designed to provide social protection. As Wright observes, this combination of interstitial strategies will likely be necessary to build alternative economic models of production and consumption and to ensure corresponding and supportive strategies from the state, which should play a role in solving society's functional problems. Patricia Allen (2010) similarly reminds us that "no social advances have ever been made without a combination of social movements and legislation."

There are myriad policy options, executable on multiple scales and ranging from the voluntary to mandatory, which might be utilized to help restructure the social and economic relations that contribute to contemporary consumer capitalism. From universal carbon taxes and minimum wage protections to prohibitions on the sale of disposable, single-use products, the problem is certainly not a question of an insufficient number of alternatives. The more important question is how to motivate policy movement given contemporary political culture in the United States which is marked by significant contention and the dominance of neoliberal ideology. I have argued here that citizen engagement is necessary, but improbable as long as activism continues to be concentrated in the market realm and communicated to marketers rather than policy makers. And while the environmental movement is strong, I suggest that the kind of populist pressure needed to legitimize market regulations is more likely to gather momentum if concern for the environment is clearly linked to issues of equity and justice. These already deeply embedded democratic ideals are perhaps the only two values with sufficient strength to rival neoliberalism's appeal to freedom. Given that environmental degradation, overconsumption, and inequality can all be linked to a highly unregulated capitalist system, I suggest that scholars and activists concerned with the culture of consumption might inspire stronger support for sustained change by focusing on the connections between environmental degradation and equity.

Note

1   Note some important exceptions to this rule including, for example, the work of The Next System Project (http://thenextsystem.org).

References

Abu-Lughod, L. (1991) "Writing against culture," in Fox, R. (ed.), *Recapturing Anthropology: Working in the Present*. Santa Fe, NM: School of American Research Press, pp. 137–162.

Adorno, T. and Horkheimer, M. (2000) "The culture industry: enlightenment as mass deception," in Schor, J. and Holt, D. (eds.), *The Consumer Society Reader*. New York: New Press, pp. 3–19.

Agyman, J., Bullard, R., and Evans, B. (eds.) (2003) *Just Sustainabilities: Development in an Unequal World*. Cambridge, MA: MIT Press.

Allen, P. (2010) "Realizing justice in local food systems," *Cambridge Journal of Regions, Economy and Society* 3(2):295–308.

Arnould, E. and Thompson, C. (2005) "Consumer culture theory: 20 years of research," *Journal of Consumer Research* 31(4):862–882.

Barker, T. and Rubin, J. (2007) "Macroeconomic effects of climate policies on road transport: efficiency agreements versus fuel taxation for the United Kingdom, 2000–2010," *Transportation Research Record* 2017(1):54–60.

Barrett, J., Peters, G., Wiedmann, T., Scott, K., Lenzen, M., Roelich, K., and Le Quéré, C. (2013) "Consumption-based GHG emission accounting: a UK case study," *Climate Policy* 13(4):451–470.

Baudrillard, J. (1981) *For a Critique of the Political Economy of the Signs*. St. Louis: Telos Press.

Berthe, A. and Elie, L. (2015) "Mechanisms explaining the impact of economic inequality on environmental deterioration," *Ecological Economics* 116:191–200.

Blim, M. (2000) "Capitalisms in late modernity," *Annual Review of Anthropology* 29(1):25–38.

Block, F. (2003) "Karl Polanyi and the writing of the *Great Transformation*," *Theory and Society* 32(3):275–306.

Block, F. (2008) "Polanyi's double movement and the reconstruction of critical theory," *Revue Interventions Économiques/Papers in Political Economy* 38. https://interventionseconomiques.revues.org/274.

Block, F. and Somers, M. (2014) *The Power of Market Fundamentalism: Karl Polanyi's Critique.* Cambridge, MA: Harvard University Press.

Bourdieu, P. (1977) *Outline of a Theory of Practice.* New York: Cambridge University Press.

Castree, N., Adams, W., Barry, J., Brockington, D., Büscher, B., Corbera, E., Demeritt, D., Duffy, R., Neves, K., Newell, P., Pellizzoni, L., Rigby, K., Robbins, P., Robin, L., Rose, D., Ross, A., Schlosberg, D., Sorlin, S., West, P., Whitehead, M., and Wynn, B. (2014) "Changing the intellectual climate," *Nature Climate Change* 4(9):763–768.

Cohen, L. (1998) "The New Deal state and the making of citizen consumers," in Strasser, S. McGovern, C., and Judt, M. (eds.), *Getting and Spending: American and European Consumer Society in the Twentieth Century.* New York: Cambridge University Press, pp. 111–126.

Cross, G. (2001) "Corralling consumer culture: shifting rationales for American state intervention in free markets," in Daunton, M. and Hilton, M. (eds.), *The Politics of Consumption: Material Culture and Citizenship in Europe and America.* New York: Berg, pp. 283–300.

Davidson, J. (2012) "Citizen consumers: the Athenian democracy and the origins of Western consumption," in Trentmann, F. (ed.), *The Oxford Handbook of the History of Consumption.* New York: Oxford University Press, pp. 23–46.

de Grazia, V. (2005) *Irresistible Empire: America's Advance through 20th-Century Europe.* Cambridge, MA: Harvard University Press.

Diamond, J. (1999) *Guns, Germs, and Steel: The Fates of Human Societies.* New York: W. W. Norton.

Dietz, R., O'Neill, D., and Daly, H. (2013) *Enough Is Enough: Building a Sustainable Economy in a World of Finite Resources.* San Francisco, CA: Berrett-Koehler.

Edsforth, R. (1987) *Class Conflict and Cultural Consensus: The Making of a Mass Consumer Society in Flint, Michigan.* New Brunswick, NJ: Rutgers University Press.

Ekins, P. (1991) "The sustainable consumer society: a contradiction in terms?" *International Environmental Affairs* 3(4):243–258.

Erikson, R. (1997) *Paper or Plastic: Energy, Environment and Consumerism in Sweden and America.* Westport, CT: Praeger.

Furlough, E. and Strikwerda, C. (eds.) (1999) *Consumers Against Capitalism?* Lanham, MD: Rowman and Littlefield.

Gabriel, Y. and Lang, T. (2005) "A brief history of consumer activism," in Harrison, R. Newholm, T. and Shaw, D. (eds.), *The Ethical Consumer.* Thousand Oaks, CA: Sage, pp. 39–53.

Galbraith, J. (1958) *The Affluent Society.* New York: Houghton Mifflin.

Giddens, A. (1979) *Central Problems in Social Theory.* Malden, MA: Polity Press.

Gladwell, M. (2000) "The Coolhunt," in Schor, J. and Holt, D. (eds.), *The Consumer Society Reader.* New York: New Press, pp. 360–374.

Glickman, L. (1999) *Consumer Society in American History: A Reader.* Ithaca, NY: Cornell University Press.

Gupta, A. and Ferguson, J. (1992) "Beyond 'culture': space, identity, and the politics of difference," *Cultural Anthropology* 7(1):6–23.

Halkier, B. (1999) "Consequences of the politicization of consumption: the example of environmentally friendly consumption practices," *Journal of Environmental Policy and Planning* 1(1):25–41.

Halkier, B. (2001) "Consuming ambivalences: consumer handling of environmentally related risks in food," *Journal of Consumer Culture* 1(2): 205–224.

Harvey, D. (2005) *A Brief History of Neoliberalism*. New York: Oxford University Press.

Henrich, J., Boyd, R., Bowles, S., Camerer, C., Fehr, E., Gintis, H., and McElreath, R. (2001) "Search of homo economicus: behavioral experiments in 15 small-scale societies," *American Economic Review* 91(2):73–78.

Hilton, M. (2001) "Consumer politics in post-war Britain", in Daunton, M. and Hilton, M. (eds.), *The Politics of Consumption: Material Culture and Citizenship in Europe and America*. New York: Berg, pp. 241–260.

Hobson, K. (2002) "Competing discourses of sustainable consumption: does the 'rationalization of lifestyles' make sense?" *Environmental Politics* 11(2):95–120.

Hobson, K. (2013) "On the making of the environmental citizen," *Environmental Politics* 22(1):56–72.

Homborg, A. (2001) *The Power of the Machine: Global Inequalities of Economy, Technology, and Environment*. Lanham, MD: Rowman and Littlefield.

International Energy Agency. (2015) *Global Energy-related Emissions of Carbon Dioxide Stalled in 2014*. Paris: International Energy Agency. www.iea.org/newsroomandevents/news/2015/march/global-energy-related-emissions-of-carbon-dioxide-stalled-in-2014.html.

Intergovernmental Panel on Climate Change (IPCC) (2014) *Climate Change 2014: Synthesis Report*. Geneva: IPCC.

Isenhour, C. (2010) "On conflicted Swedish consumers: the effort to stop shopping and neoliberal environmental governance," *Journal of Consumer Behaviour* 9(6):454–469.

Isenhour, C. (2012) "On the challenges of signaling ethics without all the stuff: tales of conspicuous green consumption," in Carrier, J. and Leutchford, P. (eds.), *Ethical Consumption: Social Value and Economic Practice*. New York: Berghahn Books, pp. 164–180.

Isenhour, C. and Blackmer, T. (2015). *The Future of Materials Management in Maine*. Orono, ME: Senator George J. Mitchell Center for Sustainability Solutions. http://umaine.edu/mitchellcenter/files/2015/08/The-Future-of-Materials-Mgt-in-Maine_Expanded-Report_8-5-15.pdf.

Isenhour, C. and Feng, K. (2014) "Decoupling and displaced emissions: on Swedish consumers, Chinese producers and policy to address the climate impact of consumption," *Journal of Cleaner Production* 134(A):320–329.

Jackson, R., Canadell, J., Le Quéré, C., Andrew, R., Korsbakken, J., Peters, G., and Nakicenovic, N. (2016) "Reaching peak emissions," *Nature Climate Change* 6(1):7–10.

Jackson, T. (2004) "Towards a social psychology of sustainable consumption: a cross disciplinary survey in pursuit of the sustainable consumer," *ESRC Full Research Report*, RES-332-27-0001. Swindon: ESRC.

Jackson, T. (2009) *Prosperity with Growth: Economics for a Finite Planet*. London: Earthscan.

Jackson, T. (2015) "New economy," in D'Alisa, G. Demaria, F., and Kallis, G. (eds.), *Degrowth: A Vocabulary for a New Era*. New York: Routledge, pp. 178–181.

Jenkins, J., Nordhaus, T., and Shellenberger, M. (2011) *Energy Emergence: Rebound and Backfire as Emergent Phenomena*. Berkeley, CA: Breakthrough Institute.

Johnston, J. (2008). "The citizen-consumer hybrid: ideological tensions and the case of Whole Foods Market," *Theory and Society* 37(3):229–270.

Kennedy, E. and Bateman, J. (2015) "Environmental civic practices: synthesizing individual and collective sustainable consumption," in Cohen, M., Brown, H., and Vergragt, P. (eds.), *Putting Sustainability into Practice: Applications and Advances in Research on Sustainable Consumption*. Northampton, MA: Edward Elgar, pp. 47–66.

Kolbert, E. (2014) *The Sixth Extinction: An Unnatural History*. New York: Henry Holt.

Leach, W. (1993) *Land of Desire: Merchants, Power and the Rise of a New American Culture*. New York: Pantheon.

Lorenzoni, I. and Hulme, M. (2009) "Believing is seeing: laypeople's views of future socioeconomic and climate change in England and in Italy," *Public Understanding of Science* 18(4):383–400.

Lorenzoni, L. and Pidgeon, N. (2006) "Public views on climate change: European and USA perspectives," *Climatic Change* 77(1):73–95.

MacBride, S. (2012) *Recycling Reconsidered: The Present Failure and Future Promise of Environmental Action in the United States*. Cambridge, MA: MIT Press.

Maniates, M. (2002) "Individualization: plant a tree, buy a bike, save the world?" in Princen, T., Maniates, M., and Conca, K. (eds.), *Confronting Consumption*. Cambridge, MA: MIT Press, pp. 43–66.

Matti, S. (2009) Exploring public policy legitimacy: a study of belief-system correspondence in Swedish environmental policy. Unpublished PhD dissertation, Luleå Technical University.

McGovern, C. (1998) *Consumption and Citizenship in the United States*. New York: Cambridge University Press.

Micheletti, M. (2003) *Political Virtue and Shopping: Individuals, Consumerism, and Collective Action*. New York: Palgrave Macmillan.

Middlemiss, L. (2011) "The power of community: how community-based organizations stimulate sustainable lifestyles among participants," *Society and Natural Resources* 24(11):1157–1173.

Morgan, H. (1985 [1877]) *Ancient Society*. Tucson: University of Arizona Press.

Nader, L. (1981) "Barriers to thinking new about energy," *Physics Today* 34(2):9.

O'Dell, T. (1997) *Culture Unbound: Americanization and Everyday Life in Sweden*. Lund: Nordic Academic Press.

Peters, G., Davis, S., and Andrew, R. (2012). "A synthesis of carbon in international trade," *Biogeosciences* 9(8):3247–3276.

Pew Research Center (2011). "The American-Western European values gap," Pew Research Center, November 11. www.pewglobal.org/2011/11/17/the-american-western-european-values-gap.

Pew Research Center (2016) Most Americans say U.S. economic system is unfair, but high-income Republicans disagree. Pew Research Center. www.pewresearch.org/fact-tank/2016/02/10/most-americans-say-u-s-economic-system-is-unfair-but-high-income-republicans-disagree/.

Piven, F. (2008) "Can power from below change the world?" *American Sociological Review* 73(1):1–14.

Polanyi, K. (1957 [1944]) *The Great Transformation*. Boston, MA: Beacon Press.

Princen, T., Maniates, M., and Conca, K. (eds.) (2002) *Confronting Consumption*. Cambridge, MA: MIT Press.

Reichel, A., Mortensen, L., Asquith, M., and Bogdanovic, J. (2014) *Environmental Indicator Report: Environmental Impacts of Production and Consumption Systems in Europe.* Copenhagen: European Environment Agency.

Richards, T. (1991) *The Commodity Culture of Victorian England: Advertising and Spectacle, 1851–1914.* Palo Alto, CA: Stanford University Press.

Rockström, J., Steffen, W., Noone, K., Persson, Å., Stuart, F., Lambin, E., Lenton, T., Scheffer, M., Folke, C., Schellnhuber, H., Nykvist, B., De Wit, C., Hughes, T., van der Leeuw, S., Rodhe, H., Sörlin, S., Snyder, P., Costanza, R., Svedin, U., Falkenmark, M., Karlberg, L., Corell, R., Fabry, V., Hansen, J., Walker, B., Liverman, D., Richardson, K., Crutzen, P., and Foley, J. (2009) "Planetary boundaries: exploring the safe operating space for humanity," *Ecology and Society* 14(2):1–33.

Sassatelli, R. (2007) *Consumer Culture: History, Theory and Politics.* Thousand Oaks, CA: Sage.

Schor, J. (2008) "Tackling turbo consumption: an interview by Jo Littler," *Cultural Studies* 22(5):588–598.

Sigmund, K., Fehr, E., and Nowak, M. (2002) "The economics of fair play," *Scientific American* 286(1):82–87.

Slater, D. (1997) *Consumer Culture and Modernity.* Malden, MA: Polity Press.

Strasser, S. (1999) *Waste and Want: A Social History of Trash.* New York: Metropolitan Books.

Strasser, S., McGovern, C., and Judt, M. (1998) *Getting and Spending: European and American Consumer Societies in the Twentieth Century.* New York: Cambridge University Press.

Thaler, R. (2000) "From Homo economicus to Homo sapiens," *Journal of Economic Perspectives* 14(1):131–141.

Thøgersen, J. and Olander, F. (2006) "To what degree are environmentally beneficial choices reflective of a general conservation stance?" *Environment and Behavior* 38(4):550–569.

Trentmann, F. (2004) "Beyond consumerism: new historical perspectives on consumption," *Journal of Contemporary History* 39(3):373–401.

Trentmann, F. (ed.) (2012) *The Oxford Handbook of the History of Consumption.* New York: Oxford University Press.

Trumbull, G. (2006) *Consumer Capitalism: Politics, Product Markets, and Firm Strategy in France and Germany.* Ithaca, NY: Cornell University Press.

Weber, M. and Kalberg, S. (2001 [1904]) *The Protestant Ethic and the Spirit of Capitalism.* Chicago: Fitzroy Dearborn.

Welsch, H. and Kühling, J. (2009) "Determinants of pro-environmental consumption: the role of reference groups and routine behavior," *Ecological Economics* 69(1):166–176.

White, L. (2010 [1959]) *Evolution of Culture.* Walnut Creek, CA: Left Coast Press.

Wilk, R. (2010) "Consumption embedded in culture and language: implications for finding sustainability," *Sustainability: Science, Practice, and Policy* 6(2):38–48.

World Meteorological Organization. (2015) *WMO Greenhouse Gas Bulletin: The State of Greenhouse Gases in the Atmosphere Based on Global Observations Through 2014.* Geneva: WMO. http://library.wmo.int/pmb_ged/ghg-bulletin_11_en.pdf.

Zwick, D., Denegri-Knott, J., and Schroeder, J. (2007) "The social pedagogy of Wall Street: Stock trading as political activism?" *Journal of Consumer Policy* 30(3):167–175.

8 Finance

An emerging issue in sustainable consumption research

Inge Røpke

Introduction

The financial crisis of 2007–2008 and the subsequent period of economic turmoil have served as a wake-up call for several research fields including sustainable consumption studies. It is notable that literature at the nexus of consumption and the environment previously devoted little attention to the financial system. Take, for instance, the anthology edited by Reisch and Røpke (2004) with no contributions on finance or Tim Jackson's (2006) comprehensive reader on sustainable consumption in which only the contribution by Juliet Schor (2006) refers briefly to financial management. When assessing the drivers of consumption, credit is often mentioned in passing as one of the factors used to attract consumers, but authors have been more apt to emphasize the importance of advertising much more than credit (e.g., Durning, 1992). This situation changed with the financial crisis that highlighted how important debt had become in many advanced economies as the means with which to ensure effective demand. Tim Jackson (2009) made the connection clear when he wrote, "One clearly identifiable feature of advanced economies in the period preceding the crisis was the rise and rise of consumer indebtedness. Over the course of more than a decade consumer debt served as a deliberate mechanism for freeing personal spending from wage income and allowing consumption to drive the dynamics of growth."

From a sustainable consumption perspective, the obvious response seems to be to curtail access to consumer credit, especially since many scholars working in the field have long argued that sustainable consumption is not only about consuming greener products and services, but also about reducing the quantity of consumption in the global North (e.g., Fuchs and Lorek, 2005) and reducing credit would be a straightforward way to constrain aggregate consumption. Unfortunately, many poor people depend on credit and the breakdown of the growth model induced by falling effective demand would lead to continued economic instability and unemployment (Jackson, 2009). Furthermore, consumer credit is an aspect of a wider financial system that has bearing on sustainability issues in many other ways. Since the response is thus not obvious, the purpose of this chapter is to explore the role of consumers in enhancing the environmental sustainability of the financial system. As a first step, I begin by discussing the problems inherent in the current financial system and the proposals thus far advanced for alternatives capable of supporting a sustainability transition.

This chapter applies a systems outlook in the sense that the point of departure is systemic aspects of finance and the interplay between finance and macroeconomic development. Simultaneously, it is acknowledged that financial systems are constituted by both professional and everyday practices that continuously reproduce and modify their functioning, including the relevant institutions and material arrangements. People's everyday practices and related consumption are thus seen as co-constituents of wider systems and this situation has implications for the conceptualization of sustainable consumption. In the literature on sustainable consumption, authors increasingly emphasize that systems of supply and modes of consumption co-evolve and constitute each other—the making and meeting of needs are inseparable (Shove, 2012). This point is important as a critique of individualist appraisals in which consumers are assigned an unjustifiable share of responsibility for achieving sustainable outcomes through their atomized consumption choices while policy makers assume insufficient responsibility (Shove, 2010). Simultaneously, it is important to emphasize that households co-construct the system not only in their traditional role as buyers of products and services, but also in other related capacities, for instance, as innovators, prosumers, and civil society organizers. Particularly in relation to the energy system, the importance of these other activities has been highlighted (Walker and Cass, 2007; Røpke, 2013). In evolving the financial system toward sustainability, the roles of finance professionals and policy makers are surely most important, but households also are engaged as co-constructors, in relation both to everyday practices involving finance and to dominant understandings and political support for change.

As brief background, the next section describes work to date on finance from a consumer vantage point, but environmental concerns are not readily evident in this literature. The confluence of financial and economic crises, coupled with growing concerns about climate change, may alter this situation and contribute to new research foci that commence from different starting points. For instance, scholars from finance may take up environmental challenges while their colleagues in sustainability studies evince greater interest in financial issues, as this chapter exemplifies. Then, in the third section, I argue that finance can be seen as an example of a system that cuts across the different provision systems that are usually at the center of studies on sustainability transitions and sustainable consumption. Just like the provision systems themselves, these cross-cutting systems need to be transformed to promote sustainable development. The fourth section outlines the problems of finance and financialization and in the fifth section I discuss how to cope with these dilemmas and foster more sustainable finance. The conclusion discusses the co-constructing role of consumers with respect to these changes.

Studies of consumption, credit, and environment

As the background for exploring consumer roles in relation to finance and the environment, I briefly highlight the main concerns of previous studies. There is, of course, a considerable amount of literature on consumption, credit, and debt, but this work is mainly motivated by various social concerns and the environment is not an explicit consideration. Together with media and advertising, scholars rightly recognize credit as an important component in the historical construction of consumer society, particularly after World War II (Kiron, 1997), and accumulating debt is understood to precipitate significant quality-of-life problems for many households. For some consumers, credit is a factor in impelling compulsive consumption (Feinberg, 1986; Achtziger et al., 2015) and certain individuals become victims of usurious interest rates because they cannot understand the complex loan contracts and end up trapped in a spiral of debt. Accordingly, researchers are motivated by a desire to defend consumer interests through legal and educational measures, not least of which is to prepare young people to manage their finances in consumer society.[1] This concern has also been important for various consumer associations that have lobbied for legislation to protect consumers, for instance, prohibitions on quick loans and limits on interest rates. Consumer research has also taken an interest in other aspects of finance such as pensions and insurance. This has become even more important with the liberalization of financial markets and the marketization of previously regulated services which imply that consumers face more complex decisions. On this front as well, consumer associations have tried to increase transparency for consumers.

There are connections between the literature on consumer credit/finance and sustainable consumption. For instance, Juliet Schor (1991) included credit in her analysis of the work-and-spend cycle and Maurie Cohen (2005) suggested that swelling concern at the time about consumer debt and personal bankruptcy could be strategically exploited by proponents of sustainable consumption. He later followed this up by exploring the dynamics behind the increasing use of credit cards and the dramatic growth in consumer debt and argued that sustainable consumption research should focus on the implications of indebtedness with respect to both the quantity and the type of consumption (Cohen, 2007). Of particular salience, the emergence of new varieties of loans called for increased attention to credit as an environmentally relevant driver of consumption. Quitzau and Røpke (2008) noted:

> [t]he upsurge in renovation activities in Denmark during the last 10–15 years is strongly correlated with income growth and especially the dramatic escalation of property values. New types of loans were introduced in the mid-1990s and early 2000s (loans with variable interest rates in 1996 and loans without amortization in 2003), which meant that a buyer could afford to pay a higher price. Obviously, because such new possibilities become capitalized in property prices over some years, already established owners earned fortunes

that could be cashed in for consumption. This was also encouraged by low real interest rates.

But it was not until the mortgage bubble burst that credit really came on the agenda of sustainability proponents, including for members of the sustainable consumption research community (Cohen, 2010). During the period leading up to the financial crisis, credit played an important role as a driver of unsustainable consumption, and financial mechanisms contributed to widening income inequalities in many countries as well as accumulation of the imbalances and vulnerabilities that exacerbated this situation. From an environmental vantage point, the collapse perversely achieved what sustainable consumption policies never did—it reduced the quantity of consumption and associated carbon emissions (see also Chapter 5). But this outcome was highly problematic because of the disproportionate way that the burden fell on households least able to carry it (as well as least responsible for creating the resultant conditions). Furthermore, political reaction to the financial crisis did not improve circumstances for sustainability transitions. Admittedly, the immediate expansionary policies involved some green investments, but with increasing budgetary deficits, austerity policies quickly replaced expansion, increased hardship for the poor, and made public investments more difficult. It is high time that we explore the financial sector much more intensively from a sustainability perspective.

Finance as a cross-cutting distribution system

Before moving on to address the problems raised by its actual development in the next section, I first suggest that finance as a whole can be conceptualized as a broad system, as well as a set of smaller and interconnected systems. Second, this section describes how finance can be characterized as a cross-cutting distribution system, an approach that draws on a typology inspired by the field of ecological economics. Finally, I assert that to promote sustainable development it is just as important to transform the cross-cutting systems as it is to redesign the more customary domains of energy, food, and transportation that are generally the focus of sustainable consumption research.[2]

Conceptualizing finance as a system begins with the criterion of "meaningfulness." There is a dominant everyday understanding that the financial sector is fulfilling various "functions" in society. Furthermore, some professionals identify as financial experts and regulators consider finance as a governance object. Various actors, institutions, and material arrangements are associated with the financial sector and theoretical debates revolve around connections and causalities within and beyond the system. More formally, systems thinking suggests that it makes sense to identify systems in the chaotic complexity of which humans are part and different approaches provide more or less precise delimitations of the systems concept. For instance, system theorist Donella Meadows (2008) defines a system as an interconnected set of elements that is coherently organized in a way that achieves an outcome. In her account, a system has constituent components, interconnections, and a function which may or may not be purposefully constructed. It thus differs from a conglomeration of elements that has no particular interconnections or purpose, such as a heap of sand. The performance of a system is latent within the structure and as long as the system itself is not changed, its potential behaviors are inherent in it, although they may be unleashed by an outside event. The coherence of a system is based on internal connections that are more intense than associations to elements in the external environment and these more intimate relationships form feedback loops within the system. Meadows emphasized that systems rarely have real boundaries and that border drawing must depend on the purpose of the analysis. The identification of a system is, thus, related to meaning and whether and how to identify its limits will always be a controversial matter.

In contemporary market economies, finance has many different functions and spans a variety of interconnected activities. For instance, its roles include the provision of payment services, currency exchange, instruments to store value over time (e.g., savings, pensions), insurance, credit, vehicles for investment, risk management, and instruments for speculation. It is common to use the systems concept to describe some of these activities such as payment services and pensions where separate regulations apply, but increasingly the functions are aggregated together as outcomes of a general financial system since many pre-existing boundaries separating different operations have disappeared. In the following discussion, finance is mostly described as a broad system with the main focus on banking and credit, but in some cases, reference is made to specific subsystems.

From a sustainability perspective, finance is a particular kind of system, namely a cross-cutting distribution system. This characterization is based on a typology for discussing sustainability transitions and comprises economic systems related to the provision and distribution of the means for making a living.[3] The outset for the typology is the pre-analytical vision from ecological economics that the global human economy can be seen as a metabolic organism embedded in the biosphere, as illustrated in Figure 8.1. The organism survives by taking in resources from and sending back waste to the biosphere, and the more the metabolism grows, the larger the threat to basic life support systems for humans becomes. This conception forms the basis for identifying two types of economic systems at the boundaries of the organism: *resource systems* that organize the input of resources into the organism and *waste systems* that manage the emissions from the organism back into the biosphere. A great deal of environmental social science research focuses on these interfaces where the problems are visible, but the dynamics behind the growing metabolism emerge to a large extent from economic systems that are far from resource extraction and waste handling. Within the organism, there are three different types of economic systems. First, *provision systems* transform resources into useful goods and services. They are more expansive than an industry or production sector and also include users, regulators, professionals, standards, and so forth. Second, *distribution systems* determine which goods and services are provided and who gets access to them. In contrast to neoclassical economics, allocation and distribution are here considered to be so closely intertwined that they are basically part of the same process, where distribution determines what goods and services are provided and, thus, how resources are allocated. Examples of distribution systems are tax systems, labor markets, social security systems, trade regulations, and finance. Finally, *geographical systems* refer to geographically and politically delimited systems that are established with governance structures such as national economies and cities. In this context, it is the economic management of the systems that is important for the global metabolism.

The theoretical distinctions among the different types of systems are not clear-cut and in practice there are always interdependent relationships. The typology is intended to serve as a heuristic device that broadens the scope for exploration of sustainability transitions. The dynamics behind environmental problems may originate far from the time and place where they are most readily visible and interaction among systems is also important to consider. In particular, the transformation of distribution systems as integral aspects of sustainability transitions has been inadequately explored to date. Sustainable consumption studies tend to focus on the systems where resources are most discernibly extracted, transformed into goods and services, consumed, and discarded as waste. For instance, researchers have repeatedly demonstrated the significant environmental impacts related to food, mobility, and housing (Spangenberg and Lorek, 2002; Tukker et al., 2010). It is much less obvious how distribution systems give rise to environmental impacts because the mechanisms are more indirect. But it is useful to widen the lens and explore the influence of distribution systems and geographical systems that cut across various provision systems and may contribute

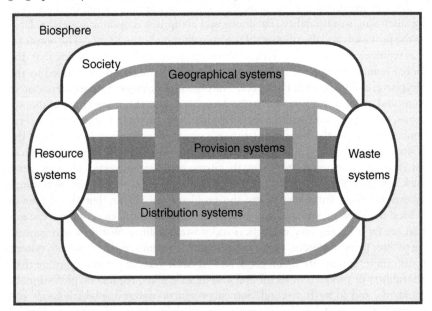

Figure 8.1 Complementary economic systems

to unsustainable production and consumption in many areas simultaneously. For instance, labor-market systems, global trade arrangements, tax systems, and so forth play important roles for both unsustainable air travel and meat consumption (Fuchs et al., 2015). As I argue in the following, the transformation of finance and the relationship between finance and the macroeconomic system are key to promoting sustainable development.

Problems of finance and financialization

The problems related to finance and financialization are overwhelming and it is a major challenge to develop effective responses. The fact that the system is so complex that only a few people can engage in the debate is a democratic problem and the situation is further amplified by the fact that the language used to discuss them can often be impenetrable. It is, however, important to try to pierce the fog.[4] Seen from a sustainability perspective, the financial system does not function well. As the recent crisis has demonstrated, the organization of finance leads to serious turbulence in the real economy and deepens inequalities. Unless one believes that a complete breakdown is needed before any real change toward sustainability can come about, transformation of finance is needed both to ensure funding for sustainability transitions of contemporary provision systems and to promote development toward more equal distribution. To discuss the character of the changes needed, it is necessary first to explore how finance contributes to recurrent crises and pronounced inequality.

To some extent, the problems pertaining to the organization of finance can be discussed in general terms that make sense over a long span of time. While a conventional account based on neoclassical economics emphasizes how the equilibrating forces of markets resolve imbalances, a systems outlook highlights how feedback mechanisms can aggravate problems and cause overshoot. For instance, credit has enabled overexuberance for centuries because when it is easy to borrow money to invest in an asset and the price is rising rapidly, there is considerable risk that the bubble will burst sooner or later. As economist Hyman Minsky (1986) described, a bubble develops through phases where cautious predispositions gradually change into very risky lending behavior. In the final phase, loans are extended to borrowers who cannot even pay the interest because the lender expects that the increase in the price of the asset will be sufficient to ensure repayment. Most banks and mortgage providers are profit-seeking institutions that have an interest in increasing debt and this prompts them to actively push customers to take on loans. The degree of vulnerability and the size of the developing bubble depend on how much leverage different actors can achieve. If the buyer of a house only has to provide a small down payment, a little decrease in the value of the property implies that the equity is lost. And the less a bank has to fund its activities through equity, the larger the risk that defaulting customers will in due course lead to bankruptcy for the financial institution. The seriousness of the impacts on the wider economy depends on how interconnected the losers are with others—either the losses are absorbed by a limited group or defaults will spread. Furthermore, the impacts depend on the level of affluence of the losers. If the losses are borne by relatively poor people with a high propensity to consume, the decline in overall demand will be relatively large and will, thus, put more pressure on the macroeconomy (Mian and Sufi, 2014).

Government regulation influences the pace at which bubbles develop and whether they can be contained before they explode. Such interventions also determine which assets can be subject to speculation, how large the bubbles are permitted to become, and what impacts they have on the real economy. But the vigilance of public oversight itself goes through phases. As Minsky (1986) argued, stability is generally destabilizing because after some time both government regulators and other economic actors forget about the previous crisis, regulation is loosened, and the stage is set for new bubbles to emerge. A particular dilemma relates to the way authorities react when a bubble bursts. If the central bank acts as the lender of last resort and makes needed money available to halt a run out of particular assets, market participants will be induced to behave irresponsibly and take large risks. But if the role of the lender of last resort is not institutionalized, market participants will struggle to save themselves by selling as quickly as possible during a panic and, thus, exacerbate the scale of the downturn. The challenge, as economic historian Charles Kindleberger (1978) observed nearly four decades ago, is that the "lender of last resort should exist, but his presence should be doubted," which requires, "a neat trick: always come to the rescue, in order to prevent needless deflation, but always leave it uncertain whether rescue will arrive in time or at all, so as to instill caution in other speculators, banks, cities, or countries."

Regulatory reaction to financial disarray has been a contentious issue for more than 200 years. All crises share some basic features, but they also differ markedly on the basis of specific historical circumstances. The collapse of 2007–2008 should, thus, be seen in the light of profound changes in global capitalism since the 1970s which has been a period characterized by widespread financialization. After the depression of the 1930s, most developed countries imposed extensive regulation on the financial sector. After World War II, domestic regulation was combined with the financial structures of the Bretton Woods system to enhance financial stability in an increasingly internationalized system. As early as the 1950s, however, financial innovations designed to evade regulation had begun to emerge, followed by elaborate interplay between new regulations and new innovations (Isenberg, 2006). Nonetheless, during the three decades following World War II, there were no bank crises. Some argue that this outcome reflects the effective financial regulation of the time, but Admati and Hellwig (2013) suggest that this period should rather be seen as the result of the generally positive economic situation in economically advanced countries and the stability in exchange and interest rates. When these fortuitous conditions came to be replaced by a much more unstable situation in the early 1970s, financial crises began to emerge even before the process of deregulation had started to gather momentum. Relating these observations to the typology of economic systems outlined above, the changes concern both distributional systems related to finance and geographical systems related to national economies. The following account, thus, illustrates the interaction between finance and macroeconomic development where the growth model shifts and alters pre-existing feedback mechanisms.

Macroeconomic instability was a consequence of the gradual breakdown of the post-war growth model where advanced countries had benefited from a virtuous cycle with wage-led growth. In other words, productivity increases enabled incomes to steadily rise and this dynamic, in turn, fueled demand and economic expansion. Full employment provided an incentive to invest and impelled further improvements in productivity. The role of finance was to provide businesses with funding to invest at low and stable interest rates, provide insurance services, and enable households to save (Palley, 2015; Dow, 2015). The virtuous circle depended on relatively strong labor unions and development of welfare states committed to full-employment policies and support for the poor, and not least, access to inexpensive energy and other raw materials (Ayres and Warr, 2005). Furthermore, the indisputable role of the United States as the dominant power in the capitalist world reduced geopolitical volatility. However, the model was vulnerable because growth in public expenditures and full employment were accompanied by an enlarging bureaucracy and increasing inflationary pressure. Moreover, different national inflation rates challenged the post-war arrangement of fixed exchange rates (Vercelli, 2011). Cost inflation additionally became manifest due to the oil-price shocks in 1973 and 1979 and the exchange rate of the dollar was undermined by public spending related to the Vietnam War and social unrest. These factors, in combination, contributed to the breakdown of the Bretton Woods agreements.

The economic crisis in the 1970s challenged the dominant understanding of the economy (a moderated version of Keynesianism) and the core ideas of monetarism and neoliberalism gradually but steadily became more influential among policy makers. The prior commitment to full employment was replaced by deepening steadfastness to contain inflation, increasing disdain for labor unions, and declining linkage between productivity improvements and wage increases (Palley, 2015). With the rise of neoliberal belief in efficient markets, the ideological foundation was laid for an unremitting process of deregulation during a period when the instability created both problems and opportunities for the financial sector. For instance, the use of derivatives emerged in the wake of the collapse of the Bretton Woods system and tax evasion became a driver in the creation of arbitrage opportunities (Wigan, 2013). The combination of instability and deregulation gathered momentum during the period 1980–2000 and triggered no shortage of turmoil. Reinhart and Rogoff (2009) describe nine international bank crises in the 1970s and more than fifty in both the 1980s and the 1990s.

In spite of this situation, the years from the early 1980s until 2007 were in many respects a golden age for finance. The size of the financial sector increased dramatically in many countries in terms of its share of gross domestic product (GDP), profits, and employment and the increased revenue opportunities encouraged businesses in non-financial sectors to upgrade their financial activities.

A critical issue involved so-called shareholder-value maximization that entailed senior managers being remunerated according to profits and share prices and motivated through stock options. This encouraged a virtually exclusive focus on share prices in the short-term at the expense of other, more long-term business concerns (Chang, 2011). The process of financialization also implied that evermore products and assets became subject to speculation and investors became preoccupied with placing bets on commodity prices (Scott, 2013) and this trend has expanded in recent years to new opportunities with respect to carbon markets, biodiversity offsetting, and so forth (Spash, 2010; Sullivan, 2013). As barriers to international capital flows fell, constituent markets became increasingly interconnected, financial innovation grew in complexity, and more transactions shifted to the shadow-banking system. New computer technologies, and in due course the Internet, initially facilitated these processes and made high-frequency trading possible.

Financialization can thus be understood as an aspect of the neoliberal growth model that replaced its wage-led predecessor after 1980 (Palley, 2015). Based on experience in the United States, economist Thomas Palley argues that the bargaining power of workers came under pressure from unemployment, increased labor-market flexibility, globalization and competition related to a new international division of labor, and less protection from the welfare state. The emerging system came to be characterized by wage stagnation and widening income inequality that created an expanding structural demand shortage because income could no longer be the engine of demand growth. Bridging this chasm by lending to consumers and inflating asset prices became the role of finance.[5] In a political context that favored deregulation, debt and asset-price inflation (e.g., through rising prices for housing) became the engines of demand growth. Palley (2015) further emphasizes that "having finance fill this 'demand gap' was not part of a grand plan: it was an unintended consequence. Neoliberal economic policymakers did not realize they were creating a demand gap, but their laissez-faire financial ideology unleashed developments that accidentally filled it."

However, the neoliberal growth model was inevitably unstable, as Minsky's general description of the mechanisms demonstrates. Over the nearly thirty years from 1980 until the financial crisis in 2007–2008, a large mountain of debt was built up. There was no shortage of turmoil over the period and central banks regularly stepped in with bailouts and reorganizations. However, the combination of lobbying from a powerful financial sector and the pervasiveness of neoliberal ideology helped to ensure continuation of deregulation while central banks maintained their role as the lender of last resort. The problem of moral hazard, thus, increased over time as successive interventions prepared the ground for future bubbles, and during the run up to the 2007–2008 crisis, financial institutions took enormous risks, and with extremely low levels of equity, banks were very vulnerable (King, 2010; Admati and Hellwig, 2013). Simultaneously, global interconnectedness increased with development of securitization of mortgage debt. The depth of the predicament was, thus, related to the wide distribution of toxic assets through financial innovation (Admati and Hellwig, 2013). In addition, less affluent groups, as mentioned above, were particularly hard hit when the housing bubble burst and this led to a steep drop in overall demand (Mian and Sufi, 2014). At first, central banks tried to handle the downturn as a liquidity crisis, but it soon became clear that it was a solvency crisis. This new awareness meant that pumping money into the financial system would not be enough, so the intervention was supplemented by bailouts to avoid an even deeper collapse in the real economy (King, 2010; Admati and Hellwig, 2013). In spite of the rescue plans and stimulation through quantitative easing, it has been difficult to restore the neoliberal growth model. Finance can no longer fill the demand gap created by inequality because the credit bubble has left behind a large debt overhang, many people and firms lack credit-worthiness, and households have increased their savings (Palley, 2015). Furthermore, quantitative easing constitutes the basis for new bubbles and subsequent financial crises.

The account above focuses on connections among aggregate elements, feedbacks, and trends, but both the systems and the changes over time rely on people performing practices. Most obvious are the professional routines carried out by bankers, investors, traders, dealers, brokers, fund managers, speculators, analysts, and many more. Scott (2013) provides a useful description of their undertakings and some of these professional activities have been carefully studied by researchers in the field of social studies of finance (e.g., Knorr Cetina and Preda, 2004; MacKenzie, 2006). It is also obvious that policy makers and central bankers play key roles in constructing and modifying the systems and are heavily influenced by lobbyists from the financial sector. Furthermore, from a consumption standpoint, it is important to emphasize that the everyday practices of households are involved in the reproduction and change of these systems. For instance, the neoliberal growth model would not have increased GDP without the inclination of consumers to rely on credit and the housing bubble would not have reached such proportions if people had not assumed mortgages and bought houses with no money down or tapped the equity in their homes through refinancing. Changing finance in a more sustainable direction, thus, involves modifying the performance of many different practices. It is, however, difficult to discuss how to redesign everyday routines without first discussing how finance should change systemically and in ways that are consistent with sustainable development.

Sustainable finance

Development during the period of financialization causes concern in many ways. First, most policy makers agree that more regulation is needed to ensure that the financial sector actually supports the real economy and that vulnerabilities have to be reduced to avoid future crises and significant public expense. In principle, this is the focus of changes in both national regulations and the Third Basel Accord,[6] but in practice the financial sector has been quite successful watering down the proposed legislation and little has been done to really deal with systemic risks (Chang, 2011; Hache, 2012; Admati and Hellwig, 2013; Turner, 2016; Kay, 2016). Industry lobbyists are still very influential and dominant understanding remains based on ideas of efficient markets. As the vigorous debate on economist Thomas Piketty's (2014) work made clear, another concern pertains to inequality that has increased considerably during the period of financialization and the concentration of capital tends to undermine democratic decision-making and impede more radical reforms.

From the standpoint of sustainability, the fact that the financial sector has succeeded in capturing such a large share of the resources available to society and has transformed them into luxurious lifestyles as well as perpetuated provision systems based on fossil fuels and unsustainable resource extraction in many parts of the world is highly problematic. Sustainability proponents also share concerns related to systemic risks, increasing inequality, and democratic retreat. Economic crises impose the largest impacts on politically and economically weaker members of society and turn attention away from addressing ecological problems. In addition, growing structural inequality amplifies and deepens unsustainable consumption aspirations because it creates more rigid social hierarchies (Cohen 2007, 2010).

A transformation toward more sustainable finance must advance at least three interrelated objectives:

1   Reduce systemic risks and dismantle the financial sector's appropriation of excessive resources at the expense of others.
2   Direct credit and investments toward radical changes with respect to resource appropriation, provisioning, and waste management that are needed for sustainability transitions.
3   Ensure interplay with a more sustainable macroeconomic system that respects biophysical boundaries.

The first of these goals is closest to mainstream concerns and thus relates to the most widely discussed issues. The second point is an emergent topic that has attracted increasing interest during the last few years and the third objective ventures into more uncharted territory. This section discusses each of these issues in turn though preponderant attention is devoted to the first one because of its more pronounced salience.

Reducing systemic risk

Since the start of the crisis in 2007, considerable discussion has been devoted to whether and how to avoid systemic crises in the financial system and how regulators and banks themselves could have prevented such a large accumulation of debt. The financial system has evolved through elaborate processes involving ideological and economic power struggles, attempts at purposeful construction, and social and technical innovation. The result is an extremely intricate system and the first precondition for improved stability entails comprehensive redesign to dramatically reduce complexity. Of course, there is no political power that has any chance of managing a detailed process of reorganization, but it is not impossible for various actors, including policy makers, to influence developments in useful ways. Unfortunately, the window of opportunity created by the crisis was not used effectively to achieve this objective. On the contrary, very detailed regulations emerged in the United States, as exemplified by the thousands of pages of the Dodd–Frank Wall Street Reform and Consumer Protection Act and subsequent interventions. With such an extensive and intrusive regulatory structure, there is an appearance of charge, but regulatory procedures have been captured by powerful players. This outcome may not be the result of corruption or ineptitude on the part of regulatory authorities, but simply because legislators and regulators view the industry through the eyes of established firms (Kay, 2016).

One problem is that the main focus of regulation has been to make the individual units of the system safer rather than to ensure the resilience of the system as a whole. Surely, there is a need to reduce the extreme leverage of financial institutions and there are good reasons to tighten capital and reserve requirements much more than present (and planned) regulation does. For instance, Admati and Hellwig (2013) suggest that all financial institutions should hold at least 20–30 percent equity capital as a share of the gross unweighted value of their assets, as this would reduce moral hazard considerably and, thus, the incentive to engage in unduly risky lending. The removal of the weighting system would reduce complexity, but incumbent banks strongly resist such efforts because prevailing arrangements make it possible for them to maintain high leverage in a largely invisible way. Small banks are at a competitive disadvantage since they do not have the resources to run the complicated computer models needed for the weighting exercise and are forced to apply less favorable standard weights. In addition to capital requirements, the excessive availability of credit can be constrained by higher reserve requirements, and in contrast to present regulation, these conditions could be based on social rather than private risk (Turner, 2016).[7] Capital and reserve requirements can also be made more flexible so they could change in a countercyclical way and therefore serve as useful automatic stabilizers (Palley, 2006), but if such a measure depends on the foresight of a regulatory authority, it may not work well.

Even if regulation of the individual units of the system could be made more effective than present regulatory initiatives imply, this approach would still suffer from a lack of systemic focus. As economist John Kay (2016) argues, the main regulatory problem relates to the interconnections within the system. Although it is useful to reduce the risk of failure of individual units, it is more important to ensure that insolvency in one unit does not diffuse to others and lead to a breakdown of the system. The overall configuration should be sufficiently robust and resilient that failures can occur without threatening the integrity of the overall system. Kay (2016) suggests that policy makers should learn from electrical engineers who know how to design systems that can cope with failures of constituent parts. To avoid system collapse, they apply modularity and redundancy so deficient parts can easily be replaced and transmission of failures avoided. Transferred to the financial system, Kay contends that functional separation would create a more durable system. This feature can be combined with the notion of diversity with regard to the units of the system—an idea that is also promoted, for instance, by UNEP (2015) which asserts that diversity can be a key feature of overall system resilience. To some extent, functional separation is included in regulatory reform in the UK calling for "ring-fencing." Under such arrangements, the retail arm of a bank would be separated from investment banking so the riskier parts could collapse without dragging down the retail side (as was previously the case in the United States under the now rescinded Glass-Steagall Act). Although this is useful, Kay and others argue that it is far from sufficient. Within investment banking, there are substantial conflicts of interest and issues of contagion among different activities such as corporate advice, proprietary trading, market making, security issuance, and asset management. Therefore, the large financial services conglomerates should be dissolved and replaced by specialist institutions. Simultaneously, this would solve the so-called "too-big-to-fail" problem. Presently, the detailed regulation favors large banks because it implies large administrative demands that are difficult for small players to fulfil. As former investment banker and now reform advocate John Fullerton (2012) maintains, it would be better to design self-regulating feedback loops that stabilize the system by creating diseconomies of scale and complexity.

Even with smaller and more specialized units, it may still be a problem that they are too interconnected to fail. The main issue revolves around the handling of risk. Many of the financial products developed before the crisis were devised as ways to diffuse risk and to let the largest risks be borne by those best prepared to do so. But actually, these strategies increased overall risk and the banks that created the complex securities no longer took responsibility for the soundness of the loans because they could sell them off. Therefore, reforms should re-establish shorter chains of intermediation from lenders to borrowers, increase transparency of financial products, regulate securitization by banning overly complex derivatives (Chang, 2011), and expand personal responsibility for senior management (Kay, 2016). A financial transactions tax, a modification of capital gains taxation to discourage short-term speculation, and imposition of restrictions on the tax deductibility of interest expense would also reduce the gambling element currently inherent in financial services (Fullerton, 2012).

In addition to a focus on the structure and behavior of the financial services industry, it is important to consider the demand side. Although much of the credit explosion was internal to the sector itself (one financial institution lending to another), increased household debt was also important in many countries, particularly related to housing. As Turner (2016) emphasizes, homes in attractive areas have become the most important consumer good with high income elasticity, and the combination of inelastic supply and ample credit leads to increasing asset prices—which then turns housing into an asset bought to achieve capital gains. To avoid bubbles and instability, it is, thus, necessary to have more effective constraints on mortgage borrowing and to tax capital gains on property. Furthermore, it would be useful to change tax regimes to reduce the bias in favor of debt finance by removing tax relief related to loans. Unfortunately, little has been done to reform the mortgage market.

The financial services industry often legitimizes itself by referring to its role funding investments in the real economy—and investment here refers to new machines, buildings, and infrastructure rather than to the purchase of existing assets. For both banks and other financial institutions, however, these activities now play a minor role compared to the funding of property acquisition and facilitating trades. Stock markets, once central to raising funds for large investments, have now become disconnected from investments in the real economy as the importance of primary issuance has decreased while the exchanges are increasingly used to facilitate equity buybacks. As Turner (2016) points out, part of the explanation for this functional shift may relate to the application of information and communication technologies that enable new businesses to get off the ground with relatively little capital. Cash that is required is now often provided by business angels. If they are successful, large fortunes can be created quickly and then the challenge is rather to find a profitable outlet for this money. A recurring theme is how to fund small- and medium-sized enterprises which calls for a return to "boring banking" rather than "roaring banking" (Epstein, 2015). In addressing this problem, local banks and values-based banks may have a very useful role to play (NEF, 2012, 2014). Fullerton and MacDonald (2013) suggest that investors such as pension funds should reconnect with businesses in a long-term relationship rather than continue to focus on short-term gains.

A final key issue related to the reduction of systemic risk in finance concerns global capital flows. The process of deregulation gave priority to free movement of money at the expense of managing exchange rates and national monetary policies. Global capital flows have played a key role in both the emergence and diffusion of various financial crises and a precondition for achieving a more stable financial system would be to reintroduce constraints on the international movement of capital, particularly exchanges of short-term duration. A financial transactions tax could play a part, but more specific measures are needed as well. While this position was utterly heretical a few years ago, even mainstream institutions increasingly acknowledge that some constraining mechanism is necessary. The large imbalances in international trading relations also call for institutional changes that place more responsibility for adjustment on surplus countries like China and Germany.

The recommendations above rely on backward-looking observations, but as Minsky and his protégés emphasize, financial innovation is a continuous process and it is important for regulators to keep in touch with new trends. Presently, digital innovation in finance (fintech) is evolving very rapidly and may engender new systemic risks that are not yet well understood.

Green investment

The reduction of systemic risk, as discussed above, is an important part of a sustainability program for finance not only because the avoidance of deep economic crises is useful for investment planning, but also such measures could dramatically reduce the attractiveness of and the possibilities for trading that is exclusively internal to the sector. Finance needs to become a servant of the real economy before it can really contribute to sustainability transitions. In addition to this precondition, determinations need to be made whether particular structural changes are needed to direct real investments toward sustainability. A common economic argument is that incentives for green investment are mostly about policies outside finance such as carbon taxes, subsidies for renewable energy, and regulatory standards concerning insulation in new housing. However, the structure within finance is also an important consideration.

Until recently, sustainability was a marginal issue within the financial sector. It is true that the Finance Initiative of the United Nations Environment Programme (UNEP) was established at the United Nations Conference on Environment and Development in Rio in 1992 and various principles for guiding responsible investments and insurance were later formulated. In addition, beginning in the 1980s an increasing number of values-based banks emerged with the aim of promoting sustainability and 2009 saw establishment of the Global Alliance for Banking on Values. However, the impact of these activities remains marginal. Within mainstream finance, two topics have lately attracted increasing interest (UNEP, 2015). In the first instance, growing awareness of environmentally related risks urges investors to demand greater openness and transparency regarding these hazards, for instance, related to stranded assets. In addition, there has been rapid growth in the issuance of so-called green bonds and climate bonds by financial institutions, governments, and non-financial firms. To scale up the market, UNEP (2015) has proposed a ten-point program involving, for instance, the development of credible and verifiable standards, aggregation of small projects, securitization, improving returns through tax credits, and preferential weighting for green bonds in capital requirements. This approach is understandable in the short term, but it seems problematic to rely on methods that perpetuate some of the systemic features that triggered the more recent financial crisis.

UNEP (2015) also suggests several other approaches to increase funding for green investments and businesses, for instance, by establishing green investment banks and funds, improving conditions for values-based financial institutions, and imposing stronger sustainability requirements in the mandates of pension funds and sovereign wealth funds. Along the same lines, Fullerton (2012) argues that public support is needed to diversify purpose-driven financial institutions such as ethical banks, cooperative banks, community development equity funds, and public banks. These institutions may be better suited to ensure a focus on long-term investments in, for example, infrastructure that is a prerequisite for sustainability transitions. Furthermore, some of these investments may not be profitable in the ordinary sense and will only be viable through public intervention.

Sustainable macroeconomy

The third objective of a transformation toward more sustainable finance is the most challenging and involves interplay between the financial sector and the macroeconomy. The challenge here arises in part from the fact that it is far from obvious what a sustainable macroeconomic system would look like.[8] A few reflections on ongoing debates are nonetheless appropriate.

Dominant political forces are primarily focused on trying to restore the neoliberal growth model, but it is becoming more and more unlikely that these endeavors will succeed. As critics argue, the ever-increasing global debt is just being shifted around, which is laying the ground for new crises (e.g., Turner, 2016). In many countries, attempts by the private sector to deleverage result in stagnation and public deficits, and when the deficits are funded by the issuance of bonds, public debt builds up. In addition to the shift of debt from the private to the public sector, global imbalances result in the transfer of debt among countries. As long as the debt overhang is not effectively reduced, inertia and the accumulation of vulnerabilities can be expected to continue.

The problem of systemic indebtedness calls for a Keynesian response. Since monetary policies focused on ample liquidity and low interest rates are not effective in stimulating demand and instead tend to create new asset bubbles, a turn to fiscal policies seems appropriate, and in some countries, it must be combined with abandonment of the restriction of an almost balanced budget. Furthermore, to avoid increasing public debt, either some of these obligations could be monetized by purchasing government securities with newly created fiat money (currency declared by a government to be legal tender, not backed by, say, gold or silver) or part of the new deficits could be funded by public money creation. As Turner (2016) explains, this is a risky strategy and has to be combined with well-conceived institutional constraints to avoid irresponsible exaggerations, but he recommends it as the only effective option. Increased use of fiat money creation, combined with strict regulation of finance as suggested above, would imply a sharp shift in the functioning of the financial system and its relationship with the macroeconomy.

If such a process were to be successful, would it then be possible and desirable to restore some sort of Keynesian growth model? Are the present problems mainly an issue of insufficient effective demand or does a return to previous growth rates meet other obstacles? One of the recurring topics in this debate concerns the role of technological innovation. On the one hand, economist Robert Gordon (2016) argues that the present wave of technological change is not comparable to previous technological revolutions and is not contributing to increased productivity and new ways of life as much as prior generations of innovation have done. In addition, he forecasts that several other headwinds in the United States will depress growth rates including inequality, education, demography, and debt repayment. On the other hand, Erik Brynjolfsson and Andrew McAfee (2014) argue that robotics and other digital technologies have an immense potential for transforming work and increasing productivity in years to come. From their vantage point, the challenge is that many people will likely lose their jobs and this eventuality implies downward pressure on wages. While technological innovation, historically, has tended to create as many or more new jobs as those replaced by machines, this may not be the case in the future. Therefore, Brynjolfsson and McAfee (2014) suggest that policies, such as earned income tax credits, are needed to ensure that the benefits of innovation are more equitably shared.

For all of their seeming diametrical differences, both of these positions can be combined with a Keynesian approach to policies (they share several recommendations), but Gordon is less optimistic with regard to opportunities for growth. Political economist Paul Mason (2015) takes a more radical position. Like Brynjolfsson and McAfee, he expects digital innovation to increase productivity dramatically, but he argues that the character of these technologies creates a problem for market economies. Since the marginal cost of information goods is basically zero, the traditional price mechanism does not work and it becomes difficult for people to earn money unless the producer succeeds in gaining some sort of monopoly position by enforcing intellectual property rights. According to Mason, this situation creates serious tensions. Using Marxist terms, he argues that capitalism has revolutionized the forces of production in such a way that they have become incompatible with capitalist relations of production. Thus, he does not envisage the emergence of a new capitalist growth model, but rather the opportunity for fundamental social change where the new technologies come to be applied in a cooperative way.

From an ecological economics perspective, the difficulties related to restoring a Keynesian growth model are primarily related to environmental and distributional challenges. It may seem that such an approach fits well with the requirements of more sustainable development because opportunities open up for public support or funding of investments in sustainability transitions of societal infrastructures and more equal distribution is encouraged both as desirable in itself and as a way to promote growth through redistribution of income and wealth toward groups with higher propensities to consume. The vision could, thus, be a green growth model, but the challenge is that the initiatives lead to multiplier and rebound effects that increase overall consumption and may undermine positive environmental achievements. These untoward effects could be counteracted by encouraging greener consumption patterns, for instance, by giving higher priority to health and education rather than energy- and material-intensive consumption goods and by implementing other policies and institutional changes that limit growth in biophysical terms (Van den Bergh, 2011). But green growth may well be an oxymoron.

How does the discussion on innovation and the potential of digital technologies figure in this appraisal? First, ecological economics emphasizes the importance of abundant, inexpensive, and high-quality energy for the long period of economic growth (Ayres and Warr, 2005; Haberl et al., 2011). It was the combination of fossil fuels and innovation that made prodigious growth possible, rather than innovation alone—a point that is strangely absent in the accounts of the authors outlined above. The transition from fossil to renewable energy, as well as the challenge of coping with several other planetary boundaries, will make it extremely difficult to re-establish agreeable conditions for growth, even with very promising technologies. In particular, economic expansion in the rich countries is impossible if more equitable global development is placed high on the international agenda. Second, current and anticipated digital technologies are heavily reliant on resources. Optimistic accounts of the potentials tend to focus on new services and the replacement of labor, while the extraction of raw materials and the use of energy in data centers and storage facilities are underemphasized. Third, on a more positive note, digital technologies can turn out to be very useful in a transition process where the rich countries have to adapt to a lower appropriation of biophysical resources and, thus, need to organize sharing and collaboration in new ways. It remains an open question whether this can happen without threatening capitalism in the way that Mason (2015) suggests.

In summary, it is improbable that a sustainable macroeconomy can be based on a new growth model in the already affluent nations. Since it is very difficult to imagine the organizational dimensions of such conditions, it is also extremely speculative to consider the role of finance. However, in the present situation it makes good sense to take the first steps in a green Keynesian direction and to regulate the financial sector in the ways suggested earlier. Along the way, adaptation will be needed to make the path more sustainable.

Conclusion: toward sustainable consumption and finance

From a sustainable consumption perspective, it is interesting to consider how everyday practices are involved in the reproduction and change of financial systems and how sustainability concerns could be integrated into these practices. As mentioned, public concerns related to financial services are mostly about how consumers can avoid being cheated or trapped in a debt spiral. Transparency in the pricing of services and the reliability of, for instance, pension schemes are key issues. But there is little awareness that consumers, through their practices, are co-responsible for maintaining systems that have problematic outcomes at a societal level. The representatives of the financial sector, often supported by mainstream economists, have been successful in persuading people that we all have shared interests in the prevailing systems. The claim is that when the financial sector is working well, we can get mortgages and credit for consumption and our pensions are safeguarded by high returns on investments. Consumer organizations focus their attention on the conflicts of interest that do not challenge the dominant framework and subscribe to free market ideals when formulating recommendations for public regulation. These proposals include efforts to secure consumer protection in case of externalities, but rarely do they seek to reconcile deeper conflicts relating to societal development. Research at the interface between finance and sustainable consumption seeks to engage with more penetrating problems and to explore, for example, dynamics of credit as a driver of consumption and environmental impacts. But it is notable that this work, at least to date, has principally focused on how finance influences consumption patterns rather than on how consumers are involved in the reproduction and evolution of financial systems.

It may seem reasonable not to devote attention to such matters because social change relies more on political measures than on consumer initiatives. For instance, it is hard to conceive of large groups of consumers refraining from taking mortgages because they understand the systemic implications. The role of citizens as supporters of political measures to change the prevailing framework, thus, appears to be more important than their role as consumers.

Changes in finance in accordance with the purposes outlined above would likely reap benefits for most people—ensuring more economic stability, equality, and most importantly, better prospects for environmental sustainability. But the related changes in everyday practices and consumption patterns are not likely to be easily achieved. To discuss the interplay between system changes and everyday life in any depth, it would be necessary to conduct case studies, also because there are considerable institutional differences among countries. A few examples may be helpful to illustrate the kind of issues that may emerge.

First, expectations regarding return on investment need to change. When societies need to simultaneously transform their provision systems and shrink in biophysical terms, lucrative profits cannot be achieved—unless they are appropriated at the expense of others which would undermine the aim of increasing equality. To ensure investments in the real economy based on "patient" capital with low remuneration, radical measures will be required to reduce the options for achieving high returns in other ways, for instance, through restrictions on banking, shadow banking, and international capital flows as mentioned above. From the standpoint of everyday life, this implies that it would become more difficult to save for retirement and a larger share of income would have to be set aside as compound interest would not be as helpful as it used to be. This challenge may also call for institutional changes in retirement systems so they do not depend on return on investments.

Second, the role of homes as objects of speculation needs to change. In addition to the systemic problems discussed earlier, current arrangements give rise to absurdities in many countries—periods when people earn more by owning their home than by doing their work and intervals when many people default on their loans. Other perverse characteristics include the outsized significance of chance that oftentimes makes life seem like a lottery and the considerable generational unfairness that becomes manifest when rent is captured by property owners due to institutional, demographic, and other factors. With constraints on mortgage borrowing and taxation of capital gains, prices may remain at a lower level, but home ownership could also decline as has already begun to occur in the United States (Mian and Sufi, 2014). In the longer term, it may be worth rethinking the priority given to homeownership.

Third, the use of credit to accelerate consumption needs to change. Adjusting the availability of consumer credit, for instance, by restricting high interest unsecured consumer lending, limiting advertising of loans (Turner, 2016), and distinguishing different purposes of credit could have considerable bearing on everyday practices. These are difficult issues as it is sometimes useful to invest in a durable product (e.g., consumer capital equipment such as a washing machine, computer, or car) that people may not be able to pay for upfront. Furthermore, in many countries loans are necessary to get an education and, due to changes in the labor market, an increasing number of people have to cope with fluctuating incomes, as reflected in discussions on the precariat (Standing, 2014). Rethinking credit availability thus has to be intertwined with social and labor market policies, for instance, by institutional changes that ensure access to education, healthcare, and basic income support.

Finally, the direction of entrepreneurial activities, investments, and innovations needs to become greener. Some citizens try to promote this change by depositing their money in environmentally oriented banks, by participating in peer-to-peer lending for eco-innovations, and by calling for divestment from fossil fuels. It is true that these activities are still relatively marginal. However, proponents of deregulation may argue that such incipient trends could be strengthened by marketization and deregulation of pensions as is currently taking place in the UK, but I would rather expect that green commitments will drown in all the difficult decisions that consumers are personally forced to make under such arrangements. Nonetheless, individual activities such as the use of green banks and pension funds may be helpful steps toward the collective decisions necessary to improve the environmental performance of key provision systems.

As these examples illustrate, a research agenda centered on sustainable consumption and finance offers many interesting topics for future case studies and could usefully bring together financial specialists and sustainable consumption researchers. In terms of theory, such work could provide opportunities for contributions to emerging discussions on how to combine studies on sustainability transitions of socio-technical systems (STRN, 2010) with a practice theory perspective on consumption and environment (Randles and Warde, 2006). Several recent publications have suggested that the two approaches are complementary and can be integrated in empirical analyses (McMeekin and Southerton, 2012; Spaargaren et al., 2012; Hargreaves et al., 2013; Cohen et al., 2013; Watson, 2013; Røpke, 2015b). Of particular interest, Seyfang and Gilbert-Squires (2016) explore whether and how values-based banks can contribute to sustainability transitions in the UK retail banking system, and through the case, they demonstrate the fruitfulness of combining transition and practice approaches. Moreover, research at the intersection of sustainable consumption and finance could highlight the importance of transforming distribution systems along with sustainability transitions of provision systems. Since there is a serious lack of research at this confluence, I hope that this chapter contributes to encouraging studies to fill the gap. If there is to be any chance of real sustainability transitions, financial systems will have to be radically changed and we need to discuss how this may be achieved.

Acknowledgment

Grateful thanks to the editors and an anonymous reviewer for useful comments and to the Velux Foundation for funding the research that gave rise to this chapter.

Notes

1 The *Journal of Consumer Policy* is especially notable in this regard with two special issues in recent years (see Micklitz, 2012; O'Mahony et al., 2015). Refer also to Mak and Braspenning (2012); Cartwright (2015).
2 This section overlaps with material in Røpke (2016).
3 A more elaborate account of the typology can be found in Røpke (2016).
4 This section overlaps with material in Røpke (2015a).
5 This account does not fit all OECD countries. For instance, the growth in Germany was export-led, but this was only possible because of the debt-fueled growth in other countries.
6 The Basel Accords are a tripartite voluntary regulatory framework on banking that includes capital and reserve requirements.
7 From the vantage point of a private bank, the risk related to mortgage lending is low because the house can be sold in case of default. But from a societal point of view, excessive mortgage lending may create a bubble and the need for bail-outs. Therefore, it would be useful to have relatively high reserve requirements in relation to loans for the acquisition of existing assets.
8 Røpke (2013) provides a very general portrayal of a sustainable macroeconomy.

References

Achtziger, A., Hubert, M., Kenning, P., Raab, G., and Reisch, L. (2015) "Debt out of control: the links between self-control, compulsive buying, and real debts," *Journal of Economic Psychology* 49:141–149.

Admati, A. and Hellwig, M. (2013) *The Bankers' New Clothes. What's Wrong with Banking and What to Do about It.* Princeton, NJ: Princeton University Press.

Ayres, R. and Warr, B. (2005) "Accounting for growth: the role of physical work," *Structural Change and Economic Dynamics* 16(2):181–209.

Brynjolfsson, E. and McAfee, A. (2014) *The Second Machine Age: Work, Progress, and Prosperity in a Time of Brilliant Technologies.* New York: W. W. Norton.

Cartwright, P. (2015) "Understanding and protecting vulnerable financial consumers," *Journal of Consumer Policy* 38:119–138.

Chang, H. (2011) *23 Things They Don't Tell You About Capitalism.* New York: Penguin Books.

Cohen, M. (2005) "Sustainable consumption American style: nutrition education, active living, and financial literacy," *International Journal of Sustainable Development and World Ecology* 12(4):407–418.

Cohen, M. (2007) "Consumer credit, household financial management, and sustainable consumption," *International Journal of Consumer Studies* 31(1):57–65.

Cohen, M. (2010) "The international political economy of (un)sustainable consumption and the global financial collapse," *Environmental Politics* 19(1):107–126.

Cohen, M., Brown, H., and Vergragt, P. (eds.) (2013) *Innovations in Sustainable Consumption. New Economics, Socio-technical Transitions, and Social Practices.* Northampton, MA: Edward Elgar.

Dow, S. (2015) "Monetary policy," in Davis, J. and Dolfsma, W. (eds.), *The Elgar Companion to Social Economics,* 2nd ed. Northampton, MA: Edward Elgar, pp. 533–547.

Durning, A. (1992) *How Much is Enough? The Consumer Society and the Future of the Earth.* London: Earthscan.

Epstein, G. (2015) "From boring banking to roaring banking. An interview with Gerald Epstein," *Dollars and Sense*, July/August. www.dollarsandsense.org/archives/2015/0715epstein.html.

Feinberg, R. (1986) "Credit cards as spending facilitating stimuli: a conditioning interpretation," *Journal of Consumer Research* 13(3):348–356.

Fuchs, D., Di Giulio, A., Glaab, K., Lorek, S., Maniates, M., Princen, T., and Røpke, I. (2015) "Power: the missing element in sustainable consumption and absolute reductions research and action," *Journal of Cleaner Production* 132:298–307.

Fuchs, D. and Lorek, S. (2005) "Sustainable consumption governance: a history of promises and failures," *Journal of Consumer Policy* 28(3):261–288.

Fullerton, J. (2012) *A Systems Approach to Financial Reform*. Greenwich, CT: Capital Institute. http://capitalinstitute.org/blog/systems-approach-financial-reform/#more-426.

Fullerton, J. and MacDonald, T. (2013) "Six reasons why our stock markets are no longer fit for purpose," *The Guardian*, October 21. www.theguardian.com/sustainable-business/stock-markets-no-longer-fit-purpose.

Gordon, R. (2016) *The Rise and Fall of American Growth: The U.S. Standard of Living Since the Civil War*. Princeton, NJ: Princeton University Press.

Haberl, H., Fischer-Kowalski, M., Krausmann, F., Martinez-Alier, J., and Winiwarter, V. (2011) "A socio-metabolic transition towards sustainability? Challenges for another Great Transformation," *Sustainable Development* 19(1):1–14.

Hache, F. (2012) *To End All Crises? Implementing Basel III in the European Union. A Position Paper on CRD IV/CRR*. Brussels: Finance Watch.

Hargreaves, T., Longhurst, N., and Seyfang, G. (2013) "Up, down, round and round: connecting regimes and practices in innovation for sustainability," *Environment and Planning A* 45(2):402–420.

Isenberg, D. (2006) "Deregulation," in Arestis, P. and Sawyer, M. (eds.), *A Handbook of Alternative Monetary Economics*. Northampton, MA: Edward Elgar, pp. 365–384.

Jackson, T. (ed.) (2006) *The Earthscan Reader in Sustainable Consumption*. London: Earthscan.

Jackson, T. (2009) *Prosperity Without Growth: Economics for a Finite Planet*. London: Earthscan.

Kay, J. (2016) *Other People's Money: Masters of the Universe or Servants of the People?* London: Profile Books.

Kindleberger, C. (1978) *Manias, Panics, and Crashes: A History of Financial Crises*. New York: Basic Books.

King, M. (2010) *Banking: From Bagehot to Basel, and Back Again*. Second Bagehot Lecture. Buttonwood Gathering, New York City, October 25. www.bis.org/review/r101028a.pdf.

Kiron, D. (1997) "Perpetuating consumer culture: media, advertising, and wants creation," in Goodwin, N., Ackerman, F., and Kiron, D. (eds.), *The Consumer Society*. Washington, DC: Island Press, pp. 229–236.

Knorr Cetina, K. and Preda, A. (eds.) (2004) *The Sociology of Financial Markets*. New York: Oxford University Press.

MacKenzie, D. (2006) *An Engine, Not a Camera: How Financial Models Shape Markets*. Cambridge MA: MIT Press.

Mak, V. and Braspenning, J. (2012) "*Errare humanum est*: financial literacy in European consumer credit law," *Journal of Consumer Policy* 35(3):307–332.

Mason, P. (2015) *Postcapitalism: A Guide to Our Future*. New York: Farrar, Straus and Giroux.

McMeekin, A. and Southerton, D. (2012) "Sustainability transitions and final consumption: practices and socio-technical systems," *Technology Analysis and Strategic Management* 24(4):345–361.

Meadows, D. (2008) *Thinking in Systems: A Primer*. White River Junction, VT: Chelsea Green.

Mian, A. and Sufi, A. (2014) *House of Debt: How They (and You) Caused the Great Recession, and How We Can Prevent It from Happening Again*. Chicago: University of Chicago Press.

Micklitz, H. (2012) "The regulation of over-indebtedness of consumers in Europe," *Journal of Consumer Policy* 35(4):417–419.

Minsky, H. (1986) *Stabilizing an Unstable Economy*. New Haven, CT: Yale University Press.

New Economics Foundation (NEF) (2012) *A Local Banking System: The Urgent Need to Reinvigorate UK High Street Banking*. London: NEF.

New Economics Foundation (NEF) (2014) *Cooperative Banks: International Evidence*. London: NEF.

O'Mahony, L., Twigg-Flesner, C., and Akinbami, F. (2015) "Conceptualizing the consumer of financial services: a new approach?" *Journal of Consumer Policy* 38(2):111–117.

Palley, T. (2006) "Monetary policy in an endogenous money economy," in Arestis, P. and Sawyer, M. (eds.), *A Handbook of Alternative Monetary Economics*. Northampton, MA: Edward Elgar, pp. 242–257.

Palley, T. (2015) Inequality, the financial crisis, and stagnation: competing stories and why they matter. Working paper. Düsseldorf: Institut für Makroökonomie und Konjunkturforschung. www.insightweb.it/web/files/inequalitythe_financial_crisis_and_stagnation.pdf.

Piketty, T. (2014) *Capital in the Twenty-First Century*. Cambridge, MA: Harvard University Press.

Quitzau, M. and Røpke, I. (2008) "The construction of normal expectations: consumption drivers for the Danish bathroom boom," *Journal of Industrial Ecology* 12(2):186–206.

Randles, S. and Warde, A. (2006) "Consumption: the view from theories of practice," in Green, K. and Randles, S. (eds.), *Industrial Ecology and Spaces of Innovation*. Northampton, MA: Edward Elgar, pp. 220–237.

Reinhart, C. and Rogoff, K. (2009) *This Time Is Different: Eight Centuries of Financial Folly*. Princeton, NJ: Princeton University Press.

Reisch, L. and Røpke, I. (eds.) (2004) *The Ecological Economics of Consumption*. Northampton, MA: Edward Elgar.

Røpke, I. (2013) "Ecological macroeconomics: implications for the roles of consumer-citizens," in Cohen, M., Brown, H., and Vergragt, P. (eds.), *Innovations in Sustainable Consumption: New Economics, Socio-technical Transitions, and Social Practices*. Northampton, MA: Edward Elgar, pp. 48–64.

Røpke, I. (2015a) Reflections on full reserve banking and sustainability in a long term perspective. Paper for the 27th Annual Conference of the European Association for Evolutionary Political Economy, Genoa, September 17–19.

Røpke, I. (2015b) "Sustainable consumption: transitions, systems and practices," in Martinez-Alier, J. and Muradian, R. (eds.), *Handbook of Ecological Economics*. Northampton, MA: Edward Elgar, pp. 332–359.

Røpke, I. (2016) "Complementary system perspectives in ecological macroeconomics: the example of transition investments during the crisis," *Ecological Economics* 121:237–245.

Schor, J. (1991) *The Overworked American: The Unexpected Decline of Leisure*. New York: Basic Books.

Schor, J. (2006) "Learning Diderot's lesson: stopping the upward creep of desire," in Jackson, T. (ed.), *The Earthscan Reader in Sustainable Consumption*. London: Earthscan, pp. 178–193.

Scott, B. (2013) *The Heretic's Guide to Global Finance: Hacking the Future of Money*. London: Pluto Press.

Seyfang, G. and Gilbert-Squires, A. (2016) Move your money? Sustainability transitions in regimes and practices in the UK retail banking sector. 3S Working Paper 2016–29. Norwich: Science, Society and Sustainability Research Group, University of East Anglia. https://uea3s.files.wordpress.com/2016/06/3s-wp-2016-291.pdf.

Shove, E. (2010) "Beyond the ABC: climate change policy and theories of social change," *Environment and Planning A* 42(6):1273–1285.

Shove, E. (2012) "Energy transitions in practice: the case of global indoor climate change," in Verbong, G. and Loorbach, D. (eds.), *Governing the Energy Transition: Reality, Illusion or Neccessity?* New York: Routledge, pp. 51–74.

Spaargaren, G., Oosterveer, P., and Loeber, A. (2012) "Sustainability transitions in food consumption, retail, and production," in Spaargaren, G., Oosterveer, P., and Loeber, A. (eds.), *Food Practices in Transition: Changing Food Consumption, Retail, and Production in the Age of Reflexive Modernity*. New York: Routledge, pp. 1–31.

Spangenberg, J. and Lorek, S. (2002) "Environmentally sustainable household consumption: from aggregate environmental pressures to priority fields of action," *Ecological Economics* 43(2):127–140.

Spash, C. (2010) "The brave new world of carbon trading," *New Political Economy* 15(2):169–195.

Standing, G. (2014) *The Precariat: The New Dangerous Class*, rev. ed. New York: Bloomsbury.

Sullivan, S. (2013) "Banking nature? The spectacular financialisation of environmental conservation," *Antipode* 45(1):198–217.

Sustainable Transitions Research Network (STRN) (2010) A mission statement and research agenda for the Sustainability Transitions Research Network. www.transitionsnetwork.org/files/STRN_research_agenda_20_August_2010.pdf.

Tukker, A., Cohen, M., Hubacek, K., and Mont, O. (2010) "The impacts of household consumption and options for change," *Journal of Industrial Ecology* 14(1):13–30.

Turner, A. (2016) *Between Debt and the Devil: Money, Credit, and Fixing Global Finance*. Princeton, NJ: Princeton University Press.

United Nations Environment Programme (UNEP) (2015) *The Financial System We Need: Aligning the Financial System with Sustainable Development*. Nairobi: UNEP.

Van den Bergh, J. (2011) "Energy conservation more effective with rebound policy," *Environmental and Resource Economics* 48(1):43–58.

Vercelli, A. (2011) "Economy and economics: the twin crises," in Brancaccio, E. and Fontana, G. (eds.), *The Global Economic Crisis: New Perspectives on the Critique of Economic Theory and Policy*. New York: Routledge, pp. 27–41.

Walker, G. and Cass, N. (2007) "Carbon reduction, 'the public,' and renewable energy: engaging with socio-technical configurations," *Area* 39(4):458–469.

Watson, M. (2013) "Building future systems of velomobility," in Shove, E. and Spurling, N. (eds.), *Sustainable Practices: Social Theory and Climate Change*. New York: Routledge, pp. 117–131.

Wigan, D. (2013) "Financial derivatives: fiscal weapons of mass destruction," *Politik* 16(4):18–25.

9 "Beyond-GDP" indicators

Changing the economic narrative for a post-consumer society?

Anders Hayden and Jeffrey Wilson

Introduction

Gross Domestic Product (GDP) is now being contested across the globe. Although the "world's most powerful number" (Fioramonti, 2013) was only intended to measure the monetary value of economic output, GDP has come to be seen as a gauge of social progress and well-being. For this purpose, its limitations are numerous; among the most important of them are GDP's failure to account for environmental costs, inequality, and the value of unpaid household and volunteer work (Wagman and Folbre, 1996; Stiglitz et al., 2009; Van den Bergh, 2009; Costanza et al., 2014). Critics of GDP also cite evidence that, beyond a threshold where core material needs are met, little if any link exists between further growth in per-capita GDP and levels of happiness, life satisfaction, or broader well-being measures (Easterlin, 1974; Donovan and Halpern, 2002; Layard, 2005; Easterlin, et al., 2010).[1] One study found that global GDP has more than tripled since 1950, but a more comprehensive well-being measure, the Genuine Progress Indicator (GPI), has fallen since 1978, while the global ecological footprint has grown beyond sustainable levels (Kubiszewski et al., 2013).

In light of such concerns, the green movement has long been a main voice demanding alternatives to GDP as a prosperity indicator—part of its wider questioning of endless output expansion (Daly and Cobb, 1989; Anderson, 1991; Meadows, 1998; Jackson, 2009; O'Neill, 2012). Recently, interest in "beyond-GDP" indicators has spread to the academic and political mainstream. Key initiatives have included: former French president Nicolas Sarkozy's establishment of the Commission on the Measurement of Economic Performance and Social Progress (Stiglitz et al., 2009), the European Union's "Beyond GDP" program (European Commission, 2009), the Organisation for Economic Co-operation and Development's Better Life Index and "green growth indicators" (OECD, 2014), and the *World Happiness Report* (Helliwell et al., 2016). Given such developments, some critics of conventional economic measurements and priorities argue that a "chance to dethrone GDP is now in sight" (Costanza et al., 2014).

Many proponents of new indicators have argued that they will have profound impacts in favor of sustainability, equity, and greater well-being—in line with the often-heard idea that "it's what you measure that matters." For example, Jonathan Porritt (2007), then-chair of the UK Sustainable Development Commission, argued that new indicators would be a "short, sharp statistical shock to the system." Meanwhile, *Limits to Growth* co-author Donella Meadows (1998) wrote that "changing indicators can be one of the most powerful and at the same time one of the easiest ways of making system changes—it does not require firing people, ripping up physical structures, inventing new technologies, or enforcing new regulations. It only requires delivering new information to new places."

Debate remains over the best alternatives to replace or complement GDP and the number of options is large and growing (Allin and Hand, 2014; Bleys, 2012; Costanza et al., 2014; McGregor, 2015; Stiglitz et al., 2009). Some alternatives adjust GDP by counting a wider range of costs and benefits—for instance, a "green GDP" includes environmental externalities and the costs of resource depletion (Boyd, 2007) and the GPI incorporates monetary estimates for a range of social and ecological factors (Talberth et al., 2006). Composite indices, such as the Human Development Index, the Social Progress Index, Bhutan's Gross National Happiness Index, and the Canadian Index of Wellbeing (CIW, 2012), combine several social and/or ecological indicators into a single number. Others privilege a dashboard of multiple measures (Stiglitz et al., 2009) and a further approach is to survey individuals about their subjective well-being (Layard, 2012). While many alternatives are presented as complements to GDP and do not directly challenge the prioritization of economic growth, some proposed indicator systems are designed to guide "degrowth" toward a sustainable, steady-state economy (O'Neill, 2012). Indeed, a distinction is evident between a radical or transformative vision of alternative indicators as a way to shift societal priorities away from GDP growth and a less expansive, reformist vision emphasizing better policy making without challenging the growth paradigm. Meanwhile, some recent interventions in the debate appear designed to turn the beyond-GDP agenda in a more conservative direction.

Development of alternative indicators has reached the point that there is now an opportunity to ask: what effect are they having in practice? Is there any evidence to date that beyond-GDP measurements have shaped policy and public priorities in ways that live up to the expectations of proponents of reform or radical transformation? What are the obstacles to fulfilling those expectations? What conditions and further changes would be needed for progress toward a transformative green vision of alternative indicators?

To answer these questions, we examine the cases of Canada, a leader in academic and nongovernmental organization (NGO) work on alternative indicators, and the United Kingdom, where the beyond-GDP debate has resulted in a new Measuring National Well-being program. We conducted semi-structured interviews (fifteen in Canada, sixteen in the UK) in 2014 and 2015 with elite respondents—political leaders, senior public servants, academics, researchers from NGOs, and activists—involved in developing and applying new indicators or advocating their use (see Appendix). Interviews generally lasted from 45 minutes to one hour. The majority (nineteen of thirty-one) took place in person while the remainder were conducted by phone or skype. Respondents were identified based on existing contacts the authors have with people working in this field, a review of websites and materials produced by organizations involved in these issues, and snowball techniques as initial interviewees provided new contacts. The study also draws on analysis of relevant documents from Canadian and British governmental and nongovernmental agencies involved in producing, using, and promoting the use of alternative indicators.

Alternative indicators, underlying visions, and a green state

While the beyond-GDP agenda is about more than environmental issues, it has links to a debate involving three main approaches to environmental challenges, each with their own vision of well-being (Hayden, 2014). First, a business-as-usual (BAU) perspective pursues endless economic expansion while downplaying or denying the severity of environmental problems. From a BAU standpoint, environmental policies often conflict with GDP growth—and the latter deserves priority (e.g., Lomborg, 2001). BAU ideas are often voiced today by libertarian conservatives, for whom the key to well-being is establishing free markets, in which pursuit of profit will lead to ever-greater material wealth and human ingenuity will overcome environmental limits (Simon, 1995). Although many libertarians originally rejected the philosophical basis and empirical claims of happiness economics and well-being politics (e.g., Norberg, 2010), more recently, "economic freedom" indices have been presented as forms of beyond-GDP well-being measurement (Fraser Institute, 2015).

Second, the theory of ecological modernization (EM) highlights the need to address environmental challenges, even as it remains committed to economic growth (Hajer, 1995; Jänicke, 2008; Mol et al., 2009). Proponents of this approach seek to decouple GDP growth from negative environmental impacts—through technological innovation and "win–win" policies that steer markets toward ecological ends while delivering economic benefits. Sustainable consumption, from this perspective, is about consuming differently—choosing greener products—and more efficiently rather than consuming less. While EM sees growth as important to well-being, some of its advocates have called for new social and ecological indicators to complement GDP and guide pursuit of "green growth" (GCEC, 2014; OECD, 2014).

Finally, in opposition to these pro-growth perspectives, a sufficiency approach asks how much is enough and questions the continued prioritization of production and consumption growth in already-affluent nations (Sachs et al., 1998; Princen, 2005; Schor, 2010; Dietz and O'Neill, 2013; D'Alisa et al., 2015). Proponents of sufficiency have criticized what they see as EM's "myth of decoupling" GDP growth from environmental damage (Jackson, 2009). They also draw on the literature, discussed above, showing a weak link between per-capita GDP and happiness in wealthy nations, while highlighting possibilities to live better while consuming less. The sufficiency perspective has been the source of a transformative green vision for alternative indicators to replace GDP as the dominant measure as part of a shift away from prioritizing economic growth (Daly and Cobb, 1989; Anderson, 1991; Jackson, 2009; O'Neill, 2012).

A transformative vision of this kind also has links to the emergence of a green (or ecological) state, whose features would include "a driving and predominant moral purpose in directing social and economic activity toward ecologically sustainable (and socially just) outcomes" (Christoff, 2005). A green state would be one that has reversed the priority between economic growth and environment, consistently favoring the latter when they conflict (Duit, 2016). Beyond-GDP measurement could be a key element of a green state's prioritization of ecological sustainability and less consumption-oriented ways of achieving well-being (Barry, 2015; Frugoli et al., 2015). A green state would also need new sustainable well-being measures to show that alternative choices, such as work-time reduction over income growth (Coote and Franklin, 2013), have social benefits that GDP's monetary focus fails to capture.

Visions and motivations behind alternative indicators

Some respondents saw their efforts to promote alternative indicators as part of a transformative green vision that challenges the growth paradigm and consumerist well-being vision. (Others saw transformative potential largely in social terms, such as a greater emphasis on equality and poverty reduction.) For example, "recognition that growth ever-lasting is not compatible with long-term wellbeing on planet earth" was the initial motivation in the late 1990s for Green Party politician Peter Bevan-Baker to help launch the Canada Wellbeing Measurement Act, which would have required the federal government to produce new economic, social, and environmental well-being indicators. He emphasized that "having more stuff" is "not the route to human satisfaction," a sentiment echoed by a British interviewee who stated, "We are trashing the planet for a failed way of making people better off." Variations on such themes have been expressed by the London-based New Economics Foundation (NEF), which launched a Well-being Manifesto in 2004 (Shah and Marks, 2004), and remains a key player in the beyond-GDP debate.

However, most respondents did not frame the issue as a challenge to a growth economy and related consumerist values. Indeed, former British cabinet secretary Gus O'Donnell argued that it was a "mistaken understanding" to link the well-being agenda to "anti-consumerism." New well-being indicators are also part of the Welsh Government's (2016) "green growth" agenda, while the Scottish Government's (2016) National Performance Framework, which includes fifty-five national indicators, identifies "increasing sustainable economic growth" as a central element of the government's purpose. On the related issue of whether the goal was to supplant or complement GDP, the latter view dominated among interviewees, as in the wider debate. "The aim is not to replace GDP, but to offer a more holistic view of wellbeing," wrote Roy Romanow (2009), former premier of the Canadian province of Saskatchewan (see also Wallace, 2013). Other respondents expressed hopes that alternative well-being measures, rather than replace GDP, "would be as prominent as GDP reports."

For proponents of the Canadian Index of Wellbeing (CIW), a key goal was to "change the conversation around the water coolers of the nation." In addition, the explicit intention was, according to one interviewee, that "governments would assume responsibility for this index and adopt it at the provincial, national, and municipal level to measure their progress," as well as to "create policy."

For many actors, the overriding objective is better policy making. In Canada, the CIW's core goals included enabling governments to "design better public policy" and "make evidence-based decisions that respond to the values and needs of Canadians" (Romanow, quoted in Grant, 2012; Romanow, 2009). "The big objective is to help make more rounded decisions focused on well-being of people," said one British public servant. "It's about better decision-making, thinking about what really matters to people."

Proponents of new indicators often emphasize the need for "a more balanced perspective" between economic goals and other objectives. Former Saskatchewan premier Roy Romanow referred to well-being indices as "a counter-balance on a teeter-totter with GDP at the other end," while former Liberal MP Joe Jordan sought to counter the "extreme bias toward economic indicators" that "do not give the total picture" (Hansard, 2003). A British public servant similarly expressed hope that when people ask how the UK is doing, "the measures of well-being and the measures of sustainable development will be as important as the economic measures that we've traditionally looked to."

Some respondents hoped that new well-being measures could produce better policy by overcoming policy "silos" and contributing to what Britons call "joined-up" government. A Canadian interviewee noted that an overarching goal of improving well-being could enable cross-sector planning "because no silo owns well-being." Similarly, a British public servant said the "personal well-being domain" is "owned by everyone, so it's a force for integration and joined-up working." Another British respondent noted that joined-up action is difficult "when you've got preventative actions that involve spending in one particular area" and the benefits or savings "then accrue to another area ... Well-being starts to allow you to do that" (see also APPGWE, 2014).

Some British interviewees working in the state sphere hoped that well-being measurement could help improve people's experience of public services. One spoke of "small changes" so that people are treated like "real human beings," adding that "it's about being a bit better about how we help people as a state." Another explained that hospitals, for example, should be concerned not only with treating illness, but also with factors that affect subjective experience such as warmth of rooms, increased contact with family and friends, or making night-time feel "more like night-time at home." A related possibility was to design policy to include elements known to improve subjective well-being, such as "a sense of control, esteem, autonomy, agency, and altruism," which could have some transformative possibilities. An NGO researcher saw opportunities to redesign public services to enhance users' autonomy and competence, and give them a role in "co-producing public services"—to "really change the power dynamics." Deep public spending cuts over the last few years in the UK have also

After an initial public consultation process in 2011 the ONS began including in regular household surveys four subjective well-being (SWB) questions that have garnered the most attention and are one of the most novel elements of the Measuring National Well-being program.[4] The program, which covers ten domains, also includes many objective measures among its forty-one indicators.[5] Several policy-specific surveys (e.g., housing, health, crime, food, youth) have incorporated the ONS's SWB questions, helping to build the evidence base on how the quality of housing, experience of crime, and so forth affect well-being. The questions have also been used to assess people's SWB before and after participation in some government programs. The "Green Book," which guides public-sector bodies in evaluating policies and proposals before committing public funds, now includes the possibility of using SWB measures in cost-benefit analysis (HM Treasury, 2011), but the methodology remains a "work in progress" according to interviewees.

Such developments have stimulated work among academics, parliamentarians, civil servants, think tanks, and NGOs on how well-being research and measurement could be used to guide policy making (APPGWE, 2014; HOCEAC, 2014; O'Donnell et al., 2014; Wallace and Schmuecker, 2012; Wallace, 2013). The government has funded a What Works Centre for Wellbeing, which gathers and synthesizes research on factors that improve well-being, and provides guidance to policy makers and others. Government interest in well-being has also had a "twin" in the work of the Behavioural Insights Team (also known as the "Nudge" unit, established in 2010 to encourage choices that benefit both individual well-being and society on the basis of behavioral insights from economics and psychology).

While the UK's well-being measurement program is well established and further developed than in most nations, overall impacts on policy choices and political priorities are "hard to pinpoint," as one public servant put it. Most UK interviewees said it was "still early days" or used similar words.

The well-being agenda in the UK has many possible trajectories. This is evident, for example, in policy proposals related to well-being such as public provision of cognitive behavioral therapy (Layard and Clark, 2014) and expansion of mindfulness programs for civil servants and others (APPGWE, 2014; MAPPG, 2015). The varying ideological orientations of Conservative, Labour, Liberal Democrat, and Green parties can lead to very different perspectives on how to promote well-being and quality of life (Conservative Party, 2010; Liberal Democrats, 2011; NEF, 2011; Quality of Life Policy Group, 2007). Competing NGO and think-tank visions are also apparent. For example, NEF has long questioned the link between consumption and happiness and promoted a less material-intensive and growth-oriented understanding of well-being (Shah and Marks, 2004; Jeffrey and Michaelson, 2015). In contrast, some groups have engaged in the beyond-GDP debate in a way that is quite compatible with continued prioritization of economic growth. In 2012, the Legatum Institute, whose slogan is "prosperity through revitalising capitalism and democracy," established a Commission on Wellbeing and Policy. Its report challenged a key element of the green critique of growth, arguing that the "effect of income on life satisfaction is significant in almost every good study" (O'Donnell et al., 2014).[6] The Legatum Institute also developed its own Prosperity Index which includes eight domains; two—"economy" and "entrepreneurship and opportunity" —are devoted to conventional economic matters and none specifically to the environment. According to one interviewee, it is a beyond-GDP index that essentially "double counts" the economy.

The distinction between advocates of relatively small changes to improve policy making and others who see socially or ecologically transformative possibilities is quite evident in the UK. The All-Party Parliamentary Group on Wellbeing Economics, for example, put forward several transformative recommendations flowing from the evidence on well-being, including: a focus on stable employment (avoiding boom-and-bust cycles) rather than maximizing growth, giving greater priority to tackling poverty and reducing inequality than to increasing aggregate income, and work-time reduction to boost quality of life for employees and job opportunities for the unemployed (APPGWE, 2014). However, such proposals have made little headway so far. Many voices in the debate have narrower ambitions of "policy change at the margins," prompting one respondent to express disappointment at the focus on doing things "a bit better" rather than broad social change.

Despite the wide range of activity related to well-being measurement and politics, interviewees noted that these issues were not a high priority for the government.[7] At no point did government adopt improving people's well-being as an overarching goal and high-level interest has appeared to wane in recent years. Well-being is "part of Toryism 2010, but I don't think it's part of Toryism 2015," said one respondent. Others suggested that the focus on deficit reduction crowded out, and ran counter to, a well-being narrative. Meanwhile, a call for political parties to "set out their approach to wellbeing in their manifestos" (APPGWE, 2014), allowing voters to choose among them, went largely unheeded in the 2015 election campaign when the issue was not a dominant theme, particularly for the two main parties.[8]

Overall assessments can vary greatly. Awareness of GDP's limits as a prosperity measure and advances in well-being measurement have reached the point that the former Cabinet Secretary (top civil servant) could speak of "the end of the GDP-only world" (O'Donnell et al., 2014). Yet a long-time critic of GDP with links to the Green Party, Victor Anderson (2013), said it was "rather depressing" to see his 1991 book *Alternative Economic Indicators* re-issued two decades later as its continued relevance was "an indication of what a short distance the world has come." In an interview, he noted the proliferation and growing awareness of proposed alternative indicators, and advances in data gathering to calculate them, but added, "We have still not dethroned GDP from its dominant place in decision-making." The differing assessments reflect the fact that it is still unclear where the beyond-GDP debate is ultimately headed, while it also appears to reflect differing views about whether the goal is simply having a wider range of information to enable better policy making or a post-growth transition.

Discussion

Although alternative indicators have had some small impacts in Canada and the UK, their proponents' hopes, whether for radical, transformative change or less expansive reforms, have yet to be fully realized. Numerous obstacles are evident.

Practical challenges

Some barriers that interviewees encountered are typical with pursuit of any reform—"inertia" that keeps the focus on GDP, the need for a "reorientation of our thinking" to see well-being in wider terms, and resistance from people who did not understand the idea and its potential, which highlights the importance of strong communications.

Challenges in producing high-quality beyond-GDP measures include overcoming resistance to the idea that well-being measurement is possible to do well, which was the "number one" obstacle according to one British respondent. Considerable work has, in fact, been done to improve subjective well-being measurement, and the OECD (2013) now offers international guidelines. That said, there remains a "difficulty of accessing high-quality data for all domains" relevant to well-being (beyond subjective measures), resulting in a need to work with the best available proxies (Wallace, 2013). A related challenge is that, unlike GDP, which is produced several times a year, relevant data are not always available on a timely basis (Jeffrey and Michaelson, 2015; Whitby et al., 2014). For example, Wales was using ecological footprint as a sustainability indicator, but updated data were not available each year, while in Canada, time-use studies of unpaid work only happen every seven years. Finding adequate resources to produce alternative measures has been a particular challenge in Canada, where governments have not taken responsibility for beyond-GDP measures and the people producing the CIW do so without secure funding, spending significant time fundraising and taking on small projects while trying to maintain focus on regular production of the Index.

Multiple alternatives, multiple agendas

Another key challenge has been lack of consensus on the best alternative measures. In Canada, the CIW emerged as the main option, but universal agreement on its merits has been lacking. One interviewee recalled disagreements over the way the various measures that make up the CIW were aggregated—a common concern with composite indices. Meanwhile, former prime minister Paul Martin favored including environmental depletion costs in a new "green GDP" or "GDP-plus," which he believed could be "measured objectively and serve as the fundamental indicator," but he was concerned that well-being and happiness indicators were more subjective and could lack credibility.

Some British respondents similarly spoke of the "lack of a clear 'winner' among alternative measures." The ONS's subjective well-being questions have had the highest profile and some observers see them as the key innovation, particularly the life-satisfaction measure (e.g., O'Donnell et al., 2014). One public servant argued that overall life satisfaction is related to all the various well-being domains and could act as something like a proxy for a single well-being index. However, others believed SWB had taken too much of the "oxygen" in the debate. One criticism was that SWB measurement could allow marginalization or poverty to appear unproblematic if people had limited aspirations or had adapted to their circumstances. Critics also expressed other concerns; namely, that SWB emphasized the individual over society as a whole, focus on individual satisfaction and fulfillment might reinforce high consumption levels rather than support a new narrative, and (as discussed further below) neither the press nor the public took SWB seriously. Many observers, including some supporters of SWB measures, saw a need to complement them with more objective measures on a dashboard of indicators (e.g., Allin and Hand, 2014) and the Measuring National Wellbeing program has adopted this approach. Other groups have developed composite indices, reflecting different value orientations, such as the aforementioned Legatum Prosperity Index weighted toward conventional economic concerns and Oxfam Scotland's (2013) Humankind Index, motivated largely by concerns that the dominant economic model "failed to address longstanding problems of poverty and inequality." Meanwhile, the Scottish government has had its own National Performance Framework indicators, and Wales planned to establish new sustainability and well-being indicators under its Wellbeing of Future Generations Act. In addition, driven by concern that the ONS measurement program had not shifted national priorities, NEF proposed five new headline indicators of national success—measuring good jobs, well-being (i.e., life satisfaction), environment, fairness, and health (Jeffrey and Michaelson, 2015).

A related challenge is that actors in the debate are pursuing many different agendas (Cassiers and Thiry, 2015; McGregor, 2015), ranging from challenging the growth paradigm to more efficient spending of limited public funds, as discussed above. Well-being is a "concept that allows people to put different things onto it," said a British interviewee. Another noted the advantage that it "brings lots of people to the table," but said it is "hard to create a conversation that is coherent … Everyone is coming at well-being from really different angles."

One British respondent argued that the well-being agenda was fundamentally "progressive" in nature, but said that, as it becomes more mainstream, "the less progressive people" try to "twist it to serve their own purposes, just as they've done with sustainability." An example is the claim by the Fraser Institute (2015)—a right-wing, Koch-brother-funded Canadian think tank—that its neoliberal Economic Freedom Index has a stronger relationship with average life satisfaction than does per-capita income or whether a country has a democratic political system.[9]

The multiple agendas at play create some challenges and concerns for those seeking a transition to an ecologically sound, equitable, and less consumption-oriented society. One concern, noted above, is that the impact of new well-being measures could be confined to small-scale change at the margins, leaving inequalities and the dominant focus on growth and consumption intact. One British interviewee with transformative hopes saw the danger of "co-opting" and "neutralizing" the agenda. She added, "I'm not ready to say yet that that's what's happened and it's a dead end, but I do see that risk being there."

More sinister possibilities have been suggested, such as dystopian *Brave New World* scenarios of happiness pills and aspiration engineering. A different sort of dystopia is actually already upon us, according to the distinct but overlapping critiques in *The Happiness Industry* (Davies, 2015) and *The Wellness Syndrome* (Cederström and Spicer, 2015). These books paint a picture of expanding corporate monitoring of employee lifestyles and attitudes; increasing pressure on individuals to present an image of health, happiness, and productivity to remain employable in stress-inducing neoliberal labor markets; and shifting of the well-being agenda away from political-economic reform toward transforming individuals, their thoughts, and behaviors. Although it is important to recognize the dangers of a depoliticized, atomizing variation on well-being politics, it is clear that many of the people involved in promoting it continue to see it as a way to work for progressive social transformation (e.g., Michaelson, 2015).

Framing and communication

An additional obstacle, most evident in the UK, has been the "sceptical and mocking" media reaction to well-being measurement (Bache and Reardon, 2013). A policy maker explained that the press tends to see it as "a bit of a sideshow" and rather "pink and fluffy." She added that "quite often it's called the 'Happiness Index,' and then people think, 'What on earth are they on about? People's happiness isn't something that government can dictate. Government should be getting on with the serious business of government.'"

Related questions remain about the most appropriate and effective terminology. In the UK, "happiness" appears particularly vulnerable to mockery (Whitby et al., 2014), although "well-being" has its own problems. One British interviewee noted that "a lot of people think about well-being purely as a health issue." Others worry about the association with what one respondent referred to as "the aromatherapy, spirit-angel side of things" since well-being is used to refer to "everything from beauticians to yoga teachers." "Quality of life," a term New Labour governments often used, is another possibility. Of course, the terminology is related to the political vision. "Happiness" and "well-being" can suggest a focus on individual solutions and lack an explicit ecological or equity dimension, prompting one interviewee to speak instead of "collective prosperity," while another respondent with a transformative green vision spoke of the need for "equitable, sustainable well-being."

Also related to communication is the debate pitting proponents of a composite index versus an indicator dashboard. An interviewee explained that, in the UK, the prevailing view has been that "you can't reduce well-being to a single number" (see also HOCEAC, 2014). The dashboard has grown to forty-one indicators, which provides statistical depth, but not an easily communicated, overarching message.

Some, however, have argued for a headline-generating indicator, or a limited number of key indicators, that can rival GDP (e.g., Jeffrey and Michaelson, 2015). One merit of the CIW is that it provides both an easily communicated single number and its percentage change can be compared to GDP trends. There is, moreover, the opportunity to look behind it to see figures for specific indicators and domains.

Additional political challenges

Who leads the way?

The need for political champions and policy entrepreneurs to take new well-being measurements to the next level, giving them a higher profile and greater impact, is also evident. In Canada, although former political leaders, as well as backbench members of parliament and the Green Party, have supported new approaches, no federal or provincial leader has prioritized introducing a beyond-GDP alternative while in power.

In the UK, David Cameron did, for a time, play the champion role, although some interviewees spoke of the need for a new political figure to rebuild momentum on the issue. The need for policy entrepreneurs, or in this case "indicator entrepreneurs," to take advantage of the existence of new measures and get them used by policy makers was noted by one of our respondents (see also Bache and Reardon, 2013; Whitby et al., 2014). In his words, "If you think of indicators as a product, it needs an entrepreneur to actually get it into the market." Indeed, some of that work was happening through the What Works Centre for Wellbeing and a Cabinet Office unit.

One factor holding back progress is that governments have faced little public pressure to calculate and use new well-being indicators. Former Canadian MP Joe Jordan saw a need for grassroots pressure to overcome the hesitancy of politicians who are unsure the issue is a "political winner," adding that "this is going to have to be something that Canadians demand." Although new indicators have elicited interest among various groups within society, no constituency with significant political force has made it a priority demand. British interviewees pointed to similar challenges, with one noting that "there has never been any real popular buy-in" for new well-being measurement (see also Whitby et al., 2014).

Anti-reflexive conservatism

One need not be left-leaning to support beyond-GDP measurement, as evidenced by former British prime minister David Cameron's actions, at least in certain time periods, to raise the profile of well-being politics and measurement. In Canada, many conservative MPs in the opposition Canadian Alliance, including its then leader Stephen Harper, voted for a parliamentary motion in 2003 calling for a new set of social, environmental, and economic indicators. An interviewee noted that one such MP was interested in ways to "measure the cost of crime and the value of work in the home."

That said, particular variations of conservatism can pose significant obstacles to new well-being measures, as seen in Canada during Harper's time in power (2006–2015). New indicator systems are premised on the idea that they can provide a valuable evidence base, whether for improved policy making or to support more transformative change. However, from canceling Canada's mandatory long-form census to silencing environmental scientists, the Harper government's dislike of evidence that could challenge its priorities was well-known, prompting criticism of the "death of evidence" (DoE, 2012) and a "war on science" (Turner, 2013). Several respondents, speaking before the October 2015 election of a center-left Liberal government, commented on this theme. For example, former prime minister Paul Martin saw obstacles from "those who battle not from an evidential basis, but from an ideological basis and do not want to have real numbers." Alternatives to GDP have been "one of many victims" of the "larger attack on evidence making," said another Canadian interviewee. "It's like ten years of being in a dark room."

In their analysis of American conservatism and its climate-science denial, McCright and Dunlap (2010) characterized the political right in the United States as a force of "anti-reflexivity." That is, it sought to undermine the social and environmental "impact science"—as well as its associated social movements—that could serve as the basis for a reflexive, ecological modernization in which society gained the capacity to critically evaluate and choose alternative paths beyond BAU industrial capitalism. The Harper government's resistance to evidence-based policy making, with regard to well-being measurement and other issues, can also be seen in this light.

The economic growth imperative vs. the radical vision for alternative indicators

While the impact of a vision of alternative indicators as a basis for better policy making has been limited to date, the more radical vision of redirecting society toward priorities other than economic growth and more consumption has faced even greater obstacles. In Canada, although some voices in the public debate express the radical critique of a growth-based economy, that appraisal has been downplayed in how the CIW has been promoted. The effort to take the demand for alternative indicators into the mainstream has involved engagement with, and advocacy by, political actors with a moderate reformist agenda rather than a radical one. As Wilson and Tyedmers (2013) wrote, "The focus has changed from using alternative metrics to question failings of GDP and economic growth toward promoting a growth platform with fewer associated environmental and social costs."

The perceived political imperative of economic growth creates a playing field heavily tilted against ideas that seek to turn away from this objective. Prince Edward Island Green Party leader Peter Bevan-Baker suspected that the radical implications of a new measurement system framed as a challenge to "the prevailing economic and business mentality of growth being good" provoked resistance: "You are challenging some very sacred cows." He also pointed to the "extraordinary power of the vested interests" who are doing well under the current system and resist change. Although he continued to promote new well-being measurements and to speak against the idea of "growth ever-lasting," he acknowledged that, as he has gone from a fringe political candidate over the years to someone with a seat in a legislature, "I'm more measured in how I bring it up now."

In the UK, while the radical green critique of growth remains part of the wider beyond-GDP debate, it is not part of the well-being politics that has entered the state sphere. Research into several European cases, including the UK, found mainstream political "resistance to Beyond GDP indicators to the extent that they are associated with 'unrealistic' steady state or de-growth proposals" (Whitby et al., 2014). As noted above, there have also been efforts to reframe the beyond-GDP agenda to make it compatible with the continued prioritization of economic growth, including pushback against the idea that rising income is not strongly associated with higher well-being in already-wealthy countries.

Distraction from the need for bigger changes?

One danger is that the focus on alternative indicators could distract those seeking green transformation from the need for a much wider and more challenging set of changes. "I've come to regard the measurement debate as, in some ways being, another distraction," said Tim Jackson, a prominent growth critic long involved in developing alternatives to GDP. He added, "All these economists coming late to the table talking about better measures, without questioning the underlying model isn't really advancing things" (Confino, 2012). An interviewee who was prepared to interrogate the underlying model and saw a need to "radically reengineer the economy"—to move beyond neoliberalism and "probably beyond capitalism"—explained that indicator changes on their own "are not going to get us a long way along that journey." He had shifted his hopes toward grassroots innovations— such as Transition Towns, the new cooperatives movement, and efforts to rebuild the commons—that aim to construct a new economy from the ground up.

New well-being measures may still be a necessary part of a transformation to a post-growth, post-consumer society, but they are far from sufficient. Respondents pointed to a range of related changes that are needed.[10] These include promotion of a new economic narrative with potential popular appeal, which might include emphasis on sustainable and equitable well-being and a focus on economic security rather than growth and rising consumption (Barry, 2015). The right indicators that "support that narrative" could make an important contribution. It is not obvious, for instance, that the UK's well-being measures, particularly the SWB questions, bolster an alternative narrative of the kind mentioned—hence the continued efforts by NEF and others to promote new headline indicators (Jeffrey and Michaelson, 2015). Work is also needed to assure political leaders that public support exists for the new narrative and the policies that go with it. Governments would need not only to adopt the new indicators, but also prioritize the new narrative's core goals. In addition, theories about how to improve well-being and which policies to change in response to shifts in associated data need to be developed, as do new decision-making structures—similar to the way creation of GNP/GDP in the 1930s was accompanied by Keynesian theory and new public institutions. Beyond that, for a transformative green vision of alternative indicators to fully come to fruition, a need exists to "disentangle" current society from its dependence on economic growth to solve problems such as unemployment, and "then you can run things on the basis of some other [non-GDP] indicator," as one interviewee put it. The overall challenge is, as another respondent noted, a "nontrivial task."

Conclusion

The idea that "changing indicators can be one of the most powerful and ... easiest ways of making system changes" (Meadows, 1998) is not borne out by the Canadian or British cases. Indeed, one respondent warned of the "indicators fantasy"—the idea that simply producing new measurements will on its own change the world. In Canada, a new well-being index and related efforts have had no major impact to date on federal and provincial policy or political priorities. The UK has gone further with official adoption of new well-being measures, which has stimulated a wide range of research and behind-the-scenes activity exploring the implications of this initiative. Although innovative possibilities exist for better policy in many areas, the dominant framing of the well-being agenda in the UK is consistent with continued prioritization of economic growth and the ambitions of some key actors are limited to marginal policy change.

So where do new indicators fit in the process of social change toward an economy and culture based on sustainable consumption and production? One possibility is that new measures of well-being will be no more than a technocratic instrument for better policy making, fostering no transformative changes. Some observers would see that as a step forward, and indeed some positive policy change might result, but it would amount to cooptation of what was once a radical demand from greens and others to move beyond GDP.

An alternative possibility is that new indicators could play an important role in measuring success as defined by a new societal narrative that is no longer focused on consumption growth—as part of a much wider set of changes that, over time, could amount to the emergence of a green state. In the more immediate future, alternative indicators might help to chip away at the existing narrative and bolster the critique of current priorities, for example, by highlighting the gap between significant economic growth and limited, if any, increases in measured well-being, alongside declines in environmental indicators (e.g., CIW, 2012; Kubiszewski et al., 2013). They could also help to show the non-monetary benefits of alternative policies or grassroots initiatives that are not captured by GDP. However, the Canadian and British experiences to date suggest that new indicators are not in themselves the key agenda setters and drivers of social change. They are instead better seen as a small piece of a much bigger puzzle—one element of broader political efforts to transform society in a more ecologically sound and equitable direction.

Finally, one other factor that could boost efforts to dethrone GDP from its still-dominant position is worth mentioning. Most mainstream political leaders and policy makers currently resist such change. However, if they find themselves unable to deliver increased GDP for an extended period as a result of the "secular stagnation" that some economists believe is setting in, then there may be renewed opportunities not only to replace GDP as the dominant measure, but also to promote policy approaches that seek to improve well-being and address problems such as unemployment, poverty, and inequality without economic growth.

Notes

1 Some researchers contest this point (Stevenson and Wolfers, 2008) or see a more complex relationship (Kahneman and Deaton, 2010).
2 This section, and other points on the Canadian case, are drawn from a more detailed account in Hayden and Wilson (2016).
3 All monetary figures in this chapter are expressed in Canadian dollars.
4 The questions are: Overall, how satisfied are you with your life nowadays? Overall, to what extent do you feel the things you do in your life are worthwhile? Overall, how happy did you feel yesterday? Overall, how anxious did you feel yesterday? (Evans et al., 2015; see also Allin and Hand, 2014).
5 The domains are: economy, education and skills, governance, natural environment, personal well-being (i.e., subjective well-being), "our relationships," health, "what we do," "where we live," and personal finance (Evans et al., 2015).
6 The one citation provided to support this point is Stevenson and Wolfers (2008).
7 Similarly, Bache and Reardon (2013) concluded that "in terms of decisive action there is some way to go before well-being can be described as 'an idea whose time has come'" in the UK.
8 One interviewee counted the references to "well-being" in election manifestos: Liberal Democrats 16, Greens 13, Labour "about three," Scottish National Party "a few," UK Independence Party "a few," and the Conservatives "none."
9 See Helliwell et al. (2016) for counter-evidence to such libertarian claims.
10 This paragraph draws heavily on ideas from Charles Seaford and Victor Anderson (see also Anderson, 1991).

References

Allin, P. and Hand, D. (2014) *The Wellbeing of Nations: Meaning, Motive and Measurement*. Hoboken, NJ: Wiley.

Anderson, V. (1991) *Alternative Economic Indicators*. New York: Routledge.

Anderson, V. (2013) "Why the reissue of my book criticising GDP is depressing news," *The Guardian*, December 18. www.theguardian.com/sustainable-business/reissue-book-alternative-economic-indicators-criticising-gdp-depressing.

Anielski, M. (2001) *The Alberta GPI Blueprint: The Genuine Progress Indicator (GPI) Sustainable Well-Being Accounting System*. Drayton Valley, AB: Pembina Institute.

All-Party Parliamentary Group on Wellbeing Economics (APPGWE) (2014) *Wellbeing in Four Policy Areas*. London: APPGWE.

Bache, I. and Reardon, L. (2013) "An idea whose time has come? Explaining the rise of well-being in British politics," *Political Studies* 61(4):898–914.

Barry, J. (2015) "Beyond orthodox undifferentiated economic growth as a permanent feature of the economy," in Gabrielson, T., Hall, C., Meyer, J., and Schlosberg, D.

(eds.), *Oxford Handbook of Environmental Political Theory*. New York: Oxford University Press, pp. 304–317.

Bleys, B. (2012) "Beyond GDP: classifying alternative measures for progress," *Social Indicators Research* 109(3):355–376.

Boyd, J. (2007) "Nonmarket benefits of nature: what should be counted in green GDP?" *Ecological Economics* 61(4):716–723.

Cameron, D. (2006) *General Well-being Speech*. London: Conservative Party. www. conservatives.com/News/Speeches/2006/07/David_Cameron_General_Well-Being_ speech.aspx.

Cameron, D. (2010) *PM Speech on Wellbeing*. London: Cabinet Office. www.number10. gov.uk/news/speeches-and-transcripts/2010/11/pm-speech-on-well-being-57569.

Cassiers, I. and Thiry, G. (2015) "A high-stakes shift: turning the tide from GDP to new prosperity indicators," in Cassiers, I. (ed), *Redefining Prosperity*. New York: Routledge, pp. 22–40.

Cederström, C. and Spicer, A. (2015) *The Wellness Syndrome*. Malden, MA: Polity.

Christoff, P. (2005) "Out of chaos, a shining star? Toward a typology of green states," in J. Barry and R. Eckersley (eds.), *The State and the Global Ecological Crisis*. Cambridge, MA: MIT Press, pp. 26–52.

Canadian Index of Wellbeing (CIW) (2012) *How are Canadians Really Doing?* Waterloo, ON: Canadian Index of Wellbeing and University of Waterloo.

Confino, J. (2012) "Rio+20: Tim Jackson on how fear led world leaders to betray green economy," *The Guardian*, June 25. www.theguardian.com/sustainable-business/ rio-20-tim-jackson-leaders-green-economy.

Conservative Party (2010) *Modern Conservatism: Our Quality of Life Agenda*. London: Conservative Party.

Coote, A. and Franklin, J. (2013) *Time on Our Side: Why We All Need a Shorter Working Week*. London: New Economics Foundation.

Costanza, R., Kubiszewski, I., Giovannini, E., Lovins, H., McGlade, J., Pickett, K., Ragnarsdóttir, K., Roberts, D., De Vogli, R., and Wilkinson, R. (2014) "Time to leave GDP behind," *Nature* 505(7483):283–285.

CTV (2012) "Canadian economy grows, but quality of life on the decline," *CTV News*, October 23. www.ctvnews.ca/canada/canadian-economy-grows-but-quality-of-life-on-the-decline-1.1006524.

D'Alisa, G., Demaria, F., and Kallis, G. (2015) *Degrowth: A Vocabulary for a New Era*. New York: Routledge.

Daly, H. and Cobb, J. (1989). *For the Common Good*. Boston, MA: Beacon Press.

Davies, W. (2015) *The Happiness Industry*. London: Verso.

Dietz, R. and O'Neill, D. (2013) *Enough Is Enough*. San Francisco, CA: Berrett-Koehler.

Death of Evidence (DoE) (2012) "The death of evidence: no science, no evidence, no truth, no democracy." www.deathofevidence.ca.

Donovan, N. and Halpern, D. (2002) *Life Satisfaction: The State of Knowledge and Implications for Government*. London: Cabinet Office Strategy Unit.

Duit, A. (2016) "The four faces of the environmental state: environmental governance regimes in 28 countries," *Environmental Politics* 25(1):69–91.

Easterlin, R. (1974) "Does economic growth improve the human lot? Some empirical evidence," in David, P. and Reder, M. (eds.), *Nations and Households in Economic Growth: Essays in Honor of Moses Abramovitz*. New York: Academic Press, pp. 89–125.

Easterlin, R., McVey, L., Switek, M., Sawangfa, O., and Zweig, J. (2010) "The happiness-income paradox revisited," *Proceedings of the National Academy of Sciences* 107(52):22463–22468.

European Commission (2009). Communication from the Commission to the Council and the European Parliament – GDP and beyond: measuring progress in a changing world. Brussels: European Commission. COM/2009/0433. http://eur-lex.europa.eu/legal-content/EN/TXT/?uri=CELEX:52009DC0433.

Evans, J., Macrory, I., and Randall, C. (2015) *Measuring National Well-being: Life in the UK, 2015*. London: Office for National Statistics.

Fioramonti, L. (2013) *Gross Domestic Problem: The Politics Behind the World's Most Powerful Number*. London: Zed.

Fraser Institute (2015) *Economic Freedom of the World: 2015 Annual Report*. Vancouver: Fraser Institute.

Frugoli, P., Almeida, C., Agostinho, F., Giannetti, B., and Huisingh, D. (2015) "Can measures of well-being and progress help societies to achieve sustainable development?" *Journal of Cleaner Production* 90:370–380.

Global Commission on the Economy and Climate (GCEC) (2014) *Better Growth, Better Climate: The New Climate Economy Report—Synthesis Report*. Washington, DC: World Resources Institute.

Grant, T. (2012) "Study finds Canadians aren't feeling economic growth in their daily lives," *The Globe and Mail*, October 23.

Hajer, M. (1995) *The Politics of Environmental Discourse: Ecological Modernization and the Policy Process*. New York: Oxford University Press.

Hansard (2003) 37th Parliament, 2nd Session, edited Hansard, Number 109, June 2, 2003. Ottawa: Parliament of Canada.

Hayden, A. (2014) *When Green Growth Is Not Enough: Climate Change, Ecological Modernization, and Sufficiency*. Montreal: McGill-Queen's University Press.

Hayden, A. and Wilson, J. (2016) "Is it what you measure that really matters? The struggle to move beyond GDP in Canada," *Sustainability* 8(7):623.

Helliwell, J. (2002) *Globalization and Well-Being*. Vancouver: University of British Columbia Press.

Helliwell, J., Layard, R., and Sachs, J. (2016). *World Happiness Report 2016*. New York: Sustainable Development Solutions Network.

HM Treasury (2011) *The Green Book: Appraisal and Evaluation in Central Government*. London: HM Treasury.

House of Commons Environmental Audit Committee (HOCEAC) (2014) *Well-being*. London: HCEAC.

Jackson, T. (2009). *Prosperity without Growth: Economics for a Finite Planet*. London: Earthscan.

Jänicke, M. (2008) "Ecological modernisation: new perspectives," *Journal of Cleaner Production* 16(5):557–565.

Jeffrey, K. and Michaelson, J. (2015) *Five Headline Indicators of National Success*. London: New Economics Foundation.

Kahneman, D. and Deaton, A. (2010) "High income improves evaluation of life but not emotional well-being," *Proceedings of the National Academy of Sciences* 107(38):16489–16493.

Kubiszewski, I., Costanza, R., Franco, C., Lawn, P., Talberth, J., Jackson, T., and Aylmer, C., (2013) "Beyond GDP: measuring and achieving global genuine progress," *Ecological Economics* 93:57–68.

Layard, R. (2005) *Happiness: Lessons from a New Science*. New York: Penguin.

Layard, R. (2012) "Why measure subjective well-being?" *OECD Obsserver*. http://oecdobserver.org/news/fullstory.php/aid/3767/Why_measure_subjective_well-being_.html.

Layard, R. and Clark, D. (2014) *Thrive: The Power of Evidence-Based Psychological Therapies*. London: Allen Lane.

Liberal Democrats (2011) *A New Purpose for Politics: Quality of Life*. London: Liberal Democrats.

Lomborg, B. (2001) *The Skeptical Environmentalist: Measuring the Real State of the World*. New York: Cambridge University Press.

Mindfulness All-Party Parliamentary Group (MAPPG) (2015) *Mindful Nation UK*. London: MAPPG.

McCright, A. and Dunlap, R. (2010) "Anti-reflexivity: the American conservative movement's success in undermining climate science and policy," *Theory, Culture, and Society* 27(2–3):100–133.

McGregor, A. (2015) Global initiatives in measuring human wellbeing: convergence and divergence. CWiPP Working Paper Series No. 2. Sheffield: Centre for Wellbeing in Public Policy, University of Sheffield.

Meadows, D. (1998) *Indicators and Information Systems for Sustainable Development*. Hartland Four Corners, VT: The Sustainability Institute.

Michaelson, J. (2015) In defence of wellbeing. *Open Democracy*. www.opendemocracy.net/transformation/juliet-michaelson/in-defence-of-wellbeing.

Michalos, A. (ed.) (2014) *Encyclopedia of Quality of Life and Well-Being Research 2014 Edition*. New York: Springer.

Mittelstaedt, M. (2001) "Fat-cat Albertans struggle with happiness," *The Globe and Mail*, April 23.

Mol, A., Sonnenfeld, D., and Spaargaren, G. (eds.) (2009) *The Ecological Modernisation Reader*. New York: Routledge.

New Economics Foundation (NEF) (2011) *The Practical Politics of Well-being*. London: NEF.

Norberg, J. (2010) *GDP and its Enemies: The Questionable Search for a Happiness Index*. Brussels: Wilfried Martens Centre for European Studies.

O'Donnell, G., Deaton, A., Durand, M., Halpern, D., and Layard, R. (2014). *Wellbeing and Policy*. London: Legatum Institute.

Organisation for Economic Co-operation and Development (OECD) (2013) *Guidelines on Measuring Subjective Well-being*. Paris: OECD.

Organisation for Economic Co-operation and Development (OECD) (2014) *Green Growth Indicators 2014*. Paris: OECD.

O'Neill, D. (2012) "Measuring progress in the degrowth transition to a steady state economy," *Ecological Economics* 84:221–231.

Oxfam Scotland (2013) *Oxfam Humankind Index: The New Measure of Scotland's Prosperity, Second Results*. Oxford: Oxfam GB.

Porritt, J. (2007) *Capitalism As If The World Matters*. London: Earthscan.

Princen, T. (2005) *The Logic of Sufficiency*. Cambridge, MA: MIT Press.

Quality of Life Policy Group (2007) *Blueprint for a Green Economy*. London: Conservative Party.

Romanow, R. (2009) "There's more to life than GDP," *Toronto Star*, June 10.

Sachs, W., Loske, R., and Linz, M. (1998) *Greening the North: A Post-Industrial Blueprint for Ecology and Equity*. London: Zed.

Schor, J. (2010) *Plenitude: The New Economics of True Wealth*. New York: Penguin.

Scottish Government (2016). The Government's Purpose. www.gov.scot/About/Performance/scotPerforms/purpose.

Shah, H. and Marks, N. (2004) *A Well-Being Manifesto for a Flourishing Society*. London: New Economics Foundation.

Simon, J. (1995) "The state of humanity: steadily improving," *Cato Policy Report* 17(5).

Stevenson, B. and Wolfers, J. (2008) "Economic growth and subjective well-being: reassessing the Easterlin Paradox," *Brookings Papers on Economic Activity* 39(1):1–102.

Stiglitz, J., Sen, A., and Fitoussi, J.-P. (2009) *Report by the Commission on the Measurement of Economic Performance and Social Progress*. Paris: Commission on the Measurement of Economic Performance and Social Progress.

Talberth, J., Cobb, C., and Slattery, N. (2006) *The Genuine Progress Indicator 2006: A Tool for Sustainable Development*. Oakland, CA: Redefining Progress.

Taylor, A. (2005) *The Alberta GPI Summary Report*. Drayton Valley, AB: Pembina Institute.

Turner, C. (2013) *The War on Science: Muzzled Scientists and Wilful Blindness in Stephen Harper's Canada*. Vancouver: Greystone.

Van den Bergh, J. (2009) "The GDP paradox," *Journal of Economic Psychology* 30(2):117–135.

Wagman, B. and Folbre, N. (1996) "Household services and economic growth in the United States, 1870–1930," *Feminist Economics* 2(1):43–66.

Wallace, J. (2013) *Shifting the Dial in Scotland*. Dunfermline: Carnegie UK Trust.

Wallace, J. and Schmuecker, K. (2012). *Shifting the Dial*. Newcastle Upon Tyne: IPPR North.

Welsh Government (2016) *Green Growth Wales*. http://gov.wales/topics/business andeconomy/creating-a-sustainable-economy/green-growth-wales/?lang=en.

Whitby, A., Seaford, C., Berry, C., and BRAINPOoL Consortium Partners (2014) *BRAINPOoL Project Final Report: Beyond GDP: From Measurement to Politics and Policy*. Hamburg: World Future Council.

Wilson, J. and Tyedmers, P. (2013) "Rethinking what counts: perspectives on wellbeing and genuine progress indicator metrics from a Canadian view point," *Sustainability* 5(1):187–202.

Appendix: interviewees

Canada

Mark Anielski, Director and Co-founder, Genuine Wealth, Inc.

Peter Bevan-Baker, Member of Legislative Assembly, Green Party leader, Prince Edward Island

Anthony Charles, Director, School of the Environment, Saint Mary's University

Joe Jordan, Former Member of Parliament

Paul Martin, Former Prime Minister and Finance Minister

Hans Messinger, Former Director, Statistics Canada

Mike Nickerson, Director, 7th Generation Initiative

Charles Pascal, Professor, University of Toronto and Former Executive Director, Atkinson Charitable Foundation

Mike Pennock, Senior Epidemiologist, Office of the Provincial Health Officer, British Columbia Ministry of Health

Roy Romanow, Former Saskatchewan Premier and Advisory Board Chair, Canadian Index of Wellbeing

Katherine Scott, Vice-President for Research and Policy, Canadian Council on Social Development

Bryan Smale, Director, Canadian Index of Wellbeing

Amy Taylor, Chief Operating Officer, Green Analytics

Two anonymous interviewees

UK

Paul Allin, Visiting Professor, Imperial College London and Former Director, Measuring National Well-being Programme, Office for National Statistics

Victor Anderson, Visiting Professor, Global Sustainability Institute, Anglia Ruskin University

Joanne Evans, Head of Reporting, Measures of National Well-being, Office for National Statistics

Nancy Hey, Director, What Works Centre for Wellbeing

Roger Higman, Director, Network of Wellbeing

Juliet Michaelson, Associate Director, Wellbeing, New Economics Foundation

Gus O'Donnell, Former Cabinet Secretary and Head of the Civil Service

Dan O'Neill, Lecturer in Environmental and Ecological Economics, and David Spencer, Professor of Economics and Political Economy, University of Leeds

Jules Peck, Founder and Convenor, Real Economy Lab

Charles Seaford, Director, An Economy That Works

Rita Singh, Director of Policy, Sustain Wales

Kathryn Trebeck, Senior Researcher, Oxfam GB

Baronness Claire Tyler, Peer, House of Lords

Jennifer Wallace, Head of Policy, Carnegie UK Trust

Sam Wren-Lewis, Head of Research and Development, Happy City

One anonymous interviewee

10 Consumption, governance, and transitions

How reconnecting consumption and production opens up new perspectives for sustainable development

Derk A. Loorbach

Introduction

Contemporary society can be characterized as a consumer society that is increasingly confronted with the need to make a fundamental shift toward sustainability (Cohen et al., 2013). The decades following World War II have given rise to remarkable improvements in welfare, well-being, and technological progress. This step forward for humankind in Western nations has, however, come at great expense for the environment and communities in many parts of the world. At the same time, we should not lose sight of the fact that we have made significant improvements in innovating new technologies and, from the 1970s onwards, formulating policies to improve energy efficiency, manage risk, and achieve direct environmental objectives such as reducing emissions, banning chlorofluorocarbons, and developing waste-management systems. Nonetheless, many persistent and systemic challenges remain and new ones continue to become manifest on a massive scale.

In this chapter, I employ a transition perspective to reflect upon the emergence of contemporary society as a family of societal system changes leading to the present "regime." I argue that efforts to date to address sustainability problems have been mainly pursued within the context of this regime, especially on the institutional level, only adding to its persistence. These initiatives have included advocating for more sustainable modes of production and consumption, which have been offset by a continuous drive for growth. My argument is that in the post-war period citizens have become better educated and conditioned as consumers, and that an important aspect of the historical transition to the current age has been the separation of production and consumption to facilitate population growth and welfare improvement.

The field of transition studies began to develop approximately fifteen years ago in Western Europe as an area of inter- and transdisciplinary research intent on formulating a better understanding of complex, non-linear change in societal systems and new governance strategies to anticipate and adapt to such transitions (e.g., Rotmans et al., 2001; Grin et al., 2010). The premise is that history clearly demonstrates that complex (societal) systems periodically go through disruptive, chaotic, and widespread periods of change. Such changes are deemed necessary to achieve sustainability goals within a scientifically determined timeframe and acknowledged as effectively inevitable because of the inherent unsustainability of current pathways. Transitions research has thus had a tripartite agenda: to further our understanding of the dynamics of these societal transitions, to identify effective strategies and interventions that influence their speed and direction, and to lead us toward more sustainable futures.

In this chapter, I address questions pertaining to what types of governance might be pursued to advance an efficacious transition away from the current growth-based consumption society. Based on the emergence of alternative production–consumption practices, I contend that more radical, system innovation-oriented governance can challenge incumbent paradigms, powers, and institutions. Strategies consistent with this idea need to take into account the disruptive upheaval of transitions as well as the dynamics of restabilization and capture of innovations by incumbent regimes (see Chapter 5). I introduce the concept of "governance panarchy" which is grounded in the notion that contemporary technologies and conditions enable large-scale processes of self-organization in which numerous forms of organization and governance are used to address sustainability problems and their impacts in particular contexts (see Loorbach, 2014). The coalescing of sustainable alternative cultures, structures, and practices in specific locales through self-organization can from this perspective be seen as a process by which new future sustainable regimes might be achieved. By definition, this inextricably implies disruptive, chaotic, and conflict-laden periods of transitional change. I will first introduce the transition perspective by applying it to the emergence of the welfare state in which the separation of production and consumption has been a core feature. This discussion will illustrate both the necessity and potential of transitions and their challenges for governance.

A historical family of transitions leading to our current predicament

The foundations for the welfare state were established during the nineteenth century. Through processes of industrial revolution, modernization, and "the Great Transformation" (Polanyi, 2001) today's so-called "developed" countries moved away from decentralized, agrarian, and undemocratic systems of political organization and began to evolve into more globalized economies with diffuse and complex governance networks and institutions through which power and resources came to be divided in often unequal and nontransparent ways. Undoubtedly critical to this process was the advent of new technologies, the exploitation of fossil fuels, and the rise of democratic nation states. After decades of innovation and experimentation, only interrupted for the most part by two world wars, social changes seemed to accelerate in the twentieth century, leading to an explosion in population, consumption, welfare, and economic growth. These dynamics also led to broad democratization of decision-making, emancipation of women, human rights, and elevation of many people out of poverty through the rise of the middle class. The contemporary welfare state now faces multiple crises (ecologically, economically, and socially) and this situation has led to increasing calls to move beyond the dominant paradigm of growth and optimization (Jackson, 2011; Kallis, 2011; Costanza et al., 2014). These crises are unfolding against a background of autonomous factors such as an ageing population (in several developed countries), low levels of economic growth, unemployment, nationalism and populism, mass migration, distrust in politics and authorities, globalization of financial systems, geopolitical tensions, and development of information technology and social media.

Researchers have explored the advent of present-day society by investigating numerous historical sociotechnical transitions (e.g., Geels, 2002, 2005; Elzen et al., 2004). These events are defined and conceptualized as evolutionary revolutions involving large-scale, nonlinear changes at the level of societal (sub) systems that take decades to unfold. Drawing from these studies of historical transitions, we can understand the era of modernization as the outcome of a "family of transitions" that evolved to address persistent societal problems such as food scarcity, inadequate healthcare, unequal rights, anti-democratic politics, and so forth (Loorbach, 2014; see also Figure 10.1). A core concept for apprehending transitions is the "regime" which is deployed in the context of sociotechnical systems as the "seamless web" of factors that have co-evolved around specific technologies with the objective of entrenching them deeply in society (Rip and Kemp, 1998; Schot and Geels, 2007). Broadening the concept to include systems that are less technology-oriented, societal regimes have come to be defined as dominant cultures (paradigms, worldviews, values), structures (infrastructures, institutions, networks) and practices (behavior, routines) in a societal (sub)system (van Raak, 2016). These arrangements evolve over time and are firmly embedded, highly dynamic, continuously reinforced, and enacted through continuous improvement and optimization. This progression generates stability and predictability, but also leads to greater lock-in with respect to dominant routines and structures, processes of normalization, and vested interests that prevent or deflect fundamental critique, competition, or change (Arthur, 1989; Unruh, 2000).

Drawing from historical examples as well as theoretical understandings in disciplines such as complex system theory, demography, and ecology, a transition is identified in retrospect and defined as a regime change. Rather than abrupt discontinuity, this process entails evolutionary revolution in which a long duration of relatively gradual transformation is interrupted by a relatively short period of disruptive change as a result of the interplay among three dominant patterns of change. The most salient factor is growing tension within the prevailing regime which leads to internal crises, deep questioning of the regime, and various forms of malfunctioning (Bosman et al., 2014). These problems become amplified by a shifting societal context (landscape) in which slow trends and other changes place increasingly novel or amended demands on the regime and lead to a growing mismatch. The final stage in the process is the gradual development and emergence of alternative cultures, structures, and practices

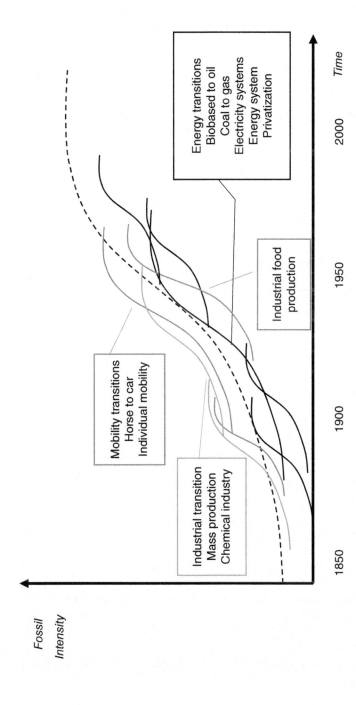

Figure 10.1 The period of modernization as a family of transitions (adapted from Loorbach, 2014)

("niches" in the terminology of transitions theory). New technologies, but also alternative visions, lifestyles, business and organizational models, and deviant practices also play a role. By definition, these niches take a long time to mature, through processes of experimentation and learning-by-doing, before they become competitive and viable alternatives. A transition ultimately occurs when these three dynamics start to reinforce each other, producing irreversible structural changes within the dominant regime. At the level of societal systems, transitions can take decades to reach the point of acceleration and reconfiguration after which a new equilibrium might be reached in ten to fifteen years (Rotmans and Loorbach, 2009).

The current regime of unsustainable production and consumption

We can describe with hindsight the historical transitions that led to contemporary society as revolutionary systemic changes, but in everyday practice they were more incremental processes of experimentation, breakthrough, institutionalization, behavioral and cultural change, and so forth. As processes of "evolutionary revolution," the transitions of modernization and industrialization completely altered society and turned it into the current capitalistic, high consumption, and unsustainable society of today. These messy, nonlinear, and complex transitions share a number of common characteristics that enable us to consider the design principles of the present-day state: centralized coordination, linear innovation, and inexpensive fossil resources. The foundations for these transitions were put into place during the second half of the nineteenth century and my argument is that they are—in spite of several decades of liberalization, globalization, and digitalization—still visible and dominant.

Central control

The rise of the nation state as central authority was accompanied by emergence of centralized systems of provisioning (Pierre and Peters, 2000; Bekkers, 2007). The new technologies of the industrial age enabled the large-scale distribution of power, food, and services on a mass basis and central planning facilitated their deployment and organization (Verbong and Loorbach, 2012). These developments were catalyzed not only by raising the necessary and enormous capital investments, but also through top-down planning and coordination. The predominant way in which societal systems have come to be constituted brings about establishment of specializations, departments, sectors, and all sorts of ordering and control mechanisms to enhance efficiency. Where it was possible for the state to enact central control, power gradually shifted to networks and industries, creating more diffuse centers of influence and devolution of control. But even in the context of a network society with liberalized markets, the logic of centralization with its special bodies of expertise, silos, hierarchies, and planning cultures has dominated contemporary bureaucracies, universities, and markets.

Linear thinking

The paradigm associated with this dominant orientation to centralized organization is top-down linear thinking. It is coupled with incremental innovation and optimization which still remain dominant today in society. This conceptual approach entails heavy reliance on control and prediction and is associated with a culture in which growth is achieved through targeted policies, specialization, and ever-continuing improvements in efficiency. The linear model of innovation has widespread consequences, most notable of which is that it gives rise to presumption of a direct causal relationship between knowledge production and material impact in the real world. It also nurtures an understanding of change as a gradual and incremental process in which innovation constitutes a step-by-step progression that builds forward from the current situation (Levinthal, 1998). The linear model of innovation has been extensively critiqued over the years but it remains dominant in research and development funding by governments and industries as well as in planning cultures where a tendency for extrapolation, optimization, and preselection of winners persists.

Fossil resources

The availability of inexpensive and abundant fossil resources, a process of co-evolution that commenced with invention and deployment of the steam engine, has been essential to the Great Transformation in many ways. The sequence of technologies—based first on coal and later on oil and natural gas—made possible proliferation of mass production, lifestyles reliant on extensive mobility, systems of industrial food distribution, centralized energy systems, and so forth. Fossil resources have also been a necessary precondition for our current economic and financial systems, creating enormous revenue flows with which to fund development of national economies and the welfare state. The availability of inexpensive energy has progressively become a social demand and requisite requirement for continued economic development, leading to co-evolution of fossil-based energy systems and structures of power and decision-making.

Current systems for producing energy, food, water services, healthcare, education, and mobility are built on these foundations that essentially form the cornerstones of contemporary societal regimes. More specifically, control over resources (fossil supplies, knowledge, money, decision-making) has facilitated exponential growth through centralized planning. These regimes helped to generate so much wealth that persistent social challenges of the early twentieth century like poverty, disease, and unsanitary conditions were largely ameliorated by developing the welfare state. An interesting feature, however, is that this process has led to the separation of production and consumption. The capitalist model of profit maximization based on control over resources and increasing efficiency and upscaling has in essence led to maximally efficient production and a complementary culture of consumerism which is continually stimulated by advertising. The transition perspective raises questions about the effectiveness of and potential for additional optimization of production (and consumption) along these lines. Further advances consistent with this pathway might exacerbate lock-in of the extant unsustainable regime, but, as I will argue below, only focusing on incremental improvement obscures the emergence of radically different niches as potential sources of far-reaching transformation.

Understanding our current lock-in as predevelopment

Acknowledging that contemporary society is presently locked in a path-dependent and unsustainable pattern of development simultaneously points to the inevitability of (undesired) fundamental systemic shifts. Highlighting these qualities of our current trajectory is obviously not a novel insight and it is even plausible to argue that by now there is a broad consensus regarding this condition. The rate of extraction of resources, the growing size of the global population and its associated consumption, and the ecological impacts of continuing economic growth were already comprehensively described in the early 1970s by the Club of Rome in *The Limits to Growth* report (Meadows et al., 1972). Due to successful environmental policies, technology development, and previously unanticipated forms of social innovation, many of the most severe negative effects have been mitigated and we have made significant strides in reducing global poverty, environmental degradation, and achieving economic development. The messages of the scientists pointing to systemic problems with respect to the economy, ecology, and society— and the need for sustainable development—have taken root in national policies, business strategies, and societal visions. Adoption of the Sustainable Development Goals (SDGs) by the United Nations and the recent Paris Climate Agreement underline this escalating awareness and sense of urgency.

But in spite of significant efforts to advance sustainable development, we are still confronted with systemic dilemmas that are deeply embedded in the fabric of the contemporary system of social organization. It seems difficult, if not impossible, to adequately address these problems through the traditional means of public regulation, economic liberalization, or political negotiation. Rather, these familiar approaches tend only to optimize existing regimes, thereby compounding their lock-in. These dynamics are evident in many societal systems that are now increasingly forced to confront a changing societal context and economic crises. Systems of ever-more efficient waste-management, healthcare, energy, food production, and construction have contributed substantially to demographic, welfare, and consumption growth, but we have reached a point where they have become completely locked-in and require still greater economic growth and efficiency improvements to maintain themselves. We are beginning to see that further iterations of this process will likely no longer be effective to support welfare states, especially in times of economic crises (Gordon, 2016).

Environmental policies, much like the discourse surrounding sustainable development, have thus become part of established regimes. Besides the fact that dominant arrangements, including policies and institutions, have developed as a response to historically entrenched societal problems and are therefore not adequate for the contemporary range of challenges, they are in themselves unsustainable because the foundations on which they are built are eroding. Both through gradual landscape changes and the maturing of alternative practices, technologies, and cultures, the groundworks of modernity are being powerfully undermined in terms of resource availability, underlying financial models, and power relationships and their performance. In practice, numerous societal regimes are experiencing existential threats and trying to develop strategies to prolong their existence including sectors such as energy (Unruh, 2000; Kern and Smith, 2007; Van den Bergh and Oosterhuis, 2008), waste (Parto et al., 2006; Yuan et al., 2006; Scholz et al., 2009) and healthcare (Van Raak, 2016).

It is perhaps unsurprising that while the focus of incumbent regimes has been on optimization, various experimental niches have begun to develop. Since the 1970s, we have witnessed the appearance of alternative currencies, renewable energy systems, local democracies, and sustainable community initiatives. For a long time, these projects were small, expensive, and often ridiculed as havens for leftist ideologues. But over time, and with experience, they have grown, developed, and matured. By now, many of these insurgent arrangements are finding their way into the mainstream in the form of urban gardens and farms, net positive energy buildings, renewable energy collaboratives, food cooperatives, credit unions, and collective insurances schemes. These examples, however local and small scale, are increasingly seen in their "translocal" context which entails organizing themselves into global networks and forging shared practices, standards, services, handbooks, conferences, and knowledge platforms (Avelino et al., 2015). These initiatives are further joined and professionalized by social entrepreneurs and startups, combining digital technologies, a societal orientation and commercial attitudes to develop and scale alternatives. The transition hypothesis is that the external pressure for systemic change now coming from the landscape level is combining with the internal tensions and stress within modernized regimes of production and the intensifying viability of alternatives is leading to tipping points that are accelerating societal transformation by triggering a multitude of complementary transitions at various levels and speeds.

A new transformation in the making?

The examples highlighted above relate to widening efforts by change-inclined actors to invest in and develop more sustainable models of production and consumption. As previously noted, these experiments focus on the conception of new diets, sustainable food systems, large-scale renewable energy generation, energy-producing buildings, and so forth. An interesting feature of many of these innovations, especially ones that operate on a community level, is the extent to which they bring consumption and production into more proximate geographic alignment. This capability is enabled by new technologies, experience, and knowledge, but also critical are novel modes of organization. This is visible in energy cooperatives where people produce, use, and exchange energy, but it also holds for food swaps, credit unions, and transition towns. But other efforts to move toward a more circular economy or smarter cities imply that production and consumption are becoming more closely interlinked, integrated, and co-productive.

These initiatives pose profound challenges to the logic of modern state-based institutions and incumbent markets as they often conflict with monopolies, central forms of coordination and taxation, vested financial interests and market structures, and the linear design of conventional production and consumption systems. To date, however, such alternatives have mainly been framed as "bottom-up" and, from a government perspective, often portrayed as part of the "Big Society" (Kisby, 2010). But because of their growing numbers, distributed network character, and ongoing professionalization, they are gradually becoming a structural force that is confronting extant regimes. This is visible in the governmental domain as well as in markets where traditional arrangements are coming under pressure. These developments are arising due to erosion of control as people and groups self-organize production, but other contributing factors include loss of tax revenues, income, and access to resources. The result is that conflicts are becoming more apparent between, on the one hand, established regimes and their interests and, on the other hand, the alternative and incipient "proto"-systems.

From a transition perspective, these ingredients will likely lead to periods of disruption and regime change, and I argue that the current crises and tensions within contemporary society are symptoms of this instability. So rather than to strive for sustainable development of existing regimes, transition governance asserts that a more effective approach is to seek strategies that disrupt inherently unsustainable regimes in such a way that their contraction and eventual demise leads to desired futures without causing unwarranted societal damage. The key question posed here is thus how to move to *sustainable stabilities* rather than to destructive transition scenarios that are haphazardly imposed on us. To denote this condition, I suggest the term "sustability" which is a portmanteau for sustainable stabilities and it can only be achieved through sweeping and disruptive transitions. Striving for *sustability* will be a critical challenge as it is not unlikely, to say the least, that the impending transitions will take us down some difficult and probably extremely unsettling roads. Climate refugees, growing inequalities, populism, civil wars, resource shortages, and food scarcity are all part of the very gloomy scenarios that may await just over the horizon. If we, however, zoom in on the sustainability alternatives outlined above, we find that many of them share common characteristics that, if enhanced and institutionalized in new ways, could lead toward the preferred *sustability* pathway. I discuss three of these criteria below: self-organization, renewable resources, and systemic innovation.

Self-organization

The now popular concept of "self-organization" points to expanding capacity in developed societies to facilitate societal functions in decentralized, distributed networks through processes of experimentation and learning (Jessop, 2002; De

Wolf and Holvoet, 2005). The accumulation of knowledge, capital, and skills in social networks augments pre-existing forms of social agency that is often only loosely connected to institutionalized and centrally coordinated forms of policy making (Voss et al., 2006). New communication technologies enable direct two-way cooperation and exchange between producers and consumers but also bypass previous managerial mechanisms. This capability leads to escalating tensions with the still dominant representative democratic systems and vast bureaucracies, challenging not only their legitimacy but also their ability to develop timely and effective solutions (Jhagroe and Loorbach, 2015).

Renewable resources

The shift from fossil resources and waste-inducing economic models toward renewable energy supplies and cyclical resource flows is still in the latter stages of its predevelopment phase but has been steadily gaining momentum in recent decades. Technologies to generate renewable energy are experiencing exponential growth in many countries, drawing enormous amounts of capital and rapidly gaining attention and support. Concomitantly, practices consistent with a circular economy are being developed and successfully implemented around the world. In many ways, the main achievements in these areas so far seem to be technological, but new business models and social innovations are steadily gaining adherents (Boons and Ludeke-Freund, 2013; Wells, 2013).

System innovation

The increasing interconnectedness of the global economy has led since the 1950s to the formation of new branches of science around complex systems theories and thinking. In recent decades, this work has begun to coalesce into a coherent paradigm and to spawn a large variety of theories, methods, and concepts to address processes of change and innovation in systemic ways (e.g., Midgley, 2003). Among researchers in this field, it is by now generally acknowledged that new technologies and products alone will not on their own be sufficient to effectively resolve our major sustainability dilemmas. In particular, the disruptive innovations associated with transitions tend to take the shape of sociotechnical or systemic change in which new socioeconomic conditions co-evolutionarily develop with inventive technologies and institutional contexts. In systemic innovation, novel societal frameworks often appear in conjunction with new knowledge and technologies, creating multi-directional flows of different forms of information ranging from scientific to practical and from entrepreneurial to institutional, with no clear point of origin. These circumstances undermine currently dominant regimes of knowledge production predicated on ownership, disciplinarity, and efficiency (Wittmayer and Schäpke, 2014).

Toward a lock-out?

Taken in combination, these three nascent drivers have the potential to confer clear sustainability benefits, but they are still marginal and obviously encounter numerous counterforces (see also Chapter 5). However, if we take the transition hypothesis seriously and anticipate the disruption of contemporary growth-based regimes, the question becomes what the social, economic, and ecological consequences might be for society at large. This is particularly critical in terms of how such transitions might affect incumbent actors with vested interests and how they might threaten middle-class jobs and mainstream consumption practices. In addition, it is not apparent what opportunities for governance and intervention are likely to be available given the inherent inertia of bureaucracies and the tendency for incrementalism and protectionism in incumbent institutions and organizations. But let us first explore the potential dynamics of such dislocation.

On the surface, most modes of sustainable development research and policy making focus on innovation and experimentation. As history shows, however, transitions are also (or perhaps even more so) about breakdown and turmoil. These features, by necessity, are related, as discussed above, to the inertia and resistance that works against systemic change, but they also relate to the disruption of social stability, structures, and future perspectives. But if our current societal regimes are indeed impossible to maintain in a world with ecological, economic, and social boundaries, then transgressing these constraints will almost certainly lead to crises. Such conditions might become most readily apparent in the pending energy transitions as regions face the impacts of climate change and emerging resource conflicts and associated political instabilities. These moments of upheaval, however intrinsic they may be to the transitions, are disadvantageous because they tend to trigger conservative and regressive counteractions. Losing stability and future orientation, in other words, fuels populism and other political attempts to revert to the old order.

This dynamic plays out at both societal and personal levels. The notion of sustainable consumption is often misunderstood by mainstream actors as "doing less" or "intervening in the freedom of choice." Not being able to eat meat every day, having to accept wind-generated electricity as a primary source of energy, lowering the thermostat, and cutting back on driving are for most people not particularly attractive alternatives and may even provide reason to ridicule neighbors that promote lifestyles consistent with these commitments (UK SDC, 2006). This situation oftentimes discourages proponents from wanting to "leave the niche" and become mainstream and for people to adapt their lifestyles or structures based on a more positive understanding of the incipient changes (Seyfang and Smith, 2007). The transition perspective itself has evolved to include greater attention to dynamics at the level of the regime and how over time they interact with forces encouraging emergence at the niche level. This tension is visualized in Figure 10.2, which suggests that different factors and patterns of change at niche and regime levels co-evolve and produce sequences of build-up and break-down.

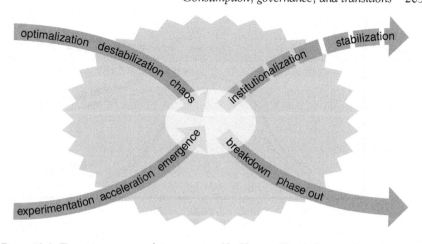

Figure 10.2 Transitions as co-evolving patterns of build-up and break-down

With respect to the energy transition, these dynamics are visible at the global, regional, and local level. The fluctuations in oil prices, international climate agreements, geopolitical tensions, and pressures on multinational oil companies are clear symptoms of spreading destabilization. At the same time, investments in renewables, system innovations in the energy system driven by outsiders like information-technology companies (e.g., smart grids), new forms of urban mobility (electric cars), and incipient ideas in the building sector (net positive energy buildings) help to scale up niches and enable local communities, cities, and networks to become more sustainable. Following the transition narrative, these developments can be interpreted as a lock-out of the path-dependent development of efficiency-oriented and centralized fossil-based energy systems. But by no means is this an inevitably sustainable transition as multiple forces are at play to defend currently dominant interests, to create new dependencies on scarce resources, and to instigate new inequalities.

The disruption of unsustainable regimes and the emergence of alternative sustainable proto-regimes could open up possibilities for strategically advancing these dynamics in a direction that enables establishment of socioeconomic regimes that are low-carbon, equitable, and resilient and thus break away from our current pathway of stabilization and unsustainable development. This process is depicted in Figure 10.3, which is similar to how the German Council for Sustainable Development conceptualized the necessary transformation in its report (WBGU, 2013). Although we are still in many domains in a situation where incumbent regimes are able to control, slow down, or adapt to alternatives, there is also an increasing number of counterparts that are being challenged by disruptive technological innovations and transformative social innovations in areas like resources, finance, energy, and governance that are indispensable to the daily functioning of the prevailing regime (see Chapters 5 and 8).

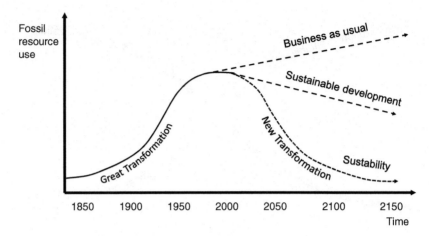

Figure 10.3 The transformation to susta(ina)bility

Government lock-in and governance panarchy

If currently dominant regimes and the actors dependent on them are not likely to proactively seek disruptive transitions, then institutionalized policies and governance systems will be unable to effectively guide and engage with transitions. But, at the same time, the large number of radical alternatives that have been incubating may not automatically scale to supplant currently unsustainable systems of consumption and production. The question then becomes what types of (meta-)governance (Jessop, 2002) might we envisage to mediate between the incremental dynamics of change at the regime level and the insurgent replacements. From this perspective, all sorts of actions undertaken by actors to influence social change are considered as elements of governance. Recent work on sustainability transitions adds a normative element of direction, notably how can we either strengthen or destabilize existing strategies, policies, and actions to move toward sustainability (Turnheim and Geels, 2012; Bosman et al., 2014)?

The dominant governance logics of state and market are at odds with sustainability which calls for context-specific solutions that are typically decentralized, flexible, adaptive, and integrated. Alternative sustainable practices, structures, and cultures that are emerging take many forms including citizen initiatives, public–private partnerships, government-funded projects, social enterprises, and network arrangements. Actors are thus becoming better able to build upon available knowledge, resources, and networks to find those governance forms that best fit their situation and perceived problems. This development has been recognized in a descriptive way as the rise of the "network society" (Castells, 1996), but it has often been interpreted as development that challenges the lack of legitimacy, transparency, and democracy. However, this rising freedom for self-organization, and co-developing sustainable modes of production and consumption, raises opportunities for transition governance.

I refer to the context in which multiple forms or regimes of governance co-exist and develop in an unplanned or centrally uncoordinated way as "panarchy." Belgian political economist and botanist Paul Émile De Puydt introduced the word "panarchy" during the 1860s (literally meaning "every order" or "meta-order") and argued for space for alternatives to the emerging nation states in the second half of the nineteenth century (Tucker and De Bellis, 2015), but it never became a serious movement or option. The basic underlying idea, however, was individual freedom of choice to accept or enact a personally desired type of governance. If we reflect on the diversity of emergent forms of governance that exists today, it is undoubtedly true that there are multiple models and people are increasingly able to develop their own contexts, be it on a very modest scale. Examples include voluntary groups, social networks, social enterprises, community initiatives, and subsidized projects. Combining this variety with the need to advance desired transitions and the potential of self-organized governance to develop context-specific and sustainable radical alternatives, "panarchy governance" then is the idea of meta-governance to direct, coordinate, and facilitate those parts of governance panarchy that contribute to desired transitions. In other words, the aim is to "steer" self-organization away from unsustainable lock-ins and to develop toward new, sustainable, regimes. To this end, insight into transition dynamics and unsustainability pathways is critical to identify those types and forms of self-organization that contribute to desired transitions.

The achievement of this outcome would, perhaps paradoxically, seem to require strong government and this observation raises at least two critical challenges for panarchy. The first relates to the neoliberal strategies that have been contributing to globalization, the (unrestrained) political influence of economic elites, and continued concentration of power and wealth that circumvents—and perhaps even dictates—state control. The second is that new forms of self-organization require skills, capacities, and resources that are not universally available. Sustainable alternatives like renewable energy cooperatives, urban farming, or car sharing are often taken up by well-educated, middle-class citizens in their own context and they tend to build on their professional experiences and networks. Therefore, panarchy governance requires the adoption and enactment of quite clear boundaries and guiding sustainability principles at a very large—preferably global—scale within which it can develop, as well as systematic support to enable the requisite skills and conditions to foster broad participation and inclusion.

Enacting governance panarchy to contribute to societal problem-solving, specifically by helping to construct a pathway to sustability, might imply a crucial transition in the current institutional landscape, possibly beyond what is currently likely or even thinkable. It would require not only adaptive policies and institutions, but also transformative ones—institutions and meta-governance principles that ensure basic values and boundaries and social conditions that encourage societal competition without prescribing solutions or outcomes. Such meta-governance principles (e.g., Derkx and Glasbergen, 2014; Fransen, 2015) would need to be embodied, enacted, and promoted by (transnational or global) organizations that are able to deal with diversity, surprise, and uncertainty while also transitioning themselves. These organizations need to be able to engage in destruction as much as they help to innovate, to facilitate as much as they direct, and to be able to work in ways that are simultaneously sensitive to context and to generic conditions. The German energy transition provides a fascinating experimental context for this new perspective in that it offers a more general policy context that sets clear long-term goals and sustainability principles but does not blueprint the implementation and short-term steps. The development of various renewable energy initiatives and structures across the country since the 1990s has been enabled by a feed-in tariff and scaled by the top-down decision to phase-out the country's nuclear power facilities. This pronouncement flew in the face of dominant interests and opened the door for the acceleration of renewables while at the same time creating a chaotic and disruptive pattern of systemic change in which a new system is reinvented "on the move." During this process, dominant logics of the incumbent energy regime have been fundamentally challenged: electricity is sold at a negative price when there is an abundance of wind and sunshine, control over energy production has shifted from incumbents to farmers and cooperatives, and energy companies have been facing big losses.

Without a possibility to plan and design sustainable futures, processes that seek to enable collective experiments that encourage movement away from unsustainability seem chaotic and uncertain, but this may be, by necessity, the only way forward. Panarchy suggests that efforts to embrace the role of providing guidance on the long-term direction, to deliberately disrupt the status quo in later transitional stages, and to ensure inclusivity and diversity in self-organization constitute the next phase in the progression from a central state model toward a reflexive government. This observation suggests three basic governance mechanisms: bottom-up innovation, top-down guidance, and phase-out support. Both transition-management theory and experiences to date have mainly focused on predevelopment dynamics and on creating the prior conditions for desirable breakthroughs via transition points. However, the interrelated task of destabilizing incumbent regimes and creating opportunities for the disruptive breakthrough of more sustainable alternatives requires not only the build-up of replacements, but also the provision of strategic guidance and managed phase-out of predecessors (Loorbach, 2010) (Figure 10.4).

While bottom-up innovation has been a staple of transitions research over the past decade, the challenges of effectively delivering top-down guidance and phase-out support have thus far attracted little attention in the literature. On the one hand, the dynamics of destabilization are beginning to draw more interest (Turnheim and Geels, 2012; Bosman et al., 2014), but how governance could actively play into such processes has yet to be conceptualized to any significant degree beyond addressing how existing policies facilitate transitions (Van Raak 2016; Kivimaa and Kern, 2016). In some respects, we can consider the recent Paris Climate Agreement to be an example of a new institutional frame with a revolutionary, long-term target that also provides short-term cycles of intermediate objectives, evaluations, and revisionary mechanisms. However, the enduring

**New institutions
and structures**

**Transitioning
and adapting**

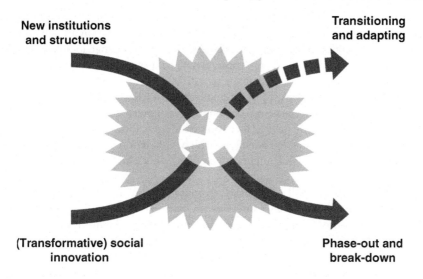

**(Transformative) social
innovation**

**Phase-out and
break-down**

Figure 10.4 Governance mix framework for transition governance

goals should be more formally established and also address issues like social equity, economic resilience, and ecological sustainability. On the other hand, phase-out policies gaining in visibility, for instance in the case of the German nuclear phase-out and the Obama administration's proposed POWER+ plan addressing the transition challenges in the fossil-energy sector.[1] Ideally, phase-out policies should be formulated to compensate the losers in transitions, to offer a relatively graceful exit from declining economic sectors, and to allow time for adaptive change. Examples could include the use of subsidies to encourage the phasing out of fossil-based mobility in cities, the reduction of meat production, and the closure of coal-burning utility plants. The possibility and necessity of such interventions is being debated, especially at a city level but also in countries like Norway and Austria that propose to stop sales of gasoline-powered cars as early as 2025. But more generally, such policies have neither been conceptualized systematically nor made an explicit part of the sketched out transition-governance portfolio.

Conclusion

I have outlined in this chapter some ideas and reflections based on fifteen years of research and experimentation on transition management. It is clear that contemporary societies are still proceeding along path-dependent developmental trajectories that are unsustainable and leading to escalating crises, tensions, and a growing sense of urgency. Attempting to address the negative externalities of the current paradigm through incremental improvements of existing systems of production and consumption seems only to be reinforcing prevailing path-dependencies. I take a different perspective and argue that the gradual build-up of pressure on the incumbent regimes and the accelerating development of sustainable alternative models provides a favorable context for destabilization and chaos and these circumstances can contribute to large-scale systems change in an acceptable timeframe. However, advancing these new proto-systems of production and consumption will require strategies that actively seek to hasten and guide the desired transitions. Such an approach implies that we stop focusing on improving either production processes or consumption practices by making them less unsustainable. Rather, we need to focus on maturing, scaling, and institutionalizing inherently more sustainable systems in which production and consumption are intimately interwoven. This might be possible by building on existing niches in which production and consumption of products and services are organized in communities (local as well as global) that often bypass incumbent regimes.

These niches and how they (self-)organize take very different shapes related to their specific contexts, engaged actors, and perceived problems. Rather than to seek harmonization and standardization, I contend that it is exactly this diversity and geographic specificity that offers possibilities to rethink what governance is and how it could be mobilized to accelerate sustainability transitions. The starting point for reconceptualizing this different role, and experimenting with it in practical transition contexts, is the combination of bottom-up social innovation that stimulates transformation, top-down collective structures and institutions, and phase-out policies that break down unsustainable cultures and structures. Transitions research to date has only just begun to devote attention to the design of new types of institutions and the role of cessation interventions.

In recent years, the research agenda on transition management has also shifted focus from experimentation and envisioning to phases of transitions in which all sorts of tensions, dilemmas, and new mechanisms are identified. For example, the European projects Accelerating and Rescaling Transitions to Sustainability (ARTS) and Transformative Social Innovation Theory (TRANSIT) take up new questions concerning inequalities between people who are able to develop new ways of producing products, services, and values and those who do not have the necessary skills, capital, and networks.[2] These projects also consider the friction between bottom-up initiatives and democratic principles in a representative democracy with regard to equal treatment and transparent decision making.

The thrust of this chapter is more in the spirit of offering a research agenda than a developed theory. I have sought to highlight some basic concepts and ideas that might work as the basis for experimentation on new governance hypotheses in the field of transition management. By moving beyond claims that change agents, frontrunners, new framings and visions, and transformative agendas might in and of themselves create the urgency and space for transitions, we can start to develop new formulations that build on insights regarding the development of niches into regimes, the opening up and reconfiguration of regimes, and the guidance and acceleration of productive tensions to impel desired transitions.

Finally, this chapter raises questions about the role of research with respect to innovating new systems of sustainable production and consumption. Assessing the unsustainability of existing systems and offering recommendations for incremental improvement is only one part of transition management. We also need to develop more experimental and transdisciplinary research methodologies around how to most effectively evolve toward novel provisioning systems that are able to operate within ecological, social, and economic boundaries. Given the very important issues at stake in finding a new balance between individual freedoms (to consume and pollute) and collective limits, we need to rethink the role, organization, and instruments of government and policy. Engaging with such questions by working directly with transition actors and organizations is likely the only way forward and such activities might themselves be an important element of governance panarchy for a more sustainable future.

Notes

1 Announced as part of the President's Budget for 2016, the Power+ Plan is a $10 billion multi-point proposal calling for the creation of new jobs by reclaiming abandoned coal mines, the provision of health and retirement benefits to coal miners and their families, the support of regional economic and employment diversification, and the deployment of carbon capture and sequestration technologies. For further information, see www. powerplusplan.org.
2 For details on ARTS refer to http://acceleratingtransitions.eu and for TRANSIT refer to www.transitsocialinnovation.eu.

References

Arthur, W. (1989) "Competing technologies, increasing returns and lock-in by historical events," *Economic Journal* 99(394):116–131.

Avelino, F., Dumitru, A., Longhurst, N., Wittmayer, J., Hielscher, S., Weaver, P., and Haxeltine, A. (2015) Transitions towards new economies? A transformative social innovation perspective. TRANSIT Project Working Paper No. 3. Rotterdam: Dutch Research Institute for Transitions, Erasmus University Rotterdam.

Bekkers, V. (2007) *Governance and the Democratic Deficit: Assessing the Democratic Legitimacy of Governance Practices*. Farnham, Surrey: Ashgate.

Boons, F. and Lüdeke-Freund, F. (2013) "Business models for sustainable innovation: state-of-the-art and steps towards a research agenda," *Journal of Cleaner Production* 45:9–19.

Bosman, R., Loorbach, D., Frantzeskaki, N., and Pistorius, T. (2014) "Discursive regime dynamics in the Dutch energy transition," *Environmental Innovation and Societal Transitions* 13:45–59.

Castells, M. (1996) *The Rise of the Network Society*. Malden, MA: Blackwell.

Cohen, M., Brown, H., and Vergragt, P. (eds.) (2013) *Innovations in Sustainable Consumption: New Economics, Socio-technical Transitions, and Social Practices*. Northampton, MA: Edward Elgar.

Costanza, R., Kubiszewski, I., Giovannini, E., Lovins, H., McGlade, J., Pickett, K., and Wilkinson, R. (2014). "Development: time to leave GDP behind," *Nature* 505(7483):283–285.

De Wolf, T. and Holvoet, T. (2005) "Emergence versus self-organization: different concepts but promising when combined," in S. Brueckner (ed.), *Engineering Self-organizing Systems: Methodologies and Applications*. Berlin: Springer–Verlag, pp. 1–15.

Derkx, B. and Glasbergen, P. (2014) "Elaborating global private meta-governance: an inventory in the realm of voluntary sustainability standards," *Global Environmental Change* 27:41–50.

Elzen, B., Geels, F., and Green, K. (eds.) (2004) *System Innovation and the Transition to Sustainability: Theory, Evidence, and Policy*. Northampton, MA: Edward Elgar.

Fransen, L. (2015) "The politics of meta-governance in transnational private sustainability governance," *Policy Sciences* 48(3):293–317.

Geels, F. (2002) *Understanding the Dynamics of Technological Transitions: A Co-evolutionary and Socio-technical Analysis*. Enschede: Twente University Press.

Geels, F. (2005) "The dynamics of transitions in socio-technical systems: a multi-level analysis of the transition pathway from horse-drawn carriages to automobiles (1860–1930)," *Technology Analysis and Strategic Management* 17(4):445–476.

Gordon, R. (2016) *The Rise and Fall of American Growth: The US Standard of Living Since the Civil War*. Princeton, NJ: Princeton University Press.

Grin, J., Rotmans, J., Schot, J., Geels, F., and Loorbach, D. (2010) *Transitions to Sustainable Development: New Directions in the Study of Long Term Transformative Change*. New York: Routledge.

Jackson, T. (2011) *Prosperity without Growth: Economics for a Finite Planet*. New York: Earthscan.

Jessop, B. (2002) Governance and metagovernance: on reflexivity, requisite variety, and requisite irony. Department of Sociology, Lancaster University. www.lancaster.ac.uk/fass/resources/sociology-online-papers/papers/jessop-governance-and-metagovernance.pdf.

Jhagroe, S. and Loorbach, D. (2015) "See no evil, hear no evil: the democratic potential of transition management," *Environmental Innovation and Societal Transitions* 15:65–83.

Kallis, G. (2011) "In defence of degrowth," *Ecological Economics* 70(5):873–880.

Kern, F. and Smith, A. (2007) "Restructuring energy systems for sustainability? Energy transition policy in the Netherlands," *Energy Policy* 36(11):4093–4103.

Kisby, B. (2010) "The Big Society: power to the people?" *The Political Quarterly* 81(4):484–491.

Kivimaa, P. and Kern, F. (2016) "Creative destruction or mere niche support? Innovation policy mixes for sustainability transitions," *Research Policy* 45(1):205–217.

Levinthal, D. (1998) "The slow pace of rapid technological change: gradualism and punctuation in technological change," *Industrial and Corporate Change* 7(2):217–247.

Loorbach, D. (2010) "Transition management for sustainable development: a prescriptive, complexity-based governance framework," *Governance* 23:161–183.

Loorbach, D. (2014) *To Transition! Governance Panarchy in the New Transformation*. Rotterdam: Dutch Research Institute for Transitions, Erasmus University Rotterdam.

Meadows, D., Meadows, D., Randers, J., and Behrens, W. (1972) *The Limits to Growth: A Global Challenge*. New York: Universe Books.

Midgley, G. (2003) "System thinking: an introduction and overview," in G. Midgley (ed.), *Systems Thinking*. Thousand Oaks, CA: Sage, pp. xvii–liii.

Parto, S., Loorbach, D., Lansink, A., and Kemp, R. (2006). "Transitions and institutional change: the case of the Dutch waste subsystem," in Parto, S. and Herbert-Copley, B.

(eds.), *Industrial Innovation and Environmental Regulation: Developing Workable Solutions*. Tokyo: United Nations University Press, pp. 233–257.

Pierre, J. and Peters, G. (2000) *Governance, Politics and the State*. New York: Macmillan.

Polanyi, K. (2001 [1944]) *The Great Transformation: Economic and Political Origins of Our Time*. Boston: Beacon Press.

Rip, A. and Kemp, R. (1998) "Technological change," in Rayner, S. and Malone, E. (eds.), *Human Choice and Climate Change*. Columbus, OH: Battelle Press, pp. 327–399.

Rotmans, J. and Loorbach, D. (2009) "Complexity and transition management," *Journal of Industrial Ecology* 13(2):184–196.

Rotmans, J., Kemp, R., and van Asselt, M. (2001) "More evolution than revolution: transition management in public policy," *Foresight* 3(1):15–31.

Scholz, R., Spoerri, A., and Lang, D. (2009) "Problem structuring for transitions: the case of Swiss waste management," *Futures* 41(3):171–181.

Schot, J., and Geels, F. (2007) "Niches in evolutionary theories of technical change," *Journal of Evolutionary Economics* 17(5):605–622.

Seyfang, G. and Smith, A. (2007) "Grassroots innovations for sustainable development: towards a new research and policy agenda," *Environmental Politics* 16(4):584–603.

Tucker, A. and De Bellis, G. (eds.) (2015) *Panarchy: Political Theories of Non-Territorial States*. New York: Routledge.

Turnheim, B. and Geels, F. (2012) "Regime destabilisation as the flipside of energy transitions: lessons from the history of the British coal industry (1913–1997)," *Energy Policy* 50:35–49.

UK Sustainable Development Commission (UK SDC) (2006) *I Will If You Will: Towards Sustainable Consumption*. London: UK SDC.

Unruh, G. (2000) "Understanding carbon lock-in," *Energy Policy* 28(12):817–830.

Van den Bergh, J. and Oosterhuis, F. (2008) "An evolutionary-economic analysis of energy transitions," in Van den Bergh, J. and Bruinsma, F. (eds.), *Managing the Transition to Renewable Energy: Theory and Practice from Local, Regional and Macro Perspectives*. Northampton, MA: Edward Elgar, pp. 149–173.

Van Raak, R. (2016) *Transition Policies: Connecting System Dynamics, Governance and Instruments in an Application to Dutch Healthcare*. Rotterdam: Dutch Research Institute for Transitions, Erasmus University Rotterdam.

Verbong, G. and Loorbach, D. (eds.) (2012) *Governing the Energy Transition: Reality, Illusion, or Necessity?* New York: Routledge.

Voss, J., Bauknecht, D., and Kemp, R. (eds.) (2006) *Reflexive Governance for Sustainable Development*. Northampton, MA: Edward Elgar.

Wells, P. (2013) *Business Models for Sustainability*. Northampton, MA: Edward Elgar.

Wissenschaftlicher Beirat der Bundesregierung Globale Umweltveränderungen (WBGU) (2013) *Welt im Wandel: Gesellschaftsvertrag für einer großen Transformation (World in Transition: Social Contract for a Major Transformation)*. Berlin WBGU. www.wbgu.de/fileadmin/templates/dateien/veroeffentlichungen/hauptgutachten/jg2011/wbgu_jg2011.pdf (in German).

Wittmayer, J. and Schäpke, N. (2014) "Action, research and participation: roles of researchers in sustainability transitions," *Sustainability Science* 9(4):483–496.

Yuan, Z., Bi, J., and Moriguichi, Y. (2006). "The circular economy: a new development strategy in China," *Journal of Industrial Ecology* 10(1–2):4–8.

Part IV

Social change toward post-consumer society

11 Conclusion and outlook

Philip J. Vergragt, Maurie J. Cohen, and Halina Szejnwald Brown

This final chapter revisits the original questions set forth in the Introduction, namely how might we interpret the potential of societal developments unfolding at the macro-, meso-, and micro-scales to foster a transition beyond consumer society. Do widely accepted theories of social change allow us to recognize—and possibly facilitate—incipient developments as precursors of a prospective transformation? Two broad conclusions emerge from the contributions to this volume.

The first is that social and cultural shifts to transcend consumer society are unlikely to occur without deeper changes in the macroeconomy including the financial system, dominant institutions and the state, and political priorities. The distinguished Polish sociologist Piotr Sztompka (1991), while studying the historically unprecedented post-Soviet transition in his home country to a market economy and democracy (and drawing on the work of Ralf Dahrendorf (1990) and Claus Offe (1991)), noted the "dilemma of three clocks" which metaphorically referred to the uneven rate of change in the political, economic, and sociocultural domains. Sztompka described at this pivotal historical moment how political change runs ahead, change in the economic system and its institutions follows at a much slower pace, and sociocultural change lags still further behind, evolving over a span of more than a generation. Efforts to supersede consumer society, as we contemplate the challenges in this volume, are largely concordant with the dilemma of three clocks.

This assessment is most explicit in the chapter by Cindy Isenhour which asserts that cultural change cannot happen without change in the underlying economy. The appraisal is also consistent with Inge Røpke's conclusion that deep reform of the financial system is a necessary precondition for tempering consumerism and overconsumption. A similar determination emerges from Derk Loorbach's contribution which pleads for a different governance system and the chapter by Anders Hayden and Jeffrey Wilson which shows that a shift away from gross domestic product as our dominant indicator of societal well-being is far from sufficient to induce reinvention of the dominant economic system. Emily Huddart Kennedy focuses on the Canadian local food movement and further underscores this point by highlighting the rift between a largely apolitical rank and file and a movement leadership which acknowledges that political changes in the global food system are unavoidable. The contribution by Tally Katz-Gerro, Predrag Cvetičanin, and Adrian Leguina illustrates that changes in the real economy, especially a steep economic downturn, strongly affect consumption behaviors, although it is not clear if they will eventually lead to lasting changes in the consumer cultures of the four southeastern European countries that they studied.

The second conclusion is that social experiments in niches are important but are prone to many pitfalls. Tom Bauler, Bonno Pel, and Julia Backhaus illustrate in their chapter the fine line between capture by incumbent interests and efforts to retain authenticity (at the cost of remaining politically marginal) that alternatives to the present economic system are forced to walk. The threats of capture are additionally illustrated in Kennedy's contribution as well as by Marlyne Sahakian who demonstrates how some credible initiatives in the sharing economy have been appropriated by mainstream businesses while others retain their connection to the solidarity economy but with only very modest broader impacts. Juliet Schor and Bobby Wengronowitz also demonstrate how the ecohabitus of proponents of the sharing economy could be neutralized by incumbent cultures and interests. In short, grassroots innovations, social experiments in niches, and interstitial strategies have potential to drive change, but as long as their "clock" is out of sync with the pace of evolution in the political and macroeconomic domains, impacts on the wider system are bound to be of minor consequence. This means that the question that is often posed with regard to small-scale initiatives—how to scale up or replicate—might be better reframed in terms of how to create the facilitative conditions for them to become effective instruments of social change.

To get the transition under way, there is, in Polanyi's (2001) terms, a critical need to develop a coherent "second movement." Such a movement could potentially counteract the problems created by prevalent modes of market fundamentalism, and its emergence would include the numerous social experiments to coalesce and carry forward the seeds of cultural change beyond consumerism.

This is an enormous challenge and so our conclusions may appear rather discouraging at first sight. But we should keep in mind that many changes in complex systems are nonlinear, hard to predict, and even more difficult to manage (Stroh, 2015). They are also characterized by unexpected outcomes and emergent properties that oftentimes cannot be anticipated. In this sense, it is encouraging to observe that in many parts of the world people are testing alternative lifestyles, forms of collaboration, and building new economic forms (albeit fragile and with uncertain prospects) that often bridge the distance between consumption and production in new and unexpected ways (Heinberg, 2011; Schor and Thompson, 2014; Thackara, 2015). The Internet is clearly the technological platform that enables and facilitates many of these social experiments and creates the material conditions for novel modes of interaction—in some cases across continents—that only the most prescient observers were able to envisage twenty years ago (Castells, 1996; Benkler, 2007). Also laying the foundation for profound social change is increasing urbanization that facilitates reinvention and, while attention is currently focused primarily on new social practices and cultural values, its magnitude and rapid tempo makes for a promising candidate to interface with rising forms of collective political action (Townsend, 2014; Ratti and Claudel, 2016).

It also merits recognizing, not without some irony, that systems of social organization contain the seeds of their own destruction. Several unfolding trends help to illustrate this situation. After World War II, and especially since 1975, when consumer society was in ascendance, its bedrock features—full employment, across-the-board wage increases tied to productivity gains, and the state's commitment to public investment—were starting to show signs of fatigue (Gordon 2016; Cohen, 2017). In the United States, manufacturing employment, the engine of the overall economic system, peaked in 1979 and has been in steady decline ever since. This reversal has been the result of various factors aiming at efficiency improvements—labor productivity, automation, and outsourcing to lower wage countries—all resulting in cheaper prices that have been indispensable to maintain consumption.

The demise of domestic manufacturing in the United States and most other post-industrial nations has had an insufficiently acknowledged effect on the ability of consumer society to reproduce itself, especially because the creation of jobs in the service sector has not compensated for the disappearance of well-paid industrial employment and the attendant decline of labor unions (Neumann, 2016). Furthermore, the extraordinarily rapid expansion of the financial industry had the effect of siphoning wealth from the middle class and redirecting it toward a small economic elite (Krippner, 2012; Foroohar, 2016). While these effects have been partially buffered by deregulation of financial markets and expansion of readily accessible credit, they are unmistakable indications of a pattern of gradual erosion in the prevailing system of social organization.

We are thus witnessing simultaneous landscape-level developments that are making it difficult to maintain a macroeconomy predicated on mass consumption and vast energy and material throughputs, and the situation is being exacerbated by climate change and other ecological crises. An interesting signal to monitor as we chart our way forward is the extent to which economic growth is able to continue to serve as a proxy for political success. And it may not be possible for much longer to pacify intensifying civic discontent with neoliberal palliatives based on discredited trickle-down economics, ever-expanding patterns of global trade, cascades of inexpensive consumer goods, fervent deregulation, ruthless reductions in social welfare, and increasingly hollow and disingenuous appeals to individual freedom.

It is this potent dynamic that may bring collective outrage to a tipping point and inspire social mobilization against incumbent institutions and power structures. In the United States, this movement may be propelled by deeply held core values of equity, opportunity and justice; other countries will need to rely on their own admixture of drivers. Should this reaction gain momentum, the social experiments and policy reforms that we detail in this book could provide constructive visions and field-tested approaches toward inventing a new system of social organization that transcends consumer society.

References

Benkler, Y. (2007) *The Wealth of Networks: How Social Production Transforms Markets and Freedom*. New Haven, CT: Yale University Press.

Castells, M. (1996) *The Rise of the Network Society*. Cambridge, MA: Blackwell.

Cohen, M. (2017) *The Future of Consumer Society: Prospects for Sustainability in the New Economy*. New York: Oxford University Press.

Dahrendorf, R. (1990) *Reflections on the Revolutions in Europe*. London: Chatto and Windus.

Foroohar, R. (2016) *Makers and Takers: The Rise of Finance and the Fall of American Business*. New York: Crown Business.

Gordon, R. (2016) *The Rise and Fall of American Growth: The U.S. Standard of Living Since the Civil War*. Princeton, NJ: Princeton University Press.

Heinberg, R. (2011) *The End of Growth: Adapting to Our New Economic Reality*. Gabriola Island, BC: New Society.

Krippner, G. (2012) *Capitalizing on Crisis: The Political Origins of the Rise of Finance*. Cambridge, MA: Harvard University Press.

Neumann, T. (2016) *Remaking the Rust Belt: The Postindustrial Transformation of North America*. Philadelphia: University of Pennsylvania Press.

Offe, C. (1991) "Capitalism by democratic design: democratic theory facing the triple transition in East Central Europe," *Social Research* 58(4):865–892.

Polanyi, K. (2001 [1944]) *The Great Transformation: The Political and Economic Origins of Our Time*. Boston, MA: Beacon Press.

Ratti, C. and Claudel, M. (2016) *The City of Tomorrow: Sensors, Networks, Hackers, and the Future of Urban Life*. New Haven, CT: Yale University Press.

Schor, J. and Thompson, C. (eds.) 2014. *Sustainable Lifestyles and the Quest for Plenitude: Case Studies of the New Economy*. New Haven, CT: Yale University Press.

Stroh, D. (2015) *Systems Thinking and Social Change*. White River Junction, VT: Chelsea Green.

Sztompka, P. (1991) Dilemmas of the great transition: a tentative catalogue. Paper presented at the conference on Theories and Research on Transition: Eastern Europe in a Comparative Perspective, Radziejowice, Poland, November 29–30. www.people. fas.harvard.edu/~ces/publications/docs/pdfs/CEE_WP19.pdf.

Thackara, J. (2015) *How to Thrive in the Next Economy*. London: Thames and Hudson.

Townsend, A. (2014) *Smart Cities: Big Data, Civic Hackers, and the Quest for a New Utopia*. New York: W. W. Norton.

Index

Page numbers in *italics* denote an illustration, **bold** indicates a table, n an endnote